5. £14.50

0951773208

Schools, services and special educational needs: management issues in the wake of LMS

Edited by
Tony Bowers

Perspective Press
Cambridge

Perspective Press
92 Hertford Street
Cambridge
CB4 3AQ
England

First published 1991

British Library Cataloguing in Publication Data

1. Great Britain. Special education
I. Bowers, Tony
371.9'0941

ISBN 0-9517732-0-8

Typeset and printed in Great Britain by:
Kay Jay Print, Evesham, Worcestershire.

Contents

Contributors to this book:

Tony Bowers Tutor in Psychology and Special Educational Needs, Cambridge Institute of Education

Peter Caldwell Senior Education Officer for Special Education, Bedfordshire

Gill Carter Head of Special Educational Needs Support Service, London Borough of Hounslow

Judith Charlesworth Head Teacher, Oakleigh School, Barnet

Malcolm Clayton Head Teacher, Colnbrook School, Watford

Andrea Clifford Independent Consultant in Special Educational Needs

Mel Farrar Head Teacher, Foxdenton School, Oldham

Adrian Fletcher Senior Consultant, Touche Ross Management Consultants

David Hill Senior Consultant, Cambridge Educational Associates

Michael Hunt Principal Pyschologist (research) Bedfordshire

Ruth MacConville Head of Service for Children with Sensory Impairments and Language Difficulties, London Borough of Ealing

Ann Mattey Special Educational Needs Co-ordinator, West Kent

Arno Rabinowitz Chartered Psychologist and Partner, Specialist Psychological Services

Gail Treml Assistant Director of Education, London Borough of Bromley

Introduction

A lot of assumptions that have grown up in the past two or three decades are being severely challenged. As this book is written, the challenges are being made. How they are met will depend not only on the qualities of the responses but on the informational base and foresight of those making them.

Challenging the assumptions of those working with children with special educational needs is nothing new. Ideas of the nature and causation of learning problems have undergone considerable changes, as have those relating to the appropriate places to educate children with special educational needs. Some well-embedded assumptions relating to the content and delivery of the curriculum, particularly in special schools, are now also having to be scrutinized with the advent of the National Curriculum and the imperative to provide maximum access to it for all children. These are not the ones to which I refer, however. What, then, are they?

The first is that to talk of children having 'special educational needs', particularly within mainstream schools, somehow sets them apart from the mechanism which funds those schools, providing an entitlement to additional resources. It has become common in many LEAs for schools to expect additional resources and assistance to be provided to meet the needs of children whose attainments, behaviour or related difficulties lie outside some notional view of what is 'normal'. The provision of additional teaching time and assistance in classrooms, particularly after the 1981 Education Act, was a natural response from LEAs seeking to use resources in a directed way. However, it encouraged the notion that special educational needs were somehow the province of the authority and not the school. Now the assumption that LEAs ought, or can be expected, to make such central provision is being challenged by pressures to maximize the delegation of funds under LMS and by the adoption of curriculum that is intended to be available to all. However attractive the idea may be to some schools, the bulk of children with special educational needs will no longer be able to be labelled as someone else's problem.

A second assumption, particularly among those in special schools and support services, has been that the economic principles - crudely summarizable as those of supply and demand - which now bear on mainstream schools as a result of LMS cannot be applied to them. The formula structure which has been created for special schools has encouraged this belief among some of their managers, with the presumption that a 'place-led' rather than a 'pupil-led' method of funding such schools will ensure their continuation. However, there are factors at work, as certain chapter authors suggest, which make it probable that special schools will come under increasing pressure to demonstrate their cost-effectiveness. The place element may come to be closely equated with pupil numbers, and the scrutiny which comes from being within the General Schools Budget is likely to lead to searching questions relating to 'value for money'. It is predictable that some special schools will close as a result of LMS; as in the mainstream, there will be losers and well as winners. Support service staff, too, having grown used to working for the LEA and therefore being 'free' to schools, may find that they have to reappraise some of their approaches, either as delegation of all or part of their funding occurs or as greater scrutiny of the value of what is not delegated is undertaken by schools.

Linked with the above assumption is another: that marketing is unnecessary and even distasteful. Because special schools, SEN support services and educational psychology services have worked for one central authority and have therefore, however they defined their clients, had one customer who determined their fortunes, they have not always felt a need to make themselves attractive to those whom they serve. In economic terms they have been part of a command economy, not a market economy; 'customer consciousness' and the need to set out a service's wares in ways which schools would find attractive and user-friendly have therefore been unnecessary. This does not mean that marketing has not been indulged in by such services, although it may have been targeted politically rather than educationally. Blissett (1972), for example, found marketing to be a major component of the activities of professionals whose job descriptions did not ostensibly require it. Now, however, an overt approach to marketing, with all that it entails, is likely to become increasingly necessary.

A further assumption, prevalent in the public services and first attacked within healthcare provision, is now being called into question. This is that the funder and the provider of services should be one and the same. The 1988 Education Act created a split between the two by separating LEAs (the funders) from schools (the providers) through the mechanisms of LMS; the inspection and monitoring role which accompanied funding, and therefore enabled the LEA still to set and monitor standards, is currently being challenged, thus further separating the two functions. A similar dichotomy is less easy to create within a framework where the LEA, at least for pupils who are statemented under Section 7 of the 1981 Education Act, retains the direct responsibility for ensuring that appropriate provision is made. Until now its special schools and services have been the executive arm of that provision, but moves to delegate management to governors of special schools and to establish criteria for monitoring the standards of performance of special schools have a strong flavour of the purchaser-provider relationship which the introduction of self-governing trusts has generated within healthcare services.

Looking to the future, it is now not too far-fetched to predict a situation where competitive bidding will take place, not necessarily for pupils but for an LEA's envisaged requirements for its statemented pupils. This is already happening in a subtle form as LEAs conduct their policy reviews and determine the types and numbers of place elements which attach to their special schools. The bidding process is with us. Support services, too, will find themselves bidding: either for the continued patronage of their LEA or for funds which have been delegated to schools. Because these will not have been earmarked, the bidding process may have to run hand in hand with advocacy. Such services will have a role in keeping school's awareness of their responsibilities and duties in relation to special educational needs. Competitive tendering will inevitably mean that more independent organizations will gain a significant place in the spectrum of provision. We are seeing the start of it already; some LEAs are themselves now attempting to create businesses from their services which can operate within their remit but outside their budgetary restrictions.

If special educational needs provision finds itself, almost unawares, entering the arena of competitive tendering, what does the prospect hold? A look at other industries, both private and state-controlled, suggests that we can expect to find higher levels of competition, a greater concentration on productivity (often, unfortunately, crudely measured), more attempts at cost saving, more spent on accountancy and associated services, and more mergers and 'buyouts'. Already the last of these can be seen in the merging or 'rationalization' of some special schools and the creation of larger 'integrated' support services; buyouts, too, are beginning to be contemplated as some service personnel see the potential of working more independently, but without LEA facilitation in the form of appropriate delegation this area remains problematic.

Other features which often accompany competitive tendering are a reduction in the eagerness to pursue social values, greater rewards for top management in cash and in kind, an undermining of the influence of trade unions and greater reliance on unqualified or unskilled labour. Some of these are already starting to be apparent. It is not uncommon to find special school head teachers already making cases to their governors for salary increases once their schools have delegated budgets, while at the same time considering ways to reduce staff incentive allowances and appointing new staff whose low entry levels on the salary scale make them financially attractive. Such moves may be rationalized in terms of increased managerial responsibility and good housekeeping, but their implications for teamwork and morale may need to be looked at as well.

A further outcome may be an increasing tendency to offer solutions rather than services. This is already with us in special educational needs. When, for example, unqualified staff are ascribed to children whose problems call for skilled help, simply as an incentive for their retention in a particular school, such action may present a management solution rather than an educational service. The prospect of solutions may start to become seductive. As the future unfolds, educational psychology and special educational needs support services which have until now committed themselves to consultancy and teacher empowerment may find that they come under increasing pressure to offer quick 'remedies' for the problems which are encountered in schools rather than embarking on the lengthier process of helping those schools to examine their practices and develop their own strategies for avoiding or reducing such problems.

In the working lives of most readers of this book, there has never been a time when more skilled management is required than now to ensure that children with special educational needs are given adequate attention within our education service. We have grown used to seeing consistently greater priority and resources applied to this area. Now this is no longer the case. What happens in the next year or two will determine the structures with which we work as we enter the coming millennium. The energy, tenacity, flexibility and competence of those committed to working with and for children with special educational needs will be of more importance than ever in ensuring that those structures meet the children's needs and not somebody else's. It is hoped that the contents of this book will not only assist readers in developing appropriate strategies for the practice of management, but will help them to harness the qualities which are necessary to work effectively in a changing system.

Part I

The issues in context

Part 1

The issues in context

Chapter 1

Putting Circular 7/91 into practice for special schools

Adrian Fletcher.

Introduction

Local Management of Schools (LMS), one of the reforms introduced by the Education Reform Act 1988, aims to improve the quality of education by allowing most decisions about resource allocation to be taken within schools. It is being phased in to mainstream schools over several years.

Section 43 of the 1988 Act provided for the possibility of local management of special schools (for which we coined the term 'LMSS'), though the first LMS regulations did not permit it. During 1990 the DES asked Touche Ross to consider whether it would be feasible and desirable to allow LEAs who wished to do so to introduce LMSS. We spoke to schools , LEAs , inspectors, practitioners, civil servants, academics, and teachers' professional associations. Our report, which recommended that enabling regulations should be made, was announced and welcomed by John MacGregor in October 1990, and the relevant sections of DES Circular 7/91 draw on its recommendations.

This chapter describes the key elements of the Touche Ross report, considers the relevant provisions of Circular 7/91, and discusses some matters which LEAs may need to consider in responding to the Circular.

The Touche Ross report

What follows is a very brief summary of the key elements of our report. Readers requiring any detail should refer to the full document, available free from the DES (not from Touche Ross).

The two fundamentals of LMS are the delegation of management powers to school governing bodies, and the use of a systematic, published formula to determine the budget of each school. These two elements are not inseparable; in theory either or both could be extended to special schools. We therefore considered them separately.

Delegation

The principle of delegation is an accepted part of good management practice. Delegation can lead to improved performance when a central body defines clearly *what* an operating unit must do (the task it must perform, the budget within it must work, the criteria by which it will be judged) but leaves the unit flexibility and discretion as to *how* it goes about delivering the results required.

The two main statutes which underlie LMSS, the Education Act 1981 and the Education Reform Act 1988, set the framework within which delegation must work. Under the statutes, an LEA must plan and review its provision for special education, and issue statements of special educational need for pupils who need them; it must then determine what provision is needed for each child with a statement, and see that such provision is made available. Special schools must fulfil the roles assigned to them in the LEA's plan, and must meet the individual needs specified in each child's statement. We found no difficulty in differentiating the role of the LEA (planning, assessing, providing, and ensuring quality) and that of the school (delivering the provision specified by the LEA). The LEA defines the tasks to be performed, and the school decides how best to perform them. Delegated management fits readily into the statutory framework.

Schools will not have unfettered discretion under LMSS. They must meet individual pupils' statements, and they must have regard to guidance (such as that provided by DES Circular 11/90 on staffing) in deciding how to do so. They must also work within the bounds of the LEA's LMS scheme. But there remains great scope for creativity and initiative at school level.

The special school heads we spoke to during the study were generally keen to have the opportunity to manage their own budgets. Not only could they see ways in which they could handle their resources better, for example by using the funding of vacant teaching posts for other purposes; they believed that special school heads needed the same degree of management responsibility and flexibility as the principals of mainstream schools and FE colleges. Pilot special schools who already had delegated budgets (under other parts of the 1988 Act, and with limited powers) confirmed the benefits to be gained.

Delegation may not be appropriate for some individual special schools (such as, for example, very small schools). But the interviews left us in no doubt that there were schools and LEAs who saw delegation as an opportunity they would welcome. We could find no reason why they should not be given that opportunity.

Formula funding

If schools are to receive control over their budgets, there must be some system of determining what those budgets should be. We therefore had to consider whether a formula approach was in principle desirable and, if so, what form it should take.

The 1988 Act defines a formula as 'a body of rules, methods, and principles, however expressed'. This is hardly a restrictive definition; it merely requires that funding should be allocated in some systematic, open and explicable way. The virtue of a formula is that it provides a public statement of the principles used to fund schools, which can be debated, and that it relates funding to the present needs of schools rather that their past circumstances. It is hard to make a case for funding schools without reference to rules, methods, or principles.

However, any formula for funding special schools would have to take their particular roles into account. There was general agreement that the formulae used for mainstream schools could not simply be transferred to the special sector. A particular feature of mainstream LMS formulae is that they are 'pupil-led' - primarily based on the numbers and ages of pupils at each school - in order to give mainstream schools an incentive to attract and retain pupils under the system of 'open enrolment'. Such incentives are not appropriate for special schools; their role is to serve pupils assigned to them by the LEA, and the 1981 Act requires the LEA to place pupils in mainstream rather than special schools where practical. In addition, because of the small and unpredictable roles of many special schools, any pupil-led system of funding could lead to large swings in funding as pupils came and went, making it very difficult for schools to maintain a stable organization.

After an exploration of possible funding bases (described in our report) we proposed that funding formulae for special schools should be based primarily on the number of places for each broad type of need which the LEA had decided to maintain at each special school. Thus an LEA which decided to maintain a school with places for one hundred pupils with (say) moderate learning difficulties would fund the school on the basis of those hundred places, whether or not all the places were filled at any given time. Some additional funding would be provided on the basis of the number of pupils actually enrolled at the school, but the major part of the school's funding would follow directly from the LEA's decision to maintain a given number of places of a particular kind there.

There has been some debate as to whether classifying types of provision for funding purposes - in whatever way the LEA sees fit - is similar to the practice of categorizing pupils by need, deplored by the Warnock Report (DES, 1978). We argue in our report that, whilst each pupil's special needs are unique, individual special schools necessarily cater for groups of pupils whose needs are to some extent similar, and that a clear classification of types of provision will help rather than hinder individually considered decisions about where best to place each pupil.

Need for effective LEA planning

Clearly, this funding system relies heavily on the planning of provision by the LEA. It will not work effectively unless the LEA has a clear view of what special needs it must provide for and how it will meet each type of need. But such planning of provision is not a new responsibility. Section 2(4) of the 1981 Act requires every LEA to review its SEN provision periodically, and the House of Commons Select Committee on Education, Science, and the Arts noted in 1987 that a 'successful implementation of the 1981 Act is very much dependent on the development by an LEA of a clear and coherent policy, arrived at in a way which enables it to command the support of those - parents, teachers, and voluntary organizations - who are most affected by it'. Certainly it would be hard for the public to make sense of LMSS funding allocations without a proper understanding of the LEA's underlying special education policy. Now that many operational tasks have been delegated to schools and colleges under local management, strategic planning and special needs are among the most significant remaining central responsibilities of LEAs and they should now be able to give those tasks their full attention.

The key recommendations of our report, therefore, were that LEAs should be allowed to extend LMS to their special schools if they wished; that special schools should be funded primarily on the basis of the number of places for each type of need which LEAs had decided to maintain there; and that these numbers of places should flow from the LEA's special needs policy, a statement of which should be published as part of any proposals for LMSS.

Circular 7/91

DES Circular 7/91, published in April 1991, consolidates and develops various aspects of LMS in general, and describes the Government's intentions as to LMSS. The circular does not require LEAs to delegate management to special schools, but it does oblige all LEAs to develop a place-led formula to fund their special schools, to be implemented by April 1994. Formula proposals must be accompanied by a statement of the LEA's special needs policy. In addition, the Government intends to allow individual special schools to appeal to the Secretary of State for delegated management of their budgets, even if their LEA does not wish to delegate.

The provisions of Circular 7/91 regarding LMS in general will also have an impact on LEAs' policies for special needs. Circular 7/91 imposes new limits on the proportion of LEA budgets which can be retained to provide central services, including special needs support services. It also includes new guidance on LMS formulae which gives LEAs added flexibility in delegating funds to mainstream schools for pupils with special needs. Support services and mainstream special needs largely fell outside the scope of our original report, although they are often extremely important in LEAs' overall policies for special education. LEAs will therefore need to consider the possibility of changes to their SEN support services and to their mainstream LMS formulae (by April 1993 except in Inner London) and their proposals for special school funding (by April 1994). It would clearly be sensible to review these matters together.

LEAs should therefore:

- consider whether their policy for SEN provision needs review, particularly in the light of new LMS guidance;

- review that policy if necessary;

- develop a funding formula for their special schools;

- consider whether they wish to delegate management to all, some, or none of their special schools;

- be prepared to delegate management to individual special schools as the result of appeals, even if their general policy is not to delegate;

- make the necessary preparations for special school delegation.

Special school proposals must be submitted to the Secretary of State by September for implementation in the following April. Few LEAs are likely to have proposals ready by September 1991. Most will therefore submit their proposals in September 1992 or 1993. Many may wish to conduct pilot projects or experimental schemes before submitting their final proposals.

Developing the policy statement

In our view, the most important task facing LEAs is the review and development of their overall policy for SEN provision. Special school formula development and training for delegation (if required) will require significant effort, but they should be relatively straightforward tasks provided that a clear overall policy direction has been set. By 1994 LEAs will already have considerable experience of devising formulae and introducing delegated management, and that experience should help them greatly with special schools.

Circular 7/91 (paragraph 64) requires LEAs to provide a policy statement which covers:

- the arrangements for identifying children with SEN, including the part to played by LEA central staff, schools, district health authorities, social services departments and voluntary agencies;

- the role of primary, secondary, and special schools;

- the arrangements for providing education for children in hospital and at home, and for placing and monitoring pupils in independent and non-maintained special schools;

- the arrangements for co-ordination, including the management and availability of support services, and collaboration with neighbouring LEAs, SSDs [social services departments] and DHAs [district health authorities]; and

- the arrangements for:

  (i) monitoring the performance of all special schools and support services;

  (ii) ensuring that children with statements receive the provision specified in their statement;

  (iii) reviewing the appropriateness of that provision at least annually.

Circular 7/91 also requires LEAs to describe their arrangements for SEN provision, not to review or change them. However, in drafting the statement of their policy, LEAs may well want to take the opportunity to review whether their existing policies make the best use of available resources, and whether any aspects of their special needs services could be improved. The following are some of the questions which LEAs may wish to consider in such a review.

- *What does the LEA regard as a 'special need'?* The definition of special needs in the 1981 Act is capable of a range of different interpretations. Whilst there is an agreed core of requirements which are generally regarded as 'special needs', there are certainly some needs (such as those of dyslexic children, or especially gifted children) which some LEAs regard as 'special educational needs' and others do not. An LEA should be aware if it is taking a distinctive or unusual approach to particular needs, or if the mix of special needs it has to deal with is in some way unusual.

- *What is the demand for each type of provision, and is it changing?* By examining the rolls of its different schools and units over the years, LEAs may discover whether they have excessive provision for some needs and insufficient provision for others. Since the number of places needed for any particular need is impossible to predict precisely, the LEA will set its number of places for each type of provision at a level adequate to provide a reasonable level of 'insurance' against likely demand. LEAs will need to satifsy themselves that they are not 'over-insured' for needs which occur relatively rarely, nor 'under-insured' for needs which occur frequently.

- *Are the roles of mainstream support services, special units, and special schools clearly defined?* Many impairments, though similar in nature, occur at differing levels of intensity, giving rise to different needs; for example, visual and hearing impairments vary from the mild to acute. LEAs might therefore reasonably decide to maintain different services (such as support services, special units and special schools) to cater for similar impairments. At the same time, when different services do operate in the same broad area, LEAs will wish to ensure that the role of each service is clearly defined, and that the range of services they offer neither duplicates nor omits provision for any particular type and degree of need. They may also wish to consider how well mainstream schools, support services, special units, and special schools currently co-operate, and whether further co-operation could and should be encouraged.

- *How should the LEA co-operate with neighbouring LEAs?* It may not be necessary for an LEA to maintain its own schools in order to make adequate provision for particular needs. Where a suitable school for a particular need exists in another nearby LEA, it may be beneficial to send pupils there. If many pupils are sent to another LEA's schools it may be desirable to make formal arrangements for co-operative planning between the two LEAs. And where an LEA accepts significant numbers of pupils from other authorities, it will wish to satisfy itself that its arrangements for recoupment do fully reflect the costs it incurs.

- *How should the LEA work with other agencies?* Circular 7/91 requires the LEA to state how it will co-operate with social services departments, district health authorities, and voluntary agencies. A policy review will provide the opportunity to consider how well present arrangements for co-operation are working, and whether they might be improved.

- *How should the LEA use independent or non-maintained schools?* Many LEAs have looked carefully at placements in such schools in recent years, because they are often expensive. However, the high fees charged by such schools often reflect the high level of care required by the pupils for whom they cater. If an LEA has only a few children with particularly acute needs, it will wish to consider carefully whether or not it can make adequate provision for those children at lower cost than the non-maintained sector. Independent or non-maintained placements should not be used too regularly, but they may offer LEAs the most effective option for placing some children. LEAs may find it useful to develop guidelines as to the circumstances under which they will consider such placements.

- *What role do mainstream schools play in SEN provision, and are they fully aware of their responsibilities?* The 1981 Act imposes a general duty on LEAs to educate pupils in mainstream schools where this is practical. The advent of LMS in mainstream schools has brought a new awareness among mainstream governors of the needs, and the associated costs, of pupils with SEN. To ensure that integration is encouraged, LEAs will wish to be sure that they have taken full advantage of the provisions of Circular 7/91 as regards SEN funding in mainstream schools. They may also wish to consider providing training about special needs for mainstream school governors, to ensure that they are fully aware of their duties under the 1981 Act and their schools' place in the overall plan for SEN.

- *How well does the LEA's statementing process work?* It is well known that the number of statements of special educational need issued by different LEAs varies widely (c.f. *Education*, 15 February, 1991, p.43). In part, this may reflect differing views as to what needs can and cannot be met within the resources generally available to mainstream schools. We would not necessarily advocate either a high or a low level of statementing, but we would suggest that LEAs should be aware of whether they make few or many statements relative to other LEAs, and of what the policy reasons are which underlie their position. Whether an LEA issues few or many statements, it will also wish to be satisfied that its process for issuing statements operates as rapidly and smoothly as possible, and that the statements it produces are clear and useful.

- *How well does the LEA control the quality of special education?* Many LEAs will have reconsidered the role of their inspection and advisory services in recent years, prompted by the demands of LMS and/or by the Audit Commission's report on the subject. The process of ensuring quality in special education is undoubtedly more complex, requiring (for example) additional input from the educational psychology service, careful attention to see that individual children's statements are being met and the need to ensure quality in independent or non-maintained, as well as LEA, schools. The overall principles of setting evaluation criteria for each service and organizing an efficient service to see that they are met are the same, however, and it should be possible to build on previous work in developing quality control mechanisms for special education.

5. Developing the special school formula

Much of the debate about LMSS has focused on the funding formula. However, we believe that the funding method used for special schools must follow from the special educational policies which the schools exist to fulfil, and that the formula guidelines in Circular 7/91 are sufficiently flexible to support whatever policy the LEA determines. Given a clear policy, the task of constructing the formula will be fundamentally straightforward, though it will involve detailed technical work. The following are some questions which LEAs will need to consider in drawing up the formula.

- *What role (or roles) does each of our special schools fulfil?* The policy statement should have clarified this point. It should be noted that some special schools cater for more than one type of need; where this is so, LEAs will wish to fund more than one 'type of place' at each school.

- *What are the present costs of each of our special schools?* Before the implementation of mainstream LMS, LEAs often had to perform a good deal of accounting work to identify precisely which elements of their spending were attributable to individual schools. It may be necessary to conduct a similar exercise for special schools.

- *Are schools which meet similar needs currently similarly funded?* Depending on the LEA's policy, all or some of the needs met by any given special school may be regarded as similar to those met by other schools. In principle, places for similar needs should be similarly funded, unless there is a genuine reason for the difference.

- *Are the present differences in cost for schools meeting different needs reasonable?* LEAs will need to try to assess whether the relative costs of their different types of provision are reasonable. They may, for example, wish to refer to Circular 11/90 on staffing for special educational needs, and to assess whether the relative levels of staffing (and hence cost) in their special schools resemble those suggested by the Circular.

- *How many 'types of place' should we recognise?* Unless the answers to the previous questions have produced surprises, the LEA's policy should have clarified the different types of provision made, and this question should therefore be easy to answer.

- *What resources must each pupil and place factor cover?* Circular 7/91 does not contain precise mathematical guidance on the ratio between the place and pupil elements of funding, but it does provide very clear verbal advice, and effectively rules out any possibility of a 'pupil-led' formula. The bulk of funding is to be delivered through the place factor, and the pupil factor is normally expected to be low. LEAs may need to explain carefully to schools that the low level of pupil-based funding is compensated for by the high proportion of funding delivered through the place element.

- *How will the special school formula be integrated with the mainstream formula?* Special schools necessarily receive more funding than mainstream schools, and the publication of their budgets will make this fact more apparent. LEAs will need to be able to explain to mainstream school heads, governors, and parents the reasons for differences in funding. Whilst the main basis of funding will inevitably be different for the two sectors, LEAs may wish to consider using comparable arrangements for other factors, such as premises costs, in order to show that similar needs are being similarly funded. Our report contains an Appendix suggesting how different factors might be treated in this context.

- *What transitional arrangements are necessary?* Circular 7/91 allows LEAs to operate transitional arrangements until 1996, in order to phase in any changes in the funding of individual schools over a number of years. Even for LEAs who begin their schemes earlier than required, this transitional period will be shorter than that allowed for mainstream LMS. However, the design of mainstream LMS formulae necessarily resulted in some significant changes in many schools' budgets; nothing in the design of the LMSS formula need cause budgets to change, unless the LEA's review of its provision leads it to the view that some change is desirable.

Conclusion

The 1981 Act requires all LEAs to plan and review their provision for special educational needs. Circular 7/91 provides an opportunity for LEAs to bring those plans fully up to date and, if they wish, to extend the benefits of delegation to their special schools. Perhaps most importantly, it will bring special schools - sometimes seen as remote from the rest of the education service - into the same framework as other institutions, and encourage greater public debate about special educational policies.

As in all areas of their planning, LEAs will need to strike a balance between 'bottom-up' pressures (the levels of staffing and resources they would ideally like to provide) with 'top-down' pressures (the financial demands of other services, and the need to limit the level of local taxation). LMSS will have no effect on the overall level of resources made available for special education. The combination of delegated management and effective planning should, however, help to ensure that the best educational value is obtained for whatever money is spent.

Chapter 2

Special educational needs: a shift from the centre

Tony Bowers

Just when we start getting used to something, they go and change it. I thought the teacher making that complaint was bemoaning the fate of SATs at Key Stage 1, or maybe continuous assessment in GCSE following the Prime Minister's speech on the virtues of written examinations. But no, she was talking about the waning star of the General Schools Budget (GSB) and the loss of currency of the terms which had tripped neatly from her tongue since the publication of DES Circular 7/88, the statutory guidance from the Secretary of State in local management of schools (LMS). No longer would mandatory exceptions, unlimited discretionary exceptions and limited discretionary exceptions (the last with the dread prospect of reduction from a maximum of 10 per cent to 7 per cent within three years of an LEA's formula being accepted by the DES) be enough to juggle with. The new term Potential Schools Budget - or PSB for short - had entered her vocabulary.

Most readers will not need reminding that the GSB is the total amount of money which an LEA has to spend from its overall education budget on primary and secondary schools. There have been many elements of education outside this GSB, including such things as nursery education, student grants, further education (although recent proposals will remove FE from LEA's education budgets entirely), adult education and, of course, expenditure on special schools. Any expenditure on LEA services attributable to these elements on, for example, central administration, transport, educational psychologists, education welfare services and specialist teaching support, does not have to appear in the LEA's 'Section 42' statement, the statutory document which must be made available by the LEA for inspection at its education offices and public libraries. Only apportionment of such services to primary and secondary schools needs to be set against the GSB.

This GSB then has taken from it a whole range of sums which the LEA attributes to primary and secondary education. The cost of inspectors and advisers, central administration costs (which effectively means the running of LEA's education offices and services bought in from other departments such as the Architects' Department and the Treasurer's Department), and home to school transport are just three examples of these. Others relevant to the readership of this book are educational psychology (EP) services, advisory and support services for pupils with special educational needs (SEN), support for statemented pupils in mainstream schools, and education welfare services. The sum that is left is what is available to primary and secondary schools. This, the aggregated schools budget (ASB), is now apportioned to schools using LEA's formula.

Circular 7/91 heralds a number of changes. There are still substantial mandatory exceptions (sums which cannot be delegated to schools) formed by capital expenditure on, say, new school buildings, interest payments on debts the LEA has accrued on expenditure supported by government (e.g. GEST) and EC grants. Other items can, and probably will, be excepted by LEAs from the GSB: home to school transport, school meals, and transitional excepted items. What is left constitutes the PSB, and of this the LEA must by April 1993 (or 1995 for the inner London boroughs), delegate at least 85% to schools. This delegated figure, the ASB, itself has certain restrictions placed upon it.

Given the scope of this book, I shall not look at all aspects of Circular 7/91. Its main provisions, however, will impact heavily on those working with or for children with special educational needs. For many teachers, LMS, formula funding and delegated budgets are synonymous. However, formula funding merely points to a means of arriving at the allocation of resources to schools in a way which adopts a set of methods, rules or principles rather than the 'ad hoc' arrangements that existed in the past. The decision-making power concerning what to do with that budget has not automatically passed to schools unless they have fallen within the terms of Section 39 of the 1988 Education Act and are secondary schools or primary schools with rolls of at least 200. Many LEAs delegated budgets to smaller schools, but Circular 7/91 now requires this for all primary schools by April 1994. By then all schools will be able to decide how they set their priorities and spend their money.

Special schools

Delegation
Not quite all. The Circular, as most readers will know, requires LEAs to

create proposals which will extend formula funding to special schools. By April 1994, at the very latest, they will - unless a subsequent government rescinds the order - have to be funded through a formula. Certain guidelines are laid down for this, which we will look at shortly. As a result, special schools will come into the GSB and be funded out of the ASB. In some cases this may be achieved by April 1992, meaning that an LEA will have had to submit its proposals before anyone reads this chapter. To act this quickly is in my view unwise; time for reflection and consultation is needed to create a formula which is rational, clearly interpretable and likely to work. Because the Circular requires a thought-through policy statement (in Chapter 1 Adrian Fletcher explores some of the questions which need to be addressed in this) to accompany the formula proposal and because most LEAs' policy documents are either not sufficiently detailed or up-to-date, there is a risk that LEAs which hasten to introduce local management of special schools (LMSS) for April 1992 will find themselves with a less satisfactory mechanism than would have been acquired with a further year's planning.

Although formula funding will before long go hand-in-hand with delegation of budgetary management to even the smallest primary school, Circular 7/91 makes a strange distinction between mainstream and special schools. It does not require LEAs to delegate management of the budget to special school governing bodies. This might seem logical because, as the Touche Ross (1990) report points out, 'open enrolment' does not apply to special schools: they have to accept pupils assigned to them by LEA. Since such pupils can usually be expected to possess statements of special educational need under Section 7 of the 1981 Education Act, and since the LEA is responsible for seeing that the statement's provision is made available, a case could be made for the LEA retaining overall management of expenditure on staff, equipment, materials and so on. However, the Circular leaves it open to LEAs as to whether or not to delegate management to schools but then provides a loophole for special schools which want a delegated budget but have an LEA which wants them to wait. The school may apply to the Secretary of State for delegation, who 'will be willing to do so where he considers the school capable of managing its own budget' (paragraph 98). By implication some special schools may not be sufficiently capable, although even the tiniest primary school will be expected to deal effectively with a delegated budget. It seems strange to single out special schools in this way, unless the assumption is that special school governors may prefer the LEA to make their decisions for them.

The formula

The rationale for the formula components set out in paragraphs 79 - 93 of Circular 7/91 is provided in some depth by Touche Ross (1990). Clearly the notion that such a formula should be 'pupil-led', as with an LEA's mainstream formula, would make a nonsense of special schools' efforts to support pupils in the mainstream and to return children on their rolls to ordinary schools. This formula proposal, with three (or perhaps four) elements, is intended to allow an equitable distribution of resources whilst keeping market forces out of the equation.

Special school head teachers in many LEAs can be forgiven for assuming that much of the allocation of resources, in particular staffing, is a function of historical precedent and the whim of education officers. Anomalies abound in which schools of similar designation within the same LEA enjoy very different pupil-teacher ratios and have quite disparate allocations of ancillary assistance. A formula will not bring more money to special schools as a whole; it simply provides a method of distributing resources in a way which everyone can understand - even if they do not like it. Inevitably a formula will bring winners and losers; some schools which have prospered may find themselves with financial allocations which allow them less resources than they have become used to, while others may find that they can afford more than in the past. That is the theory, anyway.

Of the factors which can be included, the principal one is the 'place element'. The Circular declares (paragraph 82) that 'The LEA should identify as many place factors as are necessary to support the range of provision which its SEN policy requires'. This means that the LEA has to decide what it is going to call or how it will categorize the kinds of places it has at its special schools. In one way there is precise guidance: the value of a place factor should reflect the costs of staffing and equipment. In another, LEAs are left to their own devices because, apart from a reference to DES Circular 11/90 on staffing for special needs, the ways in which place factors might be differentiated or mixed within a school are not set out at all.

The other elements are labelled the 'pupil element', a 'premises element' and an optional 'outreach element' which was not in the Touche Ross report and which is looked at later in this chapter and in Chapters 7 and 8. Whereas the pupil element is the main component of the mainstream LMS formula, represented by the AWPU, Circular 7/91 expects this to be small within special schools, representing items which are actually expended on individual pupils other than on the running of the school. Since it is often very difficult to separate the marginal costs of an individual pupil from the running costs of the school it might have been better to ignore the notion of the pupil element entirely. There will, of course, be times when a particular pupil requires equipment or staffing resources which are quite exceptional even for a special school to provide, although a well-designed place element which is not exceeded should take that into account. There will also be times when a special school is asked to accept pupils beyond the number for which it is staffed; by their very nature, special schools have to provide flexible resources and to deal with unplanned-for admissions. However, these events should be taken account of within the 'contingency element' (which is likely not to be a true formula component). It is, for example, quite insufficient to assume that a limited pupil element will enable children to be placed in a school where the place element allocation is already filled. The problem here is that a contingency element returns us to the situation which largely prevailed before formula funding, where officers enjoyed discretion in resource allocation.

The place element

There are two main questions. Firstly, what should the different place elements be? Second, does the creation of a place element mean that special schools will not be forced into a competitive marketplace because their funding is not 'pupil-led' or 'numbers-driven'? Let's look at the second one first.

In theory, a school with a set overall place element (whatever the designation of sub-designations of this element) could run with significantly less pupils without suffering any financial loss other than that ensuing from the lack of the low-rated pupil element. The non-pupil-driven special school would then be free to receive pupils and to redirect pupils to mainstream in a financially unfettered fashion. Circular 7/91 sums it up well. 'The bulk of each special school's funding will normally be determined by the numbers and types of places which it is planned should be available at the school for that year, whether of not these places are occupied' (paragraph 84). However, the Circular also allows LEAs to set the place elements and therefore the funding of its special schools on an annual basis. When there is an overall cash-limited budget for special schools, it seems unlikely that in an annual review an LEA will generously allocate a high place element to a school which has not had sufficient take-up of its places in the previous year. It is equally unlikely not to come under strong pressure from a governing body to enhance the place element of a school which has been full or over its numbers. Whether we like it or not, special schools are likely to find their funding 'pupil-driven', even if the relationship between pupils and money is a little less stark in their case.

Returning to the first point, the designation of place elements is perhaps less vexed than deciding, once they're arrived at, what element a particular child should take up. The Circular suggests (paragraph 82) that LEAs 'may wish to be guided' by Circular 11/90. This sets out 'considerations', not regulations, for the proportions of teacher and 'special support assistant' (presumably this term covers nursery nurses and classroom or 'welfare' assistants) time in relation to five 'bands of learning difficulty'. These bands have been categorized as ' profound and multiple learning difficulties', 'severe communication difficulties', 'severe emotional and behavioural difficulties', 'severe developmental difficulties' and 'other learning difficulties'. Each of these is defined in some detail but unfortunately, like any attempt to categorize, it is not always easy to place a child in a given band; or put another way, it is only too easy to place some children in more than one. A recent survey of five SLD schools in one LEA, asking head teachers to place pupils in those bands, showed that one considered 100% to fall in the first band, another 98%, ranging through 64% and 37% to a mere 6% in the final school. To an outside but praticed observer the populations of these schools do not differ significantly; we therefore have either a problem of reliability of judgement among the various head teachers or that of some with a vested interest in making a case for placing as many pupils as possible in a band which generates the best ratio of resources to children.

Whatever hopes we may have for a policy review changing things, the fact remains that most LEAs have special schools in place which have not been designated according to Circular 11/90. They used to have terms such as ESM(M) and ESN(S) attached to them, and most now carry such designations as MLD, SLD, EBD, etc. Using the 'bands of learning difficulty' means that there is room for debate over how many bands cut across a particular school's current population and the kinds of provision which it has geared itself to make. It is unlikely that any LEA will make a fresh start on provision; historical factors will impact upon place elements and it may be a tempting prospect simply to designate place elements which correspond to the typologies currently used within an LEA's special school system. It's quite simple: if a child attends an MLD school, then it takes up an MLD place element, and so on.

Although this is likely to happen is some LEAs, it would be a pity not to take the opportunity which a policy review presents to look very closely at what special schools offer and whether in fact schools with common designations are serving similar populations of pupils or are delivering the curriculum in similar ways. In the LEA quoted above, the unit cost of MLD school staffing varied from £3,360 to £4,730. This may be because one school was more favourably staffed than another, because they were similarly staffed but one had less expensive teachers and SSAs, or because there was a tendency to send children whose needs fell into different areas, yet still under the overall 'MLD' umbrella, to each of the schools. There is no doubt that many of the administratively convenient terms for special schools mask wide variations of needs within them. An effective formula, even if the LEA retains the terminology, should reflect the variability of the educational requirements of pupils within one type of school.

A further difficulty, not addressed directly in Circular 7/91, is that the creation of two formulae within an LEA - the mainstream LMS formula and the LMSS formula - will inevitably sharpen the distinction between special educational needs provision in the two. Special schools have come to be seen as just one part of the continuum of provision, but unless there is some commonality between any formula provision for statemented pupils in mainstream schools and in special schools, any financial continuum will be absent. Nicholson (1991) has pointed to the problem which such a rift poses for joint funding. The factors which influence placement decisions often imply that pupils attending special schools have needs which require higher levels of resourcing than those remaining in the mainstream, although this is not always the case. It would be difficult to argue reasonably for one suggestion which I have heard within an LEA: giving a set sum, regardless of need, for each statemented pupil attending either mainstream or special schools. This clearly ignores the wide range of learning difficulties and resultant needs which can lead to the maintenance of a statement. On the other hand, some form of funding comparability will need to be established for statemented pupils, not to act as a yardstick for determining placement but to allow for the monitoring of the efficiency with which resources are used.

What a place element represents is answered by Circular 7/91: staffing and equipment costs and, in the case of residential schools, the cost of 24-hour care. The critical question which follows this is how many place elements are necessary to support the range of provision which the LEA's SEN policy requires? Finally, the LEA has to determine the value which needs to be assigned to each place element. One LEA is currently considering three place elements which cut across the mainstream/special school devide. It defines these in some detail, terming them 'Significant learning difficulties', 'Severe learning difficulties' and 'Multiple learning difficulties'. The implication is that in order to be statemented, a child will have significant learning difficulties, and this band or element will encompass many of the pupils found in both mainstream and special schools. The other two elements, while they might be found within some integrated settings, are more likely to apply to special schools. This LEA expects that from an effective policy review the types and numbers of place elements which can be served by both special and mainstream schools can be arrived at and, by an analysis of the SEN budget across the spectrum of provision, a value can be attached to each place element.

The pupil element

Mainstream LMS is driven by pupil numbers and their ages. Until now at least 75% of the allocation to schools had has to be on that basis and by April 1992 that figure increases to 80%, although with some modifications to the requirements of Circular 7/88. While I have pointed earlier to the flaw in assuming that the LMSS formula will not ultimately be pupil-led I have found in some special school managers the misconception that once place element numbers have been arrived at for their schools, they will still be able to bargain over which kind of element a child entering the school will occupy. This seems to be based on the idea that more funds could arrive with one pupil that with another, returning us, of course, to a directly pupil-driven system. A more reasonable assumption is that a special school which found itself, through some shift from the LEA's SEN policy, with a population which was not reflected in its place element allocation, would make a case for a change in the annual review of the types and numbers of places provided at its schools. Any shorter-term compensation would have to be built into the pupil element or would more probably come via the contingency funds which an LEA will have to hold in reserve.

Although I have questioned whether a small pupil element can form a useful component for a formula, it will provide a vehicle for age-weighting if LEAs wish to operate this component. Age-weighting in mainstream schools, of course, tends to provide more favourable funding as pupils get older; whatever we think of the logic attaching to it, most LMS formulae provide significantly more for secondary-aged pupils than they do for primary ones, with incremental increases at particular year bands. On admission to a secondary school a pupil will not carry the funds which will be allocated for him or her in later years, but the school can make reasonable projections based on the continued attendance of most of its pupils. It would probably not be desirable to encourage special schools to make such projections or to encourage the retention of pupils because their continued attendance would bring incremental increases in funding. Also, in many cases greater staffing resources are required for younger pupils in special schools than for older ones, although the term 'young' may better be described in developmental than in chronological terms.

Outreach

The proposals in the draft circular published at the end of 1990 took little note of the work done by many special schools in providing support for children with special educational needs in mainstream schools in various ways. These include direct teaching, the provision of ancillary assistants, advice to mainstream staff, the preparation of materials and the provision of INSET. All these tend to go under the umbrella title of 'outreach'. There is often little distinction between such outreach and the work of some LEAs' support services for children with special educational needs. Indeed, in many LEAs the two have developed side by side and their efforts have not always been as well coordinated as they might have been.

As a result of representations, Circular 7/91 allows LEAs to 'designate certain places at some of all of its special schools as bearing enhanced funding in respect of special outreach work' (paragraph 88). However, much outreach of the kind described has been on an informal or semiformal basis: special school staff have often assisted pupils in mainstream schools, sometimes with statements and sometimes without, while the pupils remained on the rolls of those schools. No specific financial resources have usually been provided, although there has been a tendency for the LEA to maintain adequate staffing levels in such special schools to enable outreach to occur. In some cases, particularly where specialist outreach for, say, children with visual impairment has gone on across LEA boundaries, the process has been more formalized with money actually changing hands; but this has not been the norm. Now for outreach to be quantified through the LMSS formula, there is the implication that a pupil with SEN who is still on the roll of the school will either be 'double-funded', receiving assistance from two sources - the mainstream school and the special school - or that the requirement for outreach assistance will be written into the statement, in which case the special school's outreach service will effectively assume the role we have come to expect of a centrally-provided support service.

The advantage that special schools will have over such support services is that they are not centrally-funded. At present they are outside the GSB and it is interesting to see that some LEAs have actually amalgamated all or part of their support services with one or more of their special schools. This has the effect of removing them from the LEA's Section 42 statement at a stroke, and placing their funding outside the GSB even though they are working with schools and pupils who are subject to the provisions of LMS and to whom the GSB applies. One small north-east London borough, for example, has created a very large school for emotionally and behaviourally disturbed children within which it has administratively absorbed its support teachers working with such pupils. The effect of this is to remove such services from being designated discretionary exceptions, a move which may owe more to administrative expediency than to educational foresight. Of course, LMSS will bring special schools within the GSB, not as exceptions to it, but as part of the ASB allocation. Support services run as outreach services from special schools will therefore have a new advantage over central SEN support services: that of appearing within the ASB and not being scrutinized as exceptions to delegation, with the cash limits which that status implies.

Special schools and the GSB

At the time of writing, no special schools come within their LEA's LMS scheme. There are, of course, a number of 'pilot' schemes in different LEAs, usually involving a budget being delegated to the school and managed by the school's governors. This, as Judith Charlesworth points out in Chapter 5, is not true LMS but is more closely akin to the local financial management (LFM) which we saw in a few LEAs before the 1988 Education Act.

The effect of special schools lying outside the GSB has been to enable LEAs to hold back some of the costs of services (e.g. educational psychologists, specialist support teachers and educational welfare services) which work with special schools. In many cases this has been done conscientiously, but notional apportionment on a generous basis has also been possible; where this has been done it has enabled an LEA to reduce the size of discretionary exceptions to delegation which appear in its Section 42 statements. A survey of outer London boroughs for the year 1990/91, for example, showed two LEAs' designations of only around 20 per cent of the costs of their EP services to the GSB, while another set the whole of the cost of its EP service within the GSB. Unless there is very considerable variation in the ways in which services operate from one LEA to another, the reason for the discrepancies discovered stems from accounting procedures. This creative approach to accounting will not be as easy to adopt with the advent of LMS. What could previously be placed outside the GSB because of attribution to special schools will now have to appear as an exception to delegation within the maximum figure of 15% which can be centrally retained.

This has had the effect of causing some LEAs to look either to reduce the number of central support staff or to find ways of delegating their costs to the schools and to create mechanisms for those schools to repurchase the services. A number of chapters in this book explore these issues and I will not repeat them here. What is interesting is that while the costs of such services lie almost entirely within the GSB and so are subject to scrutiny as exceptions, money spent on placing pupils in schools maintained by other LEAs or to independent or non-maintained special schools will still remain outside the GSB and so not be the subject of regulation.

One problem which may arise for special schools in some LEAs is that potentially they can be used as a means of 'earmarking' services which are apparently delegated, with the costs which that implies. It is possible for an LEA to delegate a budget to the school but then, through the requirements of the statement, recover certain sums from the school. For example, Circular 7/91 requires (paragraph 60) special school governing bodies to 'ensure that the provision specified in statements is made available'. This is entirely reasonable, since the 1981 Education Act places this duty on the LEA: in delegating funds, as I suggest in Chapter 8, it is questionable whether it can also delegate responsibility. What this means in practice, however, is that attendance of a member of the LEA's central staff at review meetings, particularly where this is written into the statement through a phrase such as 'Should be kept under review by a member of the LEA's educational psychology service', could be chargeable to the school. Until now this may have been done on a notional basis; however, if LEAs use historical budgets to determine the pool for future formula distribution, special schools may find themselves with costs which are difficult to avoid but which have not been built into the budget from which their funding is calculated.

Delegating funds for statemented pupils

At the time of writing, most LEAs have not delegated to schools any of the funds available for making available the resources specified in statements. This means that when a child, through the statement, is provided with, say, a part-time classroom assistant, the funds for meeting the costs of that assistant are directly provided by the LEA and not debited against the school's allocation under LMS. The classroom assistant in such a case is 'earmarked' to the child, although the day-to-day management of that assistant in practice usually passes to the school and there is not always the one-to-one relationship that such earmarking might be thought to imply (c.f. Clayton, 1989). Funds for statemented pupils in mainstream schools and in most units therefore form part of the discretionary exceptions to delegation retained by the LEAs - and join the other discretionary exceptions as subject to present spending limits.

Some LEAs (10 out of those in England and Wales were quoted in a Parliamentary response on 17 December 1990) have found ways of delegating some or all of the funding for statemented pupils to schools. Circular 7/91 (paragraphs 100-102) is remarkably ambiguous: more so than in its draft state. It quotes pupils in special units and special classes as desirable targets for delegation, under the heading 'Pupils with statements'. This neglects the fact that many pupils with statements in mainstream schools are educated alongside those without and are not necessarily to be found in unit or special class provision. However, given that not delegating funds for statemented pupils will entail those funds remaining as exceptions to the PSB (i.e. within the maximum 15% which can be held centrally), we can expect may LEAs actively to consider developing the means of delivering such resources to schools. The publication of a DES league table on this seems to have concentrated the minds of many LEA officers.

Details of some models of delegation in use have already been published. Evans and Lunt (1990) give us a picture of the structure proposed by Leeds. Here schools are allocated a base budget for SEN, regardless of how many pupils have statements. This is not unusual. Circular 7/88 allowed up to 25% of the budget allocations to schools to be based on considerations other than age-weighting, and Circular 7/91, while tightening this to 20%, has allowed the SEN element (not statement-related) to be counted within the weighted pupil component (i.e. the 80%). Beyond this, children who are statemented are allocated, on the basis of the statement, a number of 'units of SEN' which can apparently range from 1 to 10, depending on the level of resourcing required. Variants of this totting-up structure, of course, have been used in Canada; problems of who is the arbiter of the number of units ascribed to a statement, and of an increasing incentive for schools to seek statementing for pupils, are two which spring readily to mind. Evans and Lunt (1990) report that the 'units of SEN can be increased or decreased in monetary terms in relation to the total number of units in the system and the budget set by the authority' (p.26). This totalizator principle means that the more units there are in a system the less each one will be worth. Unless closely monitored, one conesquence might be a demand for more units to attach to a statement to compensate for the inflationary effects of too many units within the system.

Looking at the same LEA, Evans and Lunt (1990) provide us with an account of delegated funding for special units and 'resourced schools'. A pupil-teacher ratio is set which depends on the category of learning difficulty served. In each case the first pupil attracts 25 'units of SEN', then subsequent pupils bring nothing until that ratio is achieved. After that, the next pupil attracts a further 25 and the sequence is repeated. Another model for inclusion of units , assessment classes and 'support bases' was put forward by Cleveland LEA early in 1990. In a manner reminiscent of the place element proposed in Circular 7/91, the LEA sets the capacity for each unit, sets a capitation level which is capacity-related rather that pupil-related, and provides clerical time above a certain capacity level. Additional pupils above capacity attract the usual AWPUs. A staffing formula for teachers and auxiliaries, related to capacity level, type of resource and age of pupils is converted to actual financial allocation by computing the average salary of special unit teachers (currently on Incentive 'B'path).

It is interesting to note that Cleveland's guidance points out that whilst schools have to protect the salaries of existing staff, they could in future advertise unit posts with less than Incentive B allowance. This is of course the school's prerogative; delegation implies that salaries cannot be earmarked. However, by reducing the salaries of its own unit staff, the average of unit staff salaries will become depressed, with a consequent reduction in overall allocations. This is one of the difficulties of delegation where head teachers or governors may not place high value on the activity of special needs specialists who have in the past had their salaries and other costs safeguarded by central retention. An article by Fielding (1991), a secondary school head, exemplifies this. Faced with an English vacancy, his management team has a good idea. The schools's special needs teacher is an English specialist, and so she takes over the post 'so we could use the spare capacity of several other teachers to do her job' (p.26). This view of the special needs teacher's role, often in learning support, in the mainstream being acceptably filled by teachers giving up timetabled non-teaching periods is a depressing one but one which may be expedient for many heads. In Chapter 3, Gail Treml warns against such an approach, but it may be one which we will increasingly see displayed.

The press for statementing

The generally made prediction that LMS will lead to a greater call for statementing tends to be borne out by reports from LEA officers. Published statistics are harder to draw conclusions from. Evans and Lunt's (1990) quote from their national survey an average rate of statements in relation to the school population as 2%. A year later, Mittler (1991) gives us a national average of 1.72%. Evans and Lunt's (1990) highest and lowest rates are 5.4% and 1.2% respectively, whilst Mittler (1991) offers 3.98% and 0.62%. These data do not suggest an increase over the year, although information provided by some inner London boroughs indicates that both sets of maxima are being exceeded.

There does seem to be quite compelling statistical evidence that the number of pupils being statemented is increasing in many LEAs. Nicholson (1991), for example, cities data from Sheffield and Sefton to support this. An increase in statementing for mainstream pupils can have many causes, of course. It is often attributed to parental or school pressure on the LEA, but it may simply be a shift in the balance previously established; I have spoken recently to SEN co-ordinators who, in putting pupils forward for assessment, have been told by their EPs to trim numbers considerably, and have effectively been told of the level at which the LEA will 'statement-cap' their school. This tension is probably inevitable when additional resources - and possibly delegated money - attach to a statement.

Mittler (1991) has proposed several possible reasons for the reported increase in statementing, none of them incompatible with one another: the tolerance thresholds of schools reduced by the pressures brought about by the 1988 Education Act; pupils with SEN less welcome than before; schools less willing to resource special needs from within their own budgets; a willingness to keep children with special educational needs only if they receive additional funds through the statement. From one perspective we could see any increased demand for statements as somebody's bad management: that of the head teacher for not ensuring that the school is adequately equipped and organized to meet the needs of most of the children who attend it, or that of the LEA for not providing adequate intervention or advice early enough to prevent the need for a statement. From another point of view it can be seen as appropriate for a school's head teacher who is conscientious to seek every means at his or her disposal to obtain additional resources to bolster the cash limits imposed by the LEA's formula-related distribution. In the past, negotiation, persuasion and a reliance on good relationships would suffice. Now a more legalistic approach is required.

As I explore more fully in Chapter 8, statements enjoy a legal status which, to those concerned with making legal judgements, distinguish between children with learning difficulties for whom the school must take responsibility within its own resources (those without statements) and those for whom the LEA is obliged to provide additional assistance (those with statements). This model presupposes that problems reside within the child and that all schools make similar efforts to differentiate the curriculum for all children with special educational needs. In practice, of course, the conscientious school which takes its responsibilities to all its pupils seriously will be far less likely to have children who require statements: its curriculum and staffing will be geared in such a way that additional resources are less frequently required. The apparently clear distinction between non-statemented and statemented children is a chimera; the interaction between the school and its children will determine the need for a statement, and inevitably this will be influenced by the reward system which the school perceives. If resources are seen to be dwindling, a diligent manager will probably seek ways to hold on to as many as he or she is able. A recent account by a head teacher (Adey, 1991) sums this up: effective integration is expensive.

Grant-maintained schools

These schools still only form a tiny minority of the total number of the 25,000 or so in the public sector. At the time of writing, 60 schools are grant-maintained, but now primary schools are able to apply and there are clear financial incentives for schools to 'opt out' of LEA control. Each one of them will have pupils with special educational needs.

Education Minister Michael Fallon has recently indicated (Sharron, 1991) that a fresh wave of ballots to opt out is expected after the next election (assuming the same government is in power) and has suggested that new organizational structures would be created if a significantly large number of schools attained grant-maintained status. Grant-maintained schools receive from the DES an Annual Maintenance Grant (AMG) which is made up of what it terms its 'budget share' (Circular 21/89) of the GSB determined by the LEA in which it is situated. This AMG consists of what the school would have been apportioned from the ASB if it were still within the LEA, together with a further apportionment from the GSB made on the assumption that the school is no longer in receipt of centrally-provided LEA services. The government pays the AMG to each school but receives the money from the school's former LEA. At the time of writing this figure is 16% and the cause of a number of problems for LEAs which are intent on delegating centrally-retained services. If they delegate all available funds to schools and then are faced with some schools opting to be grant-maintained, there will be insufficient money held at the centre to meet the additional apportionment to those schools.

This anomaly will clearly have to be addressed, since it militates against delegation. It does, though, provide us with an example of the low esteem with which LEAs seem currently to enjoy within government circles. Sharron's (1991) interview with Michael Fallon has produced such quotes as 'I don't think we lose much sleep fretting over the future of the LEAs', and 'It would be hard to plan the present education system worse than the councils have done since the war' (p.17).

In the field of special educational needs, LEAs still have responsibilities even when a school becomes grant-maintained. Circulars 10/88 and 21/89 spell these out in detail, but they break down to a continuing responsibility to provide educational psychology services and education welfare services to grant-maintained schools at the same level that they would to their own schools. The LEA's responsibilities apply to children who are statemented on entry or who may be statemented whilst there. Circular 21/89 puts this clearly, seeing any additional support as a result of the statement 'as a service to the individual pupil which remains the responsibility of the authority' (paragraph 61). This circular provides an incentive for LEAs to delegate some or all the costs of services and meeting statements to schools in their area through the ASB (and presumably then charging for any provision which its own services still provide) in that by doing so they will not have to meet these costs in their area's grant-maintained schools. However, the more recently announced 16% additional apportionment means that such provision will effectively be double-funded.

What happens in practice? I recently looked at one of the largest comprehensive schools (2,200+ pupils) to opt for grant-maintained status. It had, in the financial year 1990/91, 91 statemented pupils. In addition to the AWPU allowances for these, it received approximately £15,000 as additional 'per capita' monies in respect of the statements. Historically it has acted as an area resource designated as experiencing Moderate Learning Difficulties, Specific Learning Difficulties, Hearing Impairment and Speech and Language Disorders and so, in addition to the above, received a further £207,000 as departmental resource allocations. In that year the school provided the equivalent of 15 full-time teachers, 10 welfare assistants and a clerical assistant which, given that all these pupils were accessing the normal school curriculum and therefore using other resources, meant that the school was experiencing a financial shortfall. However, most of the SEN staff worked not only in support of statemented pupils, and apportionment of their time to pupils whose needs the school was directly responsible suggested that the school was a net beneficiary of the additional funding for statemented pupils.

There was an evident tension between the school's community-based approach in which they saw all pupils in their area as potential clients, and the message which parents of pupils already statemented seemed to be receiving from the LEA. They had been informed that they had no right to choose their child's school and that it was for the LEA to determine provision. While in practice many statemented pupils whose parents wanted this school actually were placed there, the school was made aware that the LEA and not the parent was the customer or, in the language used in Chapter 8, the purchasing element of the client system. After that, however, the only monitoring that went on was the receipt of reports at the review by an LEA educational psychologist.

Educational psychologists appeared to be the only service which supported the school in its work with pupils with special educational needs. LEAs have a statutory obligation, spelled out in paragraph 64 of Circular 10/88, to secure provision for both statemented and non-statemented pupils 'in such a way that they treat the pupils at a grant-maintained school no less favourably than those at schools which they maintain'. This seemed to be being done, although a move to delegate the costs of EP services through the ASB would mean that this grant-maintained school would have to purchase their services of those of other EPs - or do without them. The school seemed to value the assistance it received from two EPs with whom it had an established relationship, and it seemed likely that it would be prepared if necessary to enter into a service agreement with them or with their employers. Other specialist services seemed to be of little interest to this school;

given its ample staffing, the SEN coordinator took the view that most learning difficulties, including those arising from sensory impairment, could be dealt with internally.

While services may be able to draw some implications from the brief account above, it has to be remembered that large schools have always tended to be more self-contained because of the generosity of their resources and the opportunity to offer financial incentives to particular staff members. As smaller schools become grant-maintained, however, they may find it financially advantageous to rely on outside advice and support rather than employing their own staff.

LMS and SEN support services

Several chapters in this book look closely at the implications of LMS and the contents of Circular 7/91 for support services. I will not dwell on the issues here. There has been a tendency for support services to see full or partial delegation of their funds to schools through the ASB as the beginning of the end for them. That may be so, but as I argue in Chapter 8, central retention may in the medium term carry more risks. There are already examples of centrally-funded services for SEN being trimmed or cut entirely, their staff offered for redeployment to mainstream schools, redeployed to posts - such as those in special schools - which still lie within the management control of LEAs, or offered redundancy.

The somewhat equivocal pronouncement in paragraph 108 of Circular 7/91 that LEAs 'will wish to consider carefully the impact' of delegation of the costs of centrally managed support teams underlines what has for long been recognized: members of such teams can enable and empower schools to meet the needs of the often considerable number of pupils who have learning or emotional difficulties. In many cases, their efforts and the time allocations at their disposal prevent the need for the LEA to carry out a formal assessment of a child and to issue a statement under Section 7 of the 1981 Education Act. However, this sits uneasily with a fundamental tenet of LMS: that schools themselves, through their governing bodies, should be responsible for determining the allocation of resources within the school and should be accountable to parents for the progress of all their pupils. This applies particularly in the case of pupils for whom no statement has been issued. Unfortunatly, the drafting of the 1981 Education Act, in response to which many SEN support services have been developed, could take no account of the 'reforming' nature of the 1988 Act which was to follow it. At the beginning of the 1980s, LEAs were seen as central policy makers and planners of provision. That is no longer the case.

Even if the current policy of its LEA is to retain SEN support services centrally, a forward-looking management will be considering ways of moving that service towards a structure which can, if required, be quite easily modified to deal with future delegation. Some of the moves that can be made are:

(i) the development of operationally effective contracts or service agreements with schools;

(ii) the conduct of an internal audit, looking at what the service's members have to offer and what needs to be done;

(iii) the development of budgetary procedures which allow an awareness of the true costs of the service;

(iv) close oversight to ensure that the service's resources are used efficiently;

(v) determining what 'quality of service' means and developing ways (e.g. quality circles) of ensuring that it is sustained and improved;

(vi) creating an awareness in members of who their 'customers' are and developing an ethos of customer care;

(vii) developing a marketing plan within the service which takes account of the above points;

These are all points which are taken up within subsequent chapters and which are developed in more detail in Bowers (1991c). A service which relies on the retention of power in the centre, a situation which we became used to in the 1980s, may not find itself sufficiently flexibly placed to deal with the changes which are likely to come.

Educational psychology (EP) services

These are also considered in other chapters in this book, and many of the points made above may apply them. Interestingly, I have found EPs more ready to consider the prospect of working in a situation where their costs are delegated to schools than many SEN support teachers, although no moves so far have been made by most LEAs either to reduce their EP services or to devolve any part of them to schools. EP services have several advantages: they tend to be smaller and therefore less expensive than the sum of an LEA's SEN support services; they have established a statutory role in conducting assessments for the LEA under Section 5 of the 1981 Education Act; and some of their work has legitimately been attributable to activities which do not need to fall within the GSB and therefore do not need to be excepted from it. They have also, for many schools, retained a mystique which has not attached to other LEA services for pupils with special educational needs. This may be ascribable to their label, their role, their accessibility or to a combination of factors, but it has led, as I report in

Chapter 8 and Ruth MacConville confirms in Chapter 11, to a high level of demand for them being shown in the results of recent surveys of mainstream schools.

Much of the work which EPs do is 'non-statutory', although it is difficult at times to determine where the statutory role, in terms of assessment and advice to the LEA, separates from the non-statutory. The statutory component is based upon an assumption that a child needs assessing before prescriptive recommendations are made, although this runs counter to the prevailing view of many EPs that the child is only one element in an interactive system and that therefore other elements - for example teacher expectations, teaching style, classroom management, suitability of written materials - also bear assessment and are potentially modifiable for the benefit of the child. It would be untrue to say that all EPs see their role similarly, but many do not see themselves as clinicians whose focus is simply a particular child; a knowledge of school and classroom organization, the requirements of the National Curriculum and the educational climate and culture in which the child functions are equally important. This educational awareness is not, however, given much priority in a recent statement by Michael Fallon of the DES (Sharron, 1991) who is quoted as saying that schools will 'have the money to purchase services and if their LEA can't provide those services, they can purchase them from another public body if they like. They can use the hospital psychologist for example, they can purchase private services' (p.18). From this it seems that clinical psychologists, or indeed any psychologists, are going to be acceptable to the present government for fulfilling the role that EPs have seen as their own.

It is easy to see how the costs of EPs could be delegated to schools, but less easy to tell how the schools would use that money. One view, expressed in an article by Gold (1991), is that schools will purchase EP services which are 'useful' to them but which may not be in the best interests of the child. Another is that by paying the piper a school could call the tune on the advice resulting from a psychological assessment. By working for the LEA, the EP can view the child as client; if the school pays, it becomes the client. The first two views, however, place a low premium on the professionalism and integrity of both psychologists and teachers, while the third oversimplifies the present situation. The management structures in most LEAs are such that Principal EPs report to senior officers who are responsible for deploying resources. The ability to provide unfettered advice, and still less executive power to work in the best interests of their client the child, are not commonly enjoyed by LEA EPs.

Like SEN support services, EP services would be wise to be proactive in considering ways in which at least part of their work can be delegated to schools. It may seem safer to remain centrally funded, working in what is effectively a command economy with a group of client schools which has little choice in the service or the personnel it receives. This presupposes, however, that delegation can always be staved off; if it can't, the service may not be well placed to assist the incursion of more market-aware services in other LEAs or from the expanding private sector.

It is not always easy to differentiate between some of the non-statutory work of EP services and that of SEN support service staff. Many of the techniques and models of working employed by the two groups are similar although, as the HMI (1990) report makes clear, there is usually a greater variability in the work patterns of EPs. Unless effective lines are drawn of collaborative ways of operating are found, it is conceivable that in a delegated system we may find EP services competing with support services for the same clients. The issue of 'mission', considered in Chapters 9 and 11, is one which both sets of services will need to address.

Education welfare services

Education welfare officers (EWOs) or education social workers (ESWs) do not, of course, confine their activities to pupils with special educational needs. In nearly all LEAs they are funded as discretionary exceptions within the GSB although an apportionment can be made outside this for their work with special schools. Paragraph 78 of Circular 7/91 points out that with LMSS this apportionment will not be possible; education welfare services will then, if not delegated, form part of the maximum 15% of the PSB which may be retained centrally.

Circular 11/91 attempts to discriminate between 'authorized' and 'unauthorized' absences and is a prelude to the required publication by schools of unauthorized absences. Dry (1991) has provided a cogent critique of the draft proposals, pointing to ways in which schools can and do effectively collude with pupils to produce optimally low figures for unauthorized absence. He argues that if the costs of welfare services were delegated to schools, choice of a service might be determined not by its effectiveness in resolving poor attendance but by its willingness to turn 'a blind eye to truancy and let them get away with authorizing as many unjustified absences as possible' (p.88). What he calls for is a monitoring and inspection role for EWOs who are employed by the LEAs in which the schools are situated; but while this certainly fits in with models which we are used to, it may not be in keeping with the current government push to move inspection of schools out of the direct control of local authority personnel.

Local authorities, of which the LEA is a substantial element, have many new duties under the 1989 Children Act which came into force in 1991. A detailed examination of these lies outside the scope of this book but the Act has considerable significance to those working in the field of special educational needs. The pack produced by the National Children's Bureau (1991) provides a useful working introduction to this legislation. The bulk of the responsibilities of the local authority will fall upon its Social Services Department, but it is usually thought that the seeking and administration of Education Supervision Orders under this Act will fall upon the LEA and be delegated to its educational social work team. Although this involves considerable contact with schools, it is not part of the school inspection role alluded to by Dry (1991). The supervisor is obliged to advise, assist and befriend the child and the child's parents, giving directions that will, in his or her opinion, secure that the child is properly educated. Outside the key question of whether or not education supervision orders will work, it appears difficult for an LEA to delegate this responsibility to schools and there is a strong case for central retention of education welfare services. However, Allen (1990), pointing to the potential confusion of roles between ESWs and social workers, has indicated that Education Supervision Orders might fall within the province of Social Services personnel and not those of the LEA. Under these circumstances, delegation of the costs of education welfare services becomes possible but is likely to remain a difficult and contentious issue.

Monitoring and evaluation

Until recently, the issue of monitoring the performance of an LEA's schools had one fairly simple component. It might be complicated to find 'performance indicators' which were valid and acceptable to all, it might be ultra-simplistic to assume that attendance rates, SAT data or examination results provided suitable yardsticks of educational effectiveness, but it was quite straightforward to decide who would do it: the LEA's inspectors. Where children with special educational needs were involved, particularly in the case of special schools, the LEA's inspector for SEN would usually play a large part. Two recent developments complicate the matter now. The first is the trend in many LEAs to dispense with an inspector with a specific designation for SEN; given the requirements of the National Curriculum there is an expectation that all inspectors should have an awareness of and competence in working with pupils with special educational needs. This may or may not be true in practice, but it has become less relevant due to the second development: the announcement from the DES in August 1991 that schools would be permitted to buy in inspectors from inspection teams which could be from the private sector, which would be licensed to inspect and which should not consist exclusively of those with educational experience.

By the time this chapter is published there will doubtless be further clarification on this matter. It does, though, leave some confusion over the ways in which LEAs will set out the arrangements for monitoring the performance of their special schools as required by specifications for a policy statement set out in paragraph 64 of Circular 7/91. Do the government's intentions include special schools? Will we see schools for pupils with severe learning difficulties having their classroom organization and curriculum delivery inspected by local businessmen? How meaningful will the approaches adopted by many special schools be to those whose experience of school does not extend to working even within the mainstream?

LEAs are also required by Circular 7/91 to set out the arrangements for monitoring their support services. This has already been tackled by some authories. The London Borough of Bexley, for example, has produced a document which sets down the criteria for inspection of its support services by its own inspectorate. The details are broken down into two broad bands: *'provision'* and *'outcomes'*. Each of these bands is then applied to all *documents*, including the service development plan over a six year period, staff timetables and all records; *management and planning*, which include policy content and implementation, meetings and staff work targets; *service to clients*, which looks at policy implementation, the nature of collaborative relationships with parents and teachers, the service's own quality control procedures, and the nature of INSET provided to schools; *use of resources*, in which time allocation and budgetary planning are examined; and *relationships with other services*, where the policies and mechanisms for communication and collaboration with EPs, advisers, etc. are looked at. This particular LEA has produced an exhaustive list, and some of the information asked for (e.g. a 3-year breakdown for each service member giving the time spent with individuals, with teachers and in other activities) may seem ambitious. However, many support services have not properly addressed some of the questions of management, accountability and the efficient use of resources raised by documents such as this. Although the answers may not always be sufficiently precise to yield useful data, it is important that support services should be prepared to address the questions.

Where a school deals with children who are statemented, of course, a major criterion of appropriate performance ought to be the extent to which the provision specified in the statement is made available. Paragraph 60 of Circular 7/91 has established the responsibility of special school governors in relation to statements and there is no reason to assume that governors of mainstream schools which have funds for statemented pupils delegated to them should not be subject to similar expectations. The statement is after all a legally binding document which can be - and has been - used by the courts to determine whether an LEA is meeting its obligations under the 1981

Education Act. It should therefore provide a fundamental criterion against which to evaluate the efficacy and appropriateness of what is provided. Unfortunately, there has been a tendency for many LEAs to frame Sections 2 (special educational needs) and 3 (provision) of the statement in such a way that their accountability is limited. This is understandable: the more precise the specification in this section, the more difficult it may be to vary provision if the availability of resources makes it necessary to do so. So we often encounter bland phraseology which is open to a variety of interpretations.

Analysis of statements issued by different LEAs shows a great deal of variability in terms of what is set sown as provision . A look at one LEA's statements gives us such Section 3 provision as:

'John requires support within the classroom situation, especially in the basic skill areas'

'As far as possible, Darren should be taught in a small group situation'

'Jim needs to receive additional help and support from a specialist teacher of the deaf'

In the same section, another LEA produces such statements as:

'An environment understanding of Richard's difficulties and promoting clear guidelines for behaviour. To be kept under regular review and discussion by the educational psychologist'

'An ordinary school offering a normal curriculum within which Sharon should benefit from an individual programme with the help of welfare assistance.'

These are randomly chosen examples; there are many that are better, others that are worse. Taken in conjunction with needs which are spelled out with equal precision, they hardly form a solid base for the evaluation of a school's effectiveness. Paragraph 61 of Circular 22/89 now requires further information in Section 3 if modifications to or disapplications of the National Curriculum are to be made. Given the current drive to provide as much access as possible to the National Curriculum, though, we can probably expect this section to change little in most cases.

It may be time for HMI to look on a national scale at the operational quality of statements issued by LEAs. Until some of the disparities and ambiguities are sorted out, they provide a weak base for monitoring the quantity or quality of what is done to assist a child in meeting his or her special educational needs.

Chapter 3

'Non-statutory' special educational needs and local management in schools

Gail Treml

Introduction and definitions

The term 'non-statutory special needs', in today's context, refers to those children who have been identified as having special educational needs as defined in the 1981 Education Act who continue to be educated within the resources of their ordinary schools and do not require the Local Education Authority to determine how their needs are best met by the provision of a statement. Only a small percentage of children with more severe or complex learning difficulties require a statement to be prepared by the LEA and in most cases this is where extra resources, in terms of staffing or equipment, will be required to cater for their needs, either in an ordinary school or in a more specialized environment.

While LEAs do not have to provide statements for most pupils with special educational needs, they are required to exercise close supervision of arrangements made by governors for identifying and providing for individual pupils needs in the ordinary school. Governors of mainstream schools therefore have a duty to ensure the identification and assessment of pupils with special educational needs, whether or not they subsequently require a statement, and also to ensure that the school meets those needs. LEAs, for their part, are required to monitor the effectiveness of the provision for both statutory and non-statutory special needs,

Although the term 'non-statutory special needs' has been employed in recent pronouncements by senior government officials, pupils with special needs but without statements still fall within the statutory area. The 1981 Education Act embraced the concept of special educational needs for an identified 20 per cent of the school age population whilst recognizing that only a small percentage of these pupils would require a statement. The needs of pupils without statements are also recognized in the DES Circular 22/89. It can therefore be seen that, as there is a statutory duty to identify, assess and respond to the needs of all pupils within the notional twenty per cent put forward by the Warnock Committee (DES, 1978), no pupils can really be considered to have 'non-statutory special needs'.

Identification

Many LEAs encourage a system of identification and assessment based on the Warnock Stages of Identification (DES, 1978, 4.35). Although variations can be found from LEA to LEA, in general Stage 1 is the whole school response which relies heavily on the class teacher within the primary school or the subject specialist in the secondary school to recognize that a child has needs and to endeavour to meet those needs. Stage 2 is the school's special educational needs response whereby further advice on appropriate strategies is sought when it is decided that current approaches have not been totally successful. The response to the pupil's identified needs is co-ordinated by the school's special educational needs co-ordinator or the teacher responsible for special needs within the school. However, responsibility for meeting the needs is still that of the class teacher or subject specialist. If any review of Stage 2 strategies reveals the need for further professional advice then Stage 3 is the Local Education Authority response. Referral to professionals from other disciplines is made in order to gain advice, but the responsibility still lies within the school to meet the needs of the pupil. The children within this system all have what can euphemistically be termed non-statutory special needs.

Resourcing

At present there is a range of resources offered for pupils with non-statutory special needs. In some LEAs it is the responsibility of the head teacher and governors to provide for identified pupils from within their existing budget and from within their existing staffing. Responses to this situation range from mixed-ability teaching with no support to setting, banding or streaming. Some schools provide mainstream mixed-ability teaching or streaming together with an internal support system managed by a special educational needs co-ordinator. This system of internal support or withdrawal relies heavily on the staffing priorities and arrangements for the school.

In a system managed and resourced from within the school, the school's special educational needs co-ordinator (SENCO) should become the focal point. The SENCO has the triple role of co-ordinator, consultant and tutor. That role is explored next.

The role of the SENCO

A SENCO should co-ordinate the initial identification procedures, using the stages of assessment to encourage and aid preliminary assessment by colleagues and also co-ordinate referral to all outside agencies. Obviously the SENCO will also be responsible for the school's input for statementing, that is the school's advice as contained in Appendix C of the statement, and for annual reviews of statements. Recording systems for cross-curricular and pastoral information on identified pupils should also be co-ordinated.

Consultation with colleagues, the head teacher, outside agencies and, most importantly, parents should be within a SENCO's brief. Consultation can entail provision of specialist advice on the planning of appropriate work, specific methods of teaching, special resources and additional strategies, in addition to work carried out during identification procedures. Of course, many SENCOs also teach pupils with special needs, either by providing in-class support or specialist help during short intensive periods outside the classroom.

Ideally the SENCO will also manage a team of mainstream colleagues who also support the pupils. In a secondary school, support can either be within subject specialisms or across the curriculum. Unfortunately many managers, when devising the timetable, 'use up' extra non-contact time with special needs support. In this fashion support for pupils' special needs is relegated to - at best - second place, and is often resented by teachers who see themselves as losing free periods. Under these circumstances it is hardly surprising that such support does not always meet the needs of the pupils.

Even in LEAs where central peripatetic support is provided, a well-organized and well-established SENCO has an important role to play. Identification and assessment will still be the school's responsibility and mainstream teachers will still be required to teach all pupils. Peripatetic colleagues can share the responsibility and pass on their expertise, but cannot be available for all pupils at all times. Many LEAs have for a long time encouraged the appointment, in their mainstream schools, of a teacher with responsibility for pupils with special needs. It is important that this should continue and that governors should ensure the retention of this designation. Head teachers should recognize that SENCOs need to have appropriate specialist training or be provided with it. Centrally funded support teachers can enhance special needs provision but should not be expected to replace in-school provision. Thus LMS formulae need to provide schools with sufficient resources to fund a SENCO at an appropriate level of remuneration to take account of the responsibilities and the required level of expertise.

Role of LEA support services

Some LEAs provide support from a central team of peripatetic support teachers who either work with children who have statements or sometimes with those with non-statutory special needs. This support can be aimed specifically at certain areas of the curriculum, for instance reading support, or can be across the curriculum. Many LEAs provide learning support, especially for language, at the primary age but not at secondary. In this context 'learning support' will mean an extra classroom resource enabling the child to have greater access to the curriculum. The resource is a specialist teacher who will work directly with the child or with the class teacher to devise appropriate strategies. Other LEAs provide unit help whereby the child is withdrawn for part of the week to a reading centre or language unit. Some also provide mathematics support for primary-age pupils having difficulties in this area of the curriculum. On the whole, this type of support is of a more advisory nature rather than directed at the individual pupil, although models vary from LEA to LEA, and indeed practice within an LEA may also be variable (Gross and Gripps, 1987; Bowers, 1989a).

The majority of support has until recently been targeted on the primary sector and has providing 'learning ' support which is curriculum-centred, though some LEAs also provide separate support for pupils with emotional and behavioural needs. Whether this is a distinction which can be easily made in practice remains open to question. Behavioural support usually takes the form either of off-site part-time provision or peripatetic support. The latter aims to help the child stay in mainstream, and also supports mainstream colleagues. Some teams work a 'mixed' system of off-site units together with supporting re-entry into mainstream. The number of Stage 3 referrals for behavioural needs has been noted to be increasing, (e.g. Special Children, April 1991, p5; BBC TV 'Public Eye', May 3, 1991) and the use of centrally resourced specialist teachers can be effective way of meeting these needs in an integrated setting.

In contrast with the emphasis within learning support, in many cases the support for behavioural difficulties is aimed primarily at the child, though it may extend to advisory work in which the assumption is that in supporting the teacher to gain more expertise the child will continue to be helped once the peripatetic support has been removed. In many cases central expertise employed to maintain a pupil in the mainstream will remove the need for statementing. HMI have recognized the necessity and importance of such work, recommending that 'if pupils with SEN are to be given equitable provision and maximum curricular access, advisory work in classrooms and schools will be necessary for some time' (HMI, 1991, paragraph 73).

Delegated funding

Both peripatetic support and part-time units have central resource implications. DES Circular 7/88 provided basic guidance on LMS and recognized the continued need for special educational needs provision within the mainstream. The expectation was that LEAs would include in their formulae provision for taking account of the incidence of pupils with special needs in schools covered by their schemes (paragraph 115). These resources were not to be allocated on the basis of pupil numbers, but were to be part of the 25% of the aggregated schools budget outside the pupil factors.

In the academic year 1989/90 it was found that the majority of authorities did provide extra resources to meet special needs in mainstream schools (Evans and Lunt, 1990). About 85% provided enhanced staffing, either directly managed by the school to improve staffing ratios or by the provision of centrally managed peripatetic support teams. The latter was more common in the primary sector.

It must be emphasized that the use of funds to enhance staffing ratios directly does not always appropriately provide for individual special needs. Monitoring the effective use of staffing in this area continues to be the responsibility of the LEA. Obviously quality assurance is easier when a school maintains an efficient identification system allied to recording the subsequent provision, which underlies the appropriate use of a 'stages' system.

In one LEA, extra funding for special needs is calculated on results from standardized tests of mathematics, english and non-verbal reasoning which divide the pupils at year 6 into three bands. Secondary schools with a high proportion of pupils in the lowest band receive extra monies. It is imperative that these monies are used to resource extra staffing for these pupils. Obviously head teachers can argue that cutting the pupil-teacher ratio will aid the lowest ability pupils, but this requires monitoring. Such schools still need the services of a SENCO to maintain a 'watching brief' and to consult and advise the mainstream staff on appropriate methods for differentiation. Another LEA has used the take-up of free school meals allied to reading test results to calculate a formula for funding non-statutory special needs in all mainstream schools. In both LEAs there are centrally resourced support services comprising a mix of part-time withdrawal units and peripatetic teams. The units provide help for pupils with literacy difficulties, who do not have statements., or part-time provision for pupils with behavioural needs, again without statements. All these pupils will have been referred to an educational psychologist who will have recommended the provision.

Both LEAs employ classroom or 'welfare' assistants to support integration of children with physical needs. This extends to both the primary and secondary sectors, and is usually identified via statementing procedures. Classroom assistants are also frequently used as a means of retaining young children with emotional and behavioural difficulties within the mainstream. This appears only to occur in the primary sector. These children do not always have statements but their needs will have been identified by an educational psychologist. Non-teaching support is an increasing method of providing for special needs pupils, which can be cost-effective as the staff tend to be less qualified and therefore less expensive. At present budgets for such support are either held centrally or 'earmarked' and devolved to the schools requiring 'welfares' so that the head teacher manages the resource. Such an approach may still be possible in the future: however, it may be necessary to provide statements for such pupils, as the funds could then be earmarked to given pupils via the statement. The present and future use of welfare assistants is discussed by Clayton (1989), and it seems essential that this effective use of resources should continue.

Building SEN into LMS formulae

To date, special needs factors have counted towards the 25% of the aggregated schools budget not allocated on the basis of pupils. Some LEAs have used part of this 25% to devise a formula for weighting funding to schools with a greater incidence of special education needs pupils. Current weightings employ a variety of measures including the use of free school meals, Family Income Supplement and other social factors, together with test results from LEA-wide reading tests, mathematics and reasoning. Some authorities have devised an audit of needs or used the stages of assessment as part of their allocation formula.

Tony Dessent, speaking at a London Institute of Education conference in March 1991, has suggested that there is a strong correlation between eligibility for free school meals or Family Income Supplement and the incidence of pupils with special educational needs. However, many educationalists and politicians believe that such indicators are neither accurate or appropriate, and that social circumstances should not be used as a measure for funding education. DES Circular 7/91 (paragraph 105) allows LEAs to continue to use such 'proxy' indicators but sees them preferably only as a temporary measure.

By April 1993 all LEAs, except those in Inner London who have until 1995, must allocate a minimum of 80% of the aggregated school budget (ASB) through the pupil-led funding formula. Special educational needs factors can count towards the 80% requirement and thus the means of determining these weightings and their relative values will need to be more accurate. The government expects the weighting factors to be both valid and reliable measures of educational need (Circular 7/91, paragraph 105). In total, these additional weightings for non-statutory special needs cannot exceed 5% of the aggregated budget (ASB). Further amounts which the LEA decides to allocate on the basis of needs can continue to count against the 20% not allocated on the basis of age-weighted pupil units.

It would appears that the DES will encourage development of explicit criteria for identification of the non-statutory special needs within a school. In order that such criteria may be employed they will need to be acceptable and understood by all. Provision of a mechanism for ensuring that the judgements are consistent between schools in the same authority in respect of the same need is therefore imperative. What is significant is that any funds provided for the special educational needs of non-statemented pupils cannot be earmarked for specific pupils; they will simply be part of the total delegated budget which a school's head teacher and governors can employ for meeting the needs of such pupils and for all its other pupils within the school. Once delegated to the school, funds for special needs lie completely at the discretion of its management and can be spent as they determine.

In the future an ideal and acceptable formula might take account of the number of pupils at each stage of the identification process together with National Curriculum levels attained. Obviously the latter cannot be employed until they are standardized and used across the Key Stages. Stages of assessment also require consistent criteria for movement between stages or a 'gatekeeping' point for accounting procedures. It is possible to envisage Stage 3 as the financial cusp, with educational psychologists as the 'gate-keepers'. This would mean resourcing school psychological services appropriately. It would be necessary to identify any additional costs entailed and build them into the formula.

Negotiated and agreed criteria at Stage 3 would encourage accurate identification procedures and use of appropriate strategies. In turn this would aid effective monitoring of the quality of the whole school response to special needs. Performance indicators can then be more easily understood, equitable and, to some extent, quantifiable. Indicators can include test results, both SATs and others, together with information as to numbers of pupils at each stage of assessment and how their needs have been met from within the school's resources.

Some authorities already use complex processes to identify and fund special needs, both statutory and non-statutory. Although such processes may involve a number of elements, the division of resources is seen to equate with the requirements of pupils and schools and is therefore acceptable to head teachers and governors. Kent, for example, employs an audit of special needs with evidence from a number of sources including the school SENCO, the educational psychologists and peripatetic support teachers. Depending upon the level of need, a school may receive funding for enhanced staffing ratios plus, where necessary, provision of centrally funded support teachers. The audit could easily be developed as part of a formula for delegating funds.

Possible models for delegation

There are a number of models which could be used to devolve funds to schools. All funding for special needs could be devolved and schools offered a service level agreement which would provide a complete service identical to that received at present, or possibly even an enhanced service. This type of devolvement is already in use in many authorities for school meals services and contract cleaning of schools. The advantages of service level agreements include accurate costing and an emphasis on a negotiated level of provision. The provider is directly accountable to the school; it is a contractor-client relationship. School psychological services and special needs support services could quite easily work to this model.

Alternatively, funding could be devolved to schools, with the LEA providing a basic service which the schools are obliged to purchase. In addition, schools would have the option to buy additional services if the need arose. Again this model would be tailored for psychological and special needs support services, with the basic service applicable to statutory provision and the additional service being for non-statutory provision. The obligation to buy back would only be linked to pupils with statements; therefore the funding would not be earmarked but the expected provision would be described in the statement.

A third type of delegation would entail devolvement of all funds, with the LEA offering services which a school may choose to buy. The provider would have no means of estimating future income or demand. Such a service would have to offer unique or extremely high-quality provision in order to survive. This might be a way of encouraging excellence, but if the service then became too expensive it might not be competitive with other alternative services run by neighbouring LEAs or by newly developed service providers. Beyond this the LEA could choose not to provide any services for pupils with special needs in mainstream schools and so devolve all funds. In this case a school would have the discretion to decide whether or not to purchase services and if not, how to provide for all its pupils. At the present time this cannot be seen as an appropriate model since it would not seem to protect the legal obligations of the LEA.

Finally, it may still be possible to fund services through the kind of 'earmarking' system discussed previously. This type of arrangement offers some of the benefits of devolution by giving greater management discretion whilst ensuring an adequate level of provision for pupils with special needs. Cambridgeshire is well on the way to delegating the total Council budget for Education Service. All schools will, however, be expected to buy back into central provision for non-statutory special needs as it is felt that such a service has a 'value added' dimension (Matthews, 1991).

Within the context on non-statutory special needs, a Local Education Authority can therefore continue to provide centrally funded support services, although they will become more difficult to resource. But is this an appropriate way forward?

Non-statutory special needs should be met from within the school so that responsibility for all pupils is shared. It must be recognized that every teacher is a teacher of special needs, not just the peripatetic or unit staff from central services. We should not encourage a 'not my problem' attitude: by doing so we are 'de-skilling' mainstream teachers. However, central support services can be used to enhance that which the school provides through a consultative and supportive role. An advisory approach to special needs whereby initially peripatetic staff work with individual pupils but also help staff to devise strategies to meet the pupils' needs, then gradually withdraw the support, will lead to central support services using their expertise to facilitate the whole school approach to special needs. The centrally-resourced input could be a flexible resource used in schools on a short-term or rota basis. The expertise at present in central teams must not be dissipated or lost, but shared with all colleagues.

Pilot projects have been carried out in Croydon and Bromley which involve concentrated input into identified schools in order to raise standards of literacy. The results from such initiatives appear to be good, although they have yet to be evaluated long-term. Such work raises the status of the peripatetic staff and gives measurable results over a relatively short period of time. This can convince head teachers and governors of the benefit of central support services and could be used, prior to some types of devolvement, to encourage continued purchase of the service once it was no longer centrally resourced.

It may be possible to encourage a whole school response to special needs by delegating the money for centrally held support services to schools, either through the age-weighted pupil units (AWPU) element of the LMS formula or through the extra 5%. This money could then be used for schools to buy back into central support services, as discussed above. Alternatively, the head and governors may choose to spend this money to meet needs as they see fit, buying in their own staff for identified pupils, providing extra special needs specialists to cut class numbers. A head teacher might choose to spend all the money on such extra resources as computers or other means of making the curriculum accessible to more pupils. It is my experience that many schools at present wish to receive funds which are currently retained centrally for special needs provision, whether these are for non-statutory special needs or for pupils with statements. A number of LEAs are now carrying out feasibility pilots in this area.

The monies devolved often do not seem very large when apportioned to each school, and head teachers quickly discover that they cannot resource the same high level of expertise as they had previously received. Monitoring the use of such funding has demonstrated that head teachers sometimes use the funds inappropriately; for example, spending on supply cover occurs frequently. Future monitoring requirements may entail greater use of local Inspection and Advisory services, a move which is at odds with the drive to reduce such teams. At present some of the monitoring, when central support teams are employed, is through the line management structure. If these are reduced we will perhaps just have to trust schools to meet the needs of all their pupils.

Whatever methods we use to identify and provide for individual pupils, a fully differentiated curriculum should be in place to meet the needs of all pupils. It is not that the child should fit the curriculum; the curriculum must be tailored to meet the child's needs. The central specialist teachers may be in a position to enable their colleagues to meet children's special educational needs; however, even with their involvement, enforcement of all the requirements of the 1981 Act may be difficult. Will anyone really take the trouble? At the launching of Circular 7/91, the junior minister Michael Fallon explained that 'School governors and head teachers, who are best placed to respond to the demands of pupils and parents, will now have control over their own resources, both staffing and financial. That is essential if they are to satisfy their customers'. These customers will include many pupils with special needs. If schools accept their responsibilities then they will need to invest in strengthening their skills in providing suitable support for their pupils.

It is to be noted that the government recognizes the value of centrally managed special educational needs support teams and recommends the 'judicious use by schools of specialist teachers employed in central teams and the expertise available centrally' (DES Circular 7/91, paragraph 108). Yet however an authority chooses to fund the individual pupil's needs, the response will continue to be the responsibility of the school and the head teacher. Monitoring and evaluating the school's response to special educational needs will be a responsibility retained by the Local Education Authority. Arrangements by governors for identifying and providing for individual pupils' special needs in ordinary schools will have to be ensured. Training must continue to raise the awareness of governing bodies in order that they are able to satisfy all the requirements of the 1981 Education Act.

We cannot look in isolation at children who are not statemented. Any changes in provision for non-statutory special needs in both style and type, may lead to an imbalance in the overall contiuum of provision for special needs in a given area. I have already mentioned the increase in demands for statements. However, if care is not taken, funding formulae for non-statutory special needs my lead to a 'pre-statementing' statementing procedure which seeks to reduce resource obligations through the completion of less statements. This could be construed as a means of circumventing parental rights and LEAs might then be seen as not meeting their legal obligations. On the other hand, if the means of identification can be allied to appropriate resources, which may very well mean an increase in funding, then there should be no such accusations and no increase in statementing in order to access sparse resources.

The pupils in mainstream with special educational needs require a fair 'slice of the action' in both financial and teaching terms. It is to be hoped that both mainstream schools and local authorities will accept their responsibilities to meet such children's needs. Without this, we may see a negation of the good practice that has developed over the past ten years.

Part II

Making moves in special schools

Chapter 4

Local management of special schools

David Hill

The principle that the management of special schools is not fundamentally different from the management of mainstream schools has led the government to extend local management to special schools. Formula-funding is to be introduced for all special schools, though the delegation of powers is voluntary. Generally, this move has been welcomed by these schools, although there are a number of concerns. The likelihood is that the larger schools will volunteer first. The management issues for a very small highly-specialized school may be different and there may be major issues involved in the delegation of powers.

This chapter discusses some of the issues that have arisen out of local management of mainstream schools, especially those that are relevant to the local management of special schools. It is hoped that the chapter will help special schools as they prepare to introduce local management. In particular, it examines the changing role of governors and of school management, and the relationship between the school and the LEA.

Governors

Under local management, power rests with the governing body. In the initial phases, some mainstream schools have had problems with this new arrangement. Existing governors in some schools have thought that they may not be capable, or have the time, to exercise their statutory duties. In recent years, normal governor meetings have become lengthy and often unsatisfactory. Governors perceive that the commitment of their time and energy will increase without prospect of increase of personal reward or pleasure. They prefer, at this stage, to delegate their powers to professional educators. Also, they have not been helped by many unsatisfactory training programmes for governors.

Being a governor has to become a rewarding and enjoyable experience to ensure a satisfactory number of volunteers. Therefore the training and the organization of governing bodies must take this on board. Governing bodies also need to ensure that they represent a cross-section of the community which they serve. Special schools will have a particular problem in this respect. The homes of many of their children are often a comparatively long distance from the school which means that it often does not serve such a close community as the mainstream school. This may make it harder to attract parent governors. Another problem may be that some of the parents of the children may themselves have educational needs that would make it difficult for them to serve as governors.

The training has to meet the needs of the governors. Some of the better training provided by LEAs for mainstream schools has recognized the need for governors to work closely with school staff. This has led to governors being trained with school management teams, rather than separately. However, all governors do not need training in all aspects of school management. Special schools will probably wish to follow models that are proving successful in mainstream schools. This means dividing the responsibilities of governors into areas. These areas vary according to the wishes of individual schools but, in general, cover curriculum, personnel, finance and premises. Large schools sub-divide further. Personnel functions could become categorized as 'disciplinary', 'appointments', 'staff welfare', and 'pupils' welfare' for example, but special schools may be best advised not to have these sub-divisions. With only four areas, the governing body could form four sub-committees, each with clear terms of reference. Each governor should be expected to join only one sub-committee and specialize in this area, though the chairman of governors and head teacher may wish to be *ex-officio* on each sub-committee. Sub-committees should be encouraged to co-opt, both from the school staff and from the community. For example, the premises sub-committee, which may need to meet once or twice a year, could try to co-opt a parent or school friend with experience of buildings. Such a person may not want to serve as a full governor but would be invaluable on the sub-committee. The school caretaker is another who should be on this sub-committee.

The content of the termly full governors' meeting changes from the major item being a report from the head teacher to reports, with recommendations, from the chairs of each of the sub-committees. Experience shows that governors prefer this way of operation and find their sub-committee work to be very interesting and enjoyable, without being too onerous. In many schools, the old style of governing body meetings was most unsatisfactory for many governors. They had to endure long agendas, accompanied by many pages of paper, and listen in silence for much of the time to the head teacher. Real decision-making was a rare experience in many schools. Under local management, governors, at long last, have an opportunity to make a major impact on the quality of teaching an learning at their school.

It is worth ensuring that there is a common understanding of the broad principle by which governors should operate. Schools may wish to develop a 'Code of Practice' with their governors. An example, under five broad headings, is provided below.

Figure 4:1
Code of practice for school governors

Powers and Responsibilities

☐ Governors have responsibility for determining, monitoring and keeping under review, the aims and objectives, policies, plans and procedures within which the school operates.

☐ Governors' responsibilities include the development and implementation of a school management plan and ensuring that the requirements of the National Curriculum are met.

☐ Governors have responsibility for the financial management of the delegated budget, for personnel issues, and for premises issues at the school.

☐ Governors need to decide the extent of delegation of their powers to sub-committees and to the head teacher.

General

☐ Governors work in partnership with the school staff, parents, the LEA and other relevant agencies.

☐ All governors, although appointed by different groups, have equal status.

☐ Governors have a general duty to act fairly and without prejudice at all times.

☐ Governors should recognize, and adhere to, laws and good practices relating to employment of staff.

☐ Governors should consider carefully how their decisions might affect children in other schools.

☐ Governors should encourage open government and should be seen to do so.

Commitment

☐ Being a governor involves the commitment of significant amounts of time and energy; careful regard should be made to this when agreeing to serve on the governing body.

☐ All governors should accept a fair share of responsibilities, including service on sub-committees and working groups.

☐ Regular attendance at meetings is essential.

☐ Governors should take all opportunities to know the school well.

Confidentiality

☐ Governors should exercise the highest degree of prudence when discussing potentially contentious issues outside the governing body.

☐ Governors should observe complete confidentiality when asked to do so by the governing body, especially in relation to matters concerning individual staff or pupils.

Conduct

☐ Governing bodies should always act as a corporate body. Governors should express their views openly within meetings but accept collective responsibility for all decisions.

☐ Governors should only speak or act on behalf of the governing body when they have been specifically authorized to do so.

☐ All visits to schools should be undertaken within a framework which has been established by the governing body and agreed with the head teacher.

☐ In responding to criticism or complaints relating to the school, governors should follow procedures established by the governing body.

☐ Governors have a responsibility to maintain and develop the ethos and reputation of the school; their actions within the school community should reflect this.

Training needs to emphasize these broad principles and also concentrate on specific areas. For example, the curriculum committee needs to understand the implications of the National Curriculum and the ways this needs to be tackled and modified for pupils with special educational needs. The personnel committee needs training in industrial relations. The finance committee needs briefing on the LEA formula for the funding of schools. The premises committee needs to be aware of the regulations affecting health and safety, again especially with reference to the special needs of the school and its pupils. For the initial awareness raising session on LMS it is useful to have a whole school (governors, teaching staff and non-teaching staff) day or half-day conference, with mixed workshop sessions to discuss some of the issues. This provides a good opportunity to develop the partnership between governors and the staff.

School management

Personnel issues soon come to the fore under local management. The freedom for governors of locally-managed schools to set salaries, within a national framework, has enormous implications for school management. For example, to attract a new recruit, governors may wish to offer incentives such as an additional allowance or, for newly-qualified teachers, additional increments. It is obvious that this would have implications for the school management's relationship with existing staff and that clear criteria are needed.

School management needs, with all decisions, to ensure that the focus remains the teaching and learning of children. Therefore, under local management, schools need more than ever to be clear on their aims and objectives. This will enable them to establish policies and to set priorities very much in line with the learning situation and help to prevent sudden decisions on issues such as personnel.

In schools, and especially in special schools, teachers need support staff to enable them to achieve their objectives. Teachers find good support staff to be invaluable and have welcomed LEA efforts to appoint and train suitable staff, although many schools still feel that the training has not been adequate. Classroom support for teachers in special schools is a high priority issue. Local management also brings additional tasks to the school office and an early priority issue for school management is to ensure that the senior management and teachers in the school do not spend a great deal of time on administration. Every school needs an administrative officer, capable of being one of the senior management team, with responsibilities to include premises, financial and secretarial duties. This will probably mean a major restructuring in all school offices and, in a number of schools, the present school secretary may not be suitable for such a post. Much training is required for this enlarged roll and not all LEAs have provided opportunities for school secretaries to receive this training. On taking up their post, many secretaries in special schools were excellent 'carers', wanting to work in a place where children were the focus. They may have had little expertise as administrators and have only received initial training through their head teacher. This is an issue which has to be faced by school management.

Special schools usually form 'cluster groups' within an LEA. Under local management there is even a stronger need for such an arrangement to continue. School management teams need to meet regularly with teams from similar schools to share ideas and for training purposes. They also need, jointly, to review the LEA formula for funding their schools and should expect to be consulted at length over the formula. In this respect, it is critical that they work in a very close partnership with their LEA.

Special school management teams have an important role to play as consultants to their counterparts in the mainstream schools. In fact, colleagues in mainstream schools have much to learn from sharing of experiences and a continual dialogue does much to help children with special needs in, or in units attached to, mainstream schools. The special school and its staff can act as an excellent resources centre, assisting staff in other schools. This may help to keep some children at their mainstream school, rather than move them into a special school. Of course, in this new world of financial accountability, the special school may require payment for services rendered to mainstream schools. It is naive to think that mainstream schools will be rushing to use some of their budget in this way, but it is conceivable that a special school could provide such a high quality service that mainstream schools would give it high priority in their management plans.

A fundamental difference between LMS and LMSS is that mainstream schools need to attract and retain pupils to maintain funding levels, while a special school may try to integrate some of its children into a mainstream school without affecting its funding. Joint education of children may be another cause of a funding issue, though the two schools ought to be able to come to an agreement on what is equitable. Recharging already takes place between secondary schools and further education colleges for pupils taking 'link courses' for part of the week and this arrangement could easily be extended to special schools. More serious may be the attitude of parents of other children. Sometimes school management teams and governors are faced with the difficult decision of whether of not to retain a pupil, although this may stop other pupils choosing to go to that school. It is a moral dilemma and it is hoped that financial considerations will not be the main cause of a pupil's exclusion. However, reality suggests that this may become more of an issue under local management.

Many schools already have a good school management development programme and will have identified needs for the school, for individuals, for groups of staff and in relation to equal opportunities. As LEAs delegate more and more of their INSET budget to schools, the priority given to management development within the wider staff-development programme can become an issue. In a series of books on 'Managing Better Schools' (Paul Chapman Publishing), Agnes McMahon and Ray Bolam identify ten main task areas for school management, to which this author has added further comments in the light of local management.

(i) *Overall school policy and aims.*

As stated earlier, this is a key area for governors and school management.

(ii) *Communication, organization and decision-making structures and roles.*

Poor communication can be a major source of conflict, yet many school staff complain of a lack of good school policy in communication. Local management brings greater involvement with governors and this means there needs to be a clear policy on decision-making structures and roles.

(iii) *The curriculum, teaching methods and examinations.*

This is an area in which school management has much experience and remains, of course, a most crucial area.

(iv) *Staff and staff development.*

Morale of staff is so important, as it clearly affects teaching and learning in the school. Hopefully, local management will help school managers in their efforts to maintain high morale. Most governors see this as a priority area and welcome suggestions to improve working conditions at the school. There needs to be a pleasant, clean and tidy staff room and a working area. Some schools are increasing the hours of a mid-day supervisor or a cleaner, or bringing in a parent to look after the staff room, with tea and coffee being constantly available, free of charge, to staff. This takes a very small part indeed of the school budget but greatly enhances the working attitude of staff.

I have heard some poor reports of staff development programmes and the use of the five closure days at schools. This suggests that some school management teams have failed to match the needs of their school to their staff development programmes. Much care needs to be taken, with management teams ensuring that all participants evaluate and report on courses, visits and other development activities.

(v) *Pupils and pupil learning*

Local management must involve pupils, although this may prove to be difficult in some special schools. Pupils do like to help wherever possible and need to be aware of the aims of their education. More than ever, they need to take a pride in, and care for, their school. There are a number of school management issues in which they can be involved. For example, the maintenance of the toilet areas and the lunchtime arrangements are of great importance to school children, especially those in special schools. When introducing Drug Education into the curriculum of certain special schools some older children could well help staff, governors and parents in the formulation of the school policy.

(vi) *Finance and material resources*

Much of this area can be dealt with by the school administrative officer, leaving the head teacher time to concentrate on other matters directly related to the management of teaching and learning.

(vii) *External relations*

Special schools usually have developed strong external relations with their LEA, parents and other sections of the wider community. This is an important area and needs to continue to develop.

(viii) *Monitoring and evaluation of effectiveness*

This is an area in which our schools may not be so strong as schools in other countries. Self-evaluation is so important, with governors and school management receiving at least a short annual report from curriculum areas within the school. The DES published an *aide-memoire* in December 1989 of performance indicators from which governors and school management may wish to choose to monitor and evaluate their schools. The *aide-memoire* included sections on pupil achievement, pupil attitudes and school management. Every objective of the school needs to be monitored and evaluated.

(ix) *Change and developments*

A well-structured school, with clear aims, policies and procedures for priority-setting, will more readily adapt to change situations. It is the poorly-structured school that always seems to be responding to crisis situations, with the school's management constantly complaining about overload of administration which, in turn, leads to poor morale of the staff and pupils. This is a reason for development of school management teams to be so important.

(x) *Self-develpment*

A major task for school management is to encourage self-development. Courses on such topics as interpersonal skills, management of time and self-evaluation can assist in this process.

A school's management needs to have a clear vision for the school. All teachers and, where possible, pupils and parents, should have an opportunity to express their views on major items of school policy. Governors and their staff should not spend an excessive amount of their time on detail. Good management entails ensuring that teachers and their support staff are given the best possible chance to improve the quality of teaching and learning with the children.

Integration with mainstream schools

Since the introduction of local management in 1990, there has been a widespread increase in the number of children referred for special educational help. This increase was confirmed by the government in March 1991 (*Times Educational Supplement*, 22 March 1991) and suggests agreement with the claims of psychologists who believe that numbers have increased nationally by as much as 50%.

Under the rules of local management formula funding, this increase could have been foreseen and, indeed, was forecast by many in the education service. Every pupil is worth a sum of money to the school. In most LEA formulae, additional funds for 'special needs' children are also available, with a variety of indicators being used to measure the amount of this funding for a particular school. Instead of simply providing the extra resources as required by a statement for a special needs child, the LEA now gives the school the budget for these resources and monitors that the needs are being met. In some LEAs, statementing of children has been discouraged, the LEA preferring to allow an officer to allocate additional resources to a school without going through the full statementing process.

The new formula will be based on one or more indicators, ranging from additional funding for every pupil qualifying for a free school meal to a banding of the school based on its catchment area. Some LEAs use only one indicator, while others use a variety of indicators; in any event the formula may be too insensitive to meet the needs of a particular child.

The school will now demand a statement for that child. Another factor is that, faced with difficult problems, schools are less willing to cope than they were in the past unless they have extra resources. An issue for the LEA is the increased pressure on its educational psychologists, which makes it more difficult to start the assessment procedure on a child. This, in turn, can lead to exclusions from mainstream school, especially for children with behavioural disorders, and this means yet more pressure on the LEA to place the child in a special school.

Another problem with statementing is that the funding to meet the child's needs has to be found from the General Schools Budget. A large increase in statementing will, therefore, lead to a decrease in funds available for other children, or an increase in the General Schools Budget by the LEA. If we really, as a nation, are committed to meeting the special needs of our children, it must be recognized that additional funding is required.

The government probably does not mean to discourage integration of special needs children into mainstream schools, but there is some evidence that this is one of the side-effects of local management. The RNIB has already been alerted to cuts in services for visually-impaired pupils. Their education director fears that schools with statemented children would be looking for ones with only minor difficulties and that children with severe difficulties are more likely to be referred to special schools for financial, not educational, reasons.The RNIB wants special needs support services to be classified as mandatory exceptions, but this may not solve the financial problem for an LEA as mandatory exceptions are still part of the overall General Schools Budget.

Issues for schools entering LMS

Issues affecting the organization of the governing body and the management of the school have been considered elsewhere in this chapter. There are a number of others which face schools and their LEAs.

One is the dependency on the LEA culture ingrained into many of our schools. Governors and head teachers have, in the past, had to act like young teenagers in a family. They have been allowed a certain amount of freedom, but under a regime which has insisted on certain rules. Schools have liked to think that they have been able to argue and to modify some of the rules but have not been able to exercise the right to take a major decision against the wishes of their LEA. Under LMS, schools are able to act as older teenagers within a family. They have much more budgetary responsibility and powers of decision, with an opportunity to opt out and leave should they strongly disagree with the rules.

Under LMS, schools become very irritated by perceived inefficiency on the part of their LEA. They find it difficult to accept a lack of co-ordination between departments over the introduction of local management. This may not be the fault of their Education Officers, but schools expect the LEA to ensure such problems do not arise. They expect the Treasurer's department, the Legal department and the Property department to be customer-orientated and provide a quick and responsive service. In some LEAs, some of these departments have found it difficult to relate to the philosophy of school-based management. In other LEAs, head teachers have suddenly had to devote time to a host of previously unfamiliar officers who wish to introduce themselves in order to convince the heads that the new service will be a friendly and responsive one.

With the delegation of budgetary responsibility, many governors' finance sub-committees have been frustrated by the quality of information received from their LEA. Producing accurate historical financial information has proved to be a major problem as LEAs had not previously been required to hold such detailed information. Wise schools will try to ensure that they collect for themselves as much information as possible before entering local management. In preparation, it is sensible to ensure that the school obtains details of items such as gas, electricity and water bills, amount of after school use of building, staff salaries and short-term absence rates of teachers. They need to know the LEA policy on lettings and the repayment to be given to the school for so-called 'free' lettings. There needs to be a report on the state of internal decorations and maintenance of the building.

The total amount of resources available to the school under a new formula funding system will vary from the historical budget. A variation within 2% may not be a major issue for a school, though any loss will cause some problems. A larger variation requires careful thought and long-term planning. A number of factors can cause such a variation. It may be that the school was well-funded in the past, in comparison to similar schools. Perhaps the LEA has given the school additional resources or has funded an above-average salary bill. All teaching staff will receive an incentive allowance and many teachers in special schools are on the maximum of the main scale. The average *versus* actual salary issue could be even more pronounced than it has been in the mainstream sector. If the school has protected salaries or teachers all at the top of the incremental scale, it is probable that it will need some additional funding. If, however, the reverse is the case and the school is a 'winner' under the formula, the school still needs to be careful. There is a tendency to spend these additional resources without thinking through fully the long-term development plan. Existing teachers move up the incremental scale and may not leave. Does the school need to create some resources for the future? There are many issues that will arise from the changes to the total funding of the school.

An issue to be faced by the schools is that the financial year does not correspond with the academic year. Perhaps the govenment could allow LEAs to be more flexible with their schools? Before we had LMS, authorities allocated staffing establishments to the schools for the academic year, and in so doing they committed 80 per cent of the school's funding for the period from September to August. Officers were thus having to use estimated budgets for the April-August period of the following year. Why cannot this continue to happen and allow school financial years to match the academic year?

At present, the time scale for the governors to set their school's budget before 1st April each year is very tight. Most LEAs are unable to give a final total figure to schools before March and some have failed to do this by 1st

April. Special schools need to be aware that, on entering LMS, they will have to pay staff for 5/12th of the present academic year, planning for which would have taken place at least one year previously.

Another budget concern is that schools employ people whose salaries and wages are determined by a surprisingly large number of pay negotiating bodies. A school has to learn about pay awards and increments to teaching and non-teaching staff on a number of different months of the year. A good software program will assist with the planning (c.f. Bird, 1991).

A significant number of staff, such as social workers, physiotherapists, speech therapists and school nurses, are not employed by the LEA but work in special schools. Are the schools going to have any influence on the increase or decrease, and conditions of employment, of these staff? Will a school be able to give additional funding through its delegated budget? How do these staff fit into the management structure of the school? What will be their relationship with governors who are quasi-employers of other school staff? These are issues to be faced as a school enters local management.

The process of 'growing-up' means undertaking greater responsibility for one's affairs and a release from the dependency culture. The ability to have a greater say in one's destiny is an attraction of local management. Committed staff and governors have more influence over decisions that affect the teaching and learning at their school. The school development plan, with priorities carefully set, becomes a key to the quality of education at the school. With a friendly parent, such as the LEA, also committed to the education of children, to advise and assist with the monitoring, a locally-managed school has the potential to do well.

Chapter 5

LMSS: In-school preparation

Judith Charlesworth

Background

When our LEA began to plan its pilot scheme for Local Management of Schools in 1988 it invited volunteers from all schools to take part. Eight schools were chosen for the pilot: three secondary, four primary, and one special. At that time we were an all-age school (2-19) for children with severe learning difficulties. The school also had an outreach role in that we taught sessionally in two other settings - a small hospital and a day centre - both for profoundly and multiply handicapped adults.

However, we were already beginning to prepare for several very fundamental changes: from being an all-age school to one for children aged 2-12; from having an outreach role to adults, to taking over the LEA's home teaching service for pre-school children with special needs; and from having an entirely school-based curriculum to one set firmly within the framework of the National Curriculum. The school, many of whose pupils have sensory and physical disabilities as well as severe to profound learning difficulties, was also in need of re-equipping for its changing age range. I felt that it was therefore a good time to pilot LMS through a delegated budget since this would enable us to make the relevant changes in a more responsive and dynamic way.

One of the wondrous things about LMS is the wide variety of schemes and approaches taken by individual education authorities, and the even greater number of ways of handling financial management within individual schools. However, I do feel that there are some common principles which cut across these individual differences. LMS, and LMSS when it arrives, offers a balance between funding, management and responsibility. Whilst interrelated, these factors are separate. I will therefore consider each in turn.

Management

However much money a school has, or does not have, its expenditure still has to be managed in the best interests of the children, and to the satisfaction of the governors and staff. One of the first golden rules for a manager in introducing anything new and large into a school is: make sure that you understand it fully yourself.

When I first started to attend the various meetings, working parties and planning groups that I was inevitably drawn into, I can honestly say that I did not fully understand a large part of the early discussions that took place. Now, nearly four years on, and with LMS in mainstream schools well under way, all of us have absorbed much more of the financial terminology and ways of looking at things than we might imagine. Thus I doubt that anyone in the teaching profession will be quite as naive today as I was then. I found that the fog lifted the more I became immersed in the language and concepts surrounding LMS, and that my thinking, approach and attitude changed and moved on to a different plane. This enabled me to come back to school and feed back the major principles to the staff, who themselves started to approach in-school organization and administration in a different way. This natural growth of awareness does not always happen, however, and it may be particularly difficult for other stakeholders in the school to understand the shift of balance away from the LEA to school control, and the need for internal changes to follow. Thus the second golden rule is: make sure that everybody is involved, and consider how to heighten awareness and/or to train everybody concerned. The LEA will usually put together a cohesive training package for a number of involved people, but this is not necessarily sufficient or appropriate for everyone. In-school training, particularly on the educational implications for that school, is often best led by the head and senior management team who can then pitch it appropriately for the group in question.

Initial and update training will need to take place for at least the following groups of people: head and deputies; senior management team; teaching staff; the governing body; system manager (if not one of the foregoing); other school staff such as classroom assistants, caretaker, kitchen staff, cleaners; and of course parents and pupils.

We need also to consider such outside agencies as health authority personnel (speech therapists, physiotherapists, nurses); LEA support services (EPs, sensory impairment teachers, etc), contractors and suppliers.

Areas for training, depending on the requirements of the various groups, should include: budget production; budget management; accounting; contract/tenders; employment; accountability and legislation; computer systems; LEA systems; cost-effectiveness implications; institutional implications; the LEA/school interface; changing roles of senior staff; fund raising; accountability.

As with any in-service training, the more practical and enjoyable the sessions, led by those with a positive attitude to the subject, the better the outcome is likely to be. I was fortunate in that the LEA put on some excellent training days for a team from each of the pilot schools, comprising head, deputy, secretary, chair of governors and one other appropriate person, and we were then able to cascade our knowledge and approach to others, both within our school and to others in all sectors. As I was so positive about LMS at the time, it helped me to enthuse other members of staff who very quickly benefited from the effects of our planning and financial management.

Institutional development plans

Whilst we were learning about the principles of LMS, ready for the pilot implementation in April 1989, we were at the same time developing an in-depth institutional development plan. This was particularly geared to our forthcoming change in age range, and the implementation of the National Curriculum, and involved a massive audit of various aspects of the school. These included the following: premises; large-scale resources; furniture and equipment; small scale resources (e.g. curriculum support materials); staff expertise/INSET needs; how the staff were deployed; curriculum documentation; record keeping systems; and parental partnership and involvement.

We then constructed a time-scaled plan of action of what was needed - both physically and in terms of staff time - and decided how to fund the changes that were needed, and what our criteria of success were to be. In doing this we had our first experience of grappling with the practicalities of the budget, and how the gross sum was sub-divided into historically-based budget heads, such as teachers' salaries, electricity, capitation and maintenance. This then had to be notionally apportioned throughout the year, with regard to the fact that the financial and academic years started at different times and thus the money was just coming into school as the school year was winding down.

Whilst I am sure that all schools are now well experienced in constructing development plans, I consider it important to mention the value of a very broad audit,with a good deal of lateral thinking involved. For example, one of the areas that we looked at particularly hard in the curriculum audit was PE/gross motor skills. We felt that perhaps we were not doing enough in this subject. On analysis, we determined why.

Firstly, the hall doubled as the dining room; thus there were time-logistic problems in getting the hall ready before lunch, so cutting sessions short, and in getting the floor dry after cleaning it in time for the afternoon sessions, which often did not happen. Secondly, the walls of the hall were lined with dinner tables, thus necessitating the PE equipment to be kept in an extremely dark and poky storage room - so people tended either not to use it or store it haphazardly. Thirdly, much of the equipment was antiquated, and the wrong size for the increasing number of young children. Fourthly, the staff did not feel particularly confident in teaching this subject, and felt they needed to learn new skills to do so properly.

As a result, the following decisions and plans were made. Firstly, we decided that children should no longer eat in the hall, but eat in their class-rooms in a 'family group', an innovation appropriate to the new primary ethos of the school. This necessitated an audit of suitable eating utensils and cutlery - extra purchases being funded from the Capitation budget head. We also audited tables and chairs to ensure that every child had appropriate seating (with particular emphasis on the needs of the physically disabled) and any extra purchases were made from the Furniture and Equipment budget head.

Secondly, we decided to use money from the Maintenance budget head to decorate and shelve out the store room in order that the PE equipment could be properly stored and easily accessed. The dinner tables were then put away elsewhere, the largest of them being sent to the new school for secondary-aged pupils with severe learning difficulties.

Thirdly, from both the Furniture and Equipment head and from some substantial private donations the school had received, we ordered a range of new equipment, with the emphasis on natural wood, rounded corners and aesthetic qualities. The large equipment is now kept around the end of the hall, so that it can be moved easily and quickly into place. A mat trolley means that the new mats are stored upright, once again in the hall, and smaller folding mats and all the small equipment are kept neatly on the wide shelves in the storage room.

Fourthly, a staff training day was organized on PE skills for children with severe learning difficulties. This was held jointly with the secondary school to enable curriculum continuity.

Fifthly, a small working party led by one of the curriculum co-ordinators worked on updating our PE/gross motor skills curriculum statement, and devising the appropriate style of record sheets to accompany it. The cost of some extra staff time away from the classroom was borne by the Supply budget head, and administration/office costs funded from the Capitation head.

This is one example of how clear identification of need, plus the ability to direct one's own funds towards fulfilling those needs, has the knock-on effect of enhancing a number of aspects of the school. Previously we would have had to apply to the LEA for all but the equipment bought from capitation, and the likelihood of getting any of it would have been extremely slim. The likelihood of getting a little supply cover to enable curriculum development would have been non-existent.

Similar developments have taken place over the last two years in a wide range of areas - curricular and otherwise. By managing our own funds, we have most certainly brought the school to a point that it would have been unable to reach previously within the given time span.

Differing Schemes

Several other LEAs have experimented with giving special schools a delegated budget to manage, although the schools have had various degrees of autonomy within these schemes. Our LEA was very forward-thinking from the start in that, even in the first year of the pilot, it delegated a considerable amount of money to the schools under the given budget heads, and then gave the governing bodies of the schools a free hand in spending, and in vireing (moving notional money) from one budget head to onother. We were, from the start, given a bank account and a cheque book, and all purchases, services such as gas, bills (e.g. for replacing a window) were, and still are, settled directly.

Staff salaries were organized centrally; however, all savings made by the schools were credited to their account at the end of the financial year. Because of this we were able to benefit from what would previously have been serious misfortune. For the first time in very many years, during the pilot year two members of teaching staff suffered long-term sickness, and in fact both finally left the school. After a certain length of absence, our LEA takes over the salary costs of the sick person, leaving the school with his/her salary to pay for the supply staff. However, we were not able to find the supply teachers to cover both posts, and so had to make internal arrangements to supplement the cover from within. Consequently savings in staff costs accumulated over the summer term, and the governors agreed that this could be used over the next year to release the Incentive 'C' teachers for half a day per week for curriculum development time.

Other LEAs may not, as yet, be as free with their delegation, even under a pilot scheme. However, whilst the experience of budget management has been invaluable to our school, the underlying principles are really the most important feature of delegated budgetary management. If schools can define their overall needs now, and start to work towards them within the scope of any delegation they might currently have, they will be in a much better position to match funding with need once formula funding arrives.

In order to do this, I firmly believe that one needs a good communication and management structure within the school, with all staff involved to feed in to it. School staff are now crucial in originating change, and the responsibility for development lies with them. How each school chooses to sort out its internal management structures and how it liaises and works with its governing body are largely matters of the inter-relationships between the various personalities involved, the LEA's policies and statutory frameworks. However, it is clearly in the best interests of all concerned if decisions are based on the ideal of ensuring the best possible quality of teaching and learning, and people in special schools should strive to work co-operatively to achieve this aim in preparation for full LMSS.

Funding

All the above developments at our school took place with a budget based on historic funding, and were really the result of the school being able to optimise the use of its given resources. LMSS brings with it the notion of formula funding, and this will almost certainly cause significant modifications. Perhaps one of the most fundamentally important aspects of Circular 7/91 which, amongst other things, redefines the original Act to incorporate special schools, is the need for each LEA to carry out a review of all its special needs policy, using this as the basis of its proposed special school formula funding.

I think it fair to say that this leaves a number of us feeling vulnerable in terms of the viability of our schools. Such a radical look at overall provision in any LEA will inevitably mean that unnecessary expenditure and economies scale will be looked for. Thus at this time, heads should be looking honesty at their own schools and anticipating questions that might be asked. It is important that heads, at the very least, should be involved in the work and discussions leading to the development of the formula. Nobody else will understand the workings of their school like they do, or be able to put their case forward as easily.

In Chapter 1, Adrian Fletcher poses some key questions for us to consider, and these should be borne closely in mind by all special school heads. In parallel with these questions will need to be a consideration of the staffing of the special schools in relation to the guidance given in Circular 11/90. Whether or not they saw the categorizations as appropriate, I am sure that every head in the land looked at the children in his/her school against the number of staff recommended to see how the school fared.

It is vital that special schools start to look at themselves now, if they have not already begun to do so, and so develop a clear rationale for their existence. Once again, forward planning is essential if one wants to continue to develop. The days of trundling along as a cog in the LEA's mechanism have now gone, and the notion of schools actively driving themselves forward on very many counts has definitely arrived. Each school should now be looking at its current position in the light of the LEA's special needs policy, and planning its future. Changes in role should be carefully written into development plans, and working towards them should begin as soon as possible.

A few years ago, I identified a gap in our LEA's provision for pre-school children. There was no assessment centre for children whose needs were such that their assessment could not be carried out adequately in other establishments. Such children went out of the Borough for their assessment, and for various reasons rarely came back.

When our school took over the home teaching service, I started to plan for such an assessment centre to be housed under our roof although run as a separate establishment. Because of the transfer of our secondary-aged pupils to the other school when we were reorganized, and the fact that we received fewer primary-aged pupils in return, space and staff became available to open this centre. Judicious use of money during the first year of pilot LMS, and the fact that major building works were already planned and then carried out to give adequate facilities for the greater numbers of primary-aged children, meant that the accommodation could be extensively updated and re-equipped. The new assessment centre opened in September 1990, at the same time as we became a primary school, and has proved to be an invaluable and money-saving resource for the LEA. Further developments are planned in conjunction with a private charity to make this a really unique venture.

I am not suggesting that such a development could take place in every school, but simply illustrating the principle of identifying a need or suitable development and using the system and resources appopriately to meet that need. New developments can be costly to an LEA which is under pressure from all sides to delegate as much as possible to schools and so retain the minimum centrally. On the other hand, developments on the back of existing provision are very much cheaper and tend to be viewed positively by the DES, and are thus more likely to take place.

Lengthy discussions are currently taking place in every LEA on the nature of their particular special schools formula. These will all be different, since they should where possible be a variation of each authority's original LMS formula. However, heads should be stating their cases clearly and accurately in terms of place and pupil factors, and how various costs should be built into these components. If more that half one's school is profoundly and multiply disabled, there is no point in staying silent during the planning stages and then complaining that the school is staffed for severe learning difficulty children and that the children don't have adequate staffing to allow them access them to the curriculum. On the other hand, the head of an MLD school who feels that the children need staffing at the level suggested for severe learning difficulty children might expect a rationalization in terms of place factor during the LEA's review.

There are a variety of other aspects that will need to be considered in terms of each individual school. Much will depend on each LEA's approach to LMS and delegation, and on what services and money they intend to hold centrally. Considerable debate will go on according to one's own point of view - for example, on the buying of a service like Educational Welfare Officers. If the money for this were delegated to schools (including special schools), some of those schools would not have enough of the share to buy in the amount of the service that they need, and would have to find the balance from elsewhere. Other schools might not have used an Educational Welfare Officer for years, and would be delighted to have a share of the money to use in another capacity.

Each school should know clearly what its needs are and should be putting forward its case in the general debate. This self-identification of need does not come out of thin air, but is the result of in-school discussion and consultation, backed up by evidence and clear justification.

Marketing

In some ways, special schools have always had to market themselves, since they have had to promote a positive image to the public and parents. The notion of the marketplace as it applies to ordinary schools, who are being encouraged to compete for their children, does not apply in quite the same way in special schools, where all the children are placed by the LEA itself. However, marketing is assuming a greater and greater importance for us. Just as ordinary schools acquire a higher profile in the public's eye, with glossier buildings, brochures and curricula, so in turn must our schools if we are not to be left behind. Furthermore, if more than one school in an LEA covers the same place factor and parents make sufficient demands, then the market economy will certainly start to apply.

Marketing can be considered at several levels. As I have already said, we need to promote a positive image in the public's eye to kill the myths that still exist about children with special needs, and to enable us to attract the financial support that we need in order to augment our budgets. Very few special schools have their large-scale specialist facilities, such as hydrotherapy pools, coaches, soft play or sensory rooms, put in by the their

LEA. These will have been the result of fund-raising on the part of the school and parents' groups. However, ordinary schools are now turning increasingly to the business sector for help, and we will thus have to work harder in future.

We need to market ourselves positively in the eyes of the parents - once again on the two levels. We have to demonstrate that we are helping their children learn to the best of their ability and that our curricula are set within the National Curriculum framework, placing us on a par with ordinary schools. This means ensuring that each school is working well, and to return to the theme at the beginning of this chapter, to do this calls for an extensive in-school audit to bring up weaker areas and to augment others as developments take place.

We also have to show parents that our environment is ideal for the needs of their children: that it is welcoming, modern, educational and well-resourced. It is a considerable blow for many parents that their child has to attend a special school; it is our job to reframe their feelings positively, and positive marketing is the way forward. Once again, environmental audit will ensure that their initial misapprehensions and misconceptions are dissipated, and that they see the school and the package it is offering as the best possible place for their child's education.

I have always believed that our school should have an 'open door' policy, and that we should educate a wide variety of people about the nature of our work. This, too, is positive, marketing and raises the profile of the school and special schools in general. Special schools are closely connected with a wide range of professionals and outside agencies. Tighter controls and financial appraisal are everywhere, and at the moment the country is in recession. If we are to continue to grow, and to receive the statutory and voluntary services which may provide these people, special schools must be considered worthwhile places in which to invest (financially and in terms of people's time). This can only be done by being a top-rate establishment in all aspects, and letting others know about it. Reputations take a long time to build up - and very little time indeed to slide down.

In a similar way, it is important to ensure that one's own LEA is properly aware of the work of the school. Misconceptions - albeit benevolent - can prevail at bureaucratic levels, and assumptions can be made about what is or is not needed in a school based on out-of-date or misconceived facts. Invite people in to see the school at work. Make sure that the Director, Assistant Directors, financial controllers, and key elected members are familiar with your school and see it as a positive educational environment. It is too easy to be forgotten otherwise.

Finally, one can easily improve aspects of the school which create good and lasting first impressions. Over the last year, we have re-floored and repainted classrooms (part of a rolling programme); repainted the entrance hall in a fairly innovative way; added some cane furniture and plants to the waiting area; mounted children's art work in proper glassed frames instead of putting up the usual art display; re-vamped the P.E. hall in the way I explained; had new notepaper and compliments slips printed with the school logo in the corner and, to extend this, are using the school logo on all documents written by the school. We have also produced a very extensive ring binder for each set of parents, containing a full description of the school, its curriculum, working procedures, what help we and the community can offer and so on. It has specific sections for the termly individual programmes of work, reports and the photographs of progress that we frequently send home. This is the Parents' Information and Record of Progress Pack, and has been well received. As each new child joins the school, the class teacher does an immediate initial home visit to go through the pack with the parents and explain its importance in the child's time at school.

All the above are important developments and updates in their own right. However, taken together they contribute to our policy of positive marketing which we see as vital if we are to survive.

Responsibility

All the way through this chapter I have referred to 'the school' and made little mention of the governing body. This is based on my personal experiences and is because our governing body is really an integral part of the school, and is 'with us' all the way. Communication is frequent and positive; the members are supportive and helpful, and the various sub-committees meet as and when appropriate. Much superficial decision-making about expenditure has been delegated to me, and the finance sub-committee is prepared to meet at any time to discuss larger proposals, perhaps formulated by the senior management team.

With LMSS comes greater responsibility for staffing, and with this comes the head's responsibility for ensuring that the staff are carrying out their jobs properly. We have already been experimenting with informal appraisal in preparation for the formal scheme to be introduced at national level. The LEA is also about to implement its own local quality assurance mechanisms, through the inspectorate, and I consider it only fair to give the staff some experience in having their teaching, records and evidence of the children's learning looked at through outside eyes - albeit mine.

Schools have always been responsible for the education of children, but I feel that the responsibility has never weighed so heavily as it does today, and will do increasingly in the future. We are responsible for ensuring the best possible education of the children in our care, but mechanisms have now been set up to see that this happens in reality. The National Curriculum has been established to ensure given standards, and we must show a variety of inspectors that we are working appropriately for the needs of our children. All the above should pose no problems if the school is doing as it should. Responsibility falls into two categories - legal and moral. The legal responsibilities of schools and governing bodies are being increased all the time, but the moral responsibilities have always been there.

In conclusion

The basic principle underlying LMS is that it should enable the delivery of the best quality education to take place in a locally responsive way. The needs of each individual school should be met by that school directing its own resources appropriately. It is the responsibility of schools to identify their needs in an honest and positive way, and to plan ways of meeting these needs. These can be done immediately and provide the easiest preparation for LMSS that can take place since they rest entirely within the domain of the school's management. Everyone can and should be involved, and will therefore feel part of the developments.

It is also vitally important that consideration is given to the externally impinging aspects of LMSS; to how the formula should be developed, what place each school has in the LEA's special needs provision, and what is unique about each school that should be reflected in its funding. Heads should be involved as much as possible in the formula development work and associated activities, to represent their school and branch of education, to maintain a high profile and to ensure that they are fully aware of all the ramifications of LMSS.

LMSS is here, whether we like it or not. In my experience the management of our own budget has been exceptionally beneficial to our school. We do not 'do' LMS at given times: it has affected our whole way of working and thinking, and the extra work caused has been amply compensated for in seeing the school develop so favourably. However, management is one thing, the funding is very much another, and this I cannot predict for anyone. If the school and its work is successfully marketed, if it takes its responsibilities seriously and is a good educational establishment that is not duplicating or costing a great deal more than similar provision elsewhere, and if the head is able to contribute properly to LEA-wide debate, then one would hope that LMSS will bring all schools the benefits that we have found so far.

Chapter 6

Close to the customer: a modus supervivendi for the special school

Mel Farrar

This chapter draws on an action research project extending over six years (and still continuing) in one special school for youngsters with special needs arising from a physical disability. It considers the nature of the marketplace in education, the notion of the customer as it applies to the special school or support service, some of the drawbacks of special schools, and looks at the management issues and consequences for schools of putting the customer first.

Background

The school on which this chapter is based has been in an educational market-place since it opened in 1973. It is sited in a heavily urbanised area where over a million people live within easy travelling distance. It serves up to eight LEAs and takes over 55% of its children from other districts. Most of those children have historically had a choice of three or four similar schools within the same travelling distance. The school has always had as one of its aims the provision of a quality service to children and the development of strong links with parents but for the last six years has engaged in a struc-tured dialogue with its customers as part of an internal research project. That dialogue has incorporated surveys, discussions, and various formal and informal contacts with them and others perceived as having purchasing power. The results have been fed back into the system to promote a service which, it is felt, is truly 'close to the customer.'

Education in the marketplace

'What matters most are the attitudes of teachers to parents and parents to teachers - whether there is a genuine mutual respect,whether parents understand what the schools are doing for their individual children and teachers realize how dependent they are on parental support' (DES, 1967 p.40).

Though now more than twenty years old, the above quotation from the Plowden Report has been given added significance by developments in the 1980s which give more power to parents and make teachers (and others working in schools) realize that job security, not simply job satisfaction, is dependent on parental support. The activities of many education professionals in the past two decades - especially as observed at the annual conferences of the National Associations - could well have appeared to give credence to Adam Smith's dictum that whenever professionals gather together the result is either a conspiracy against the public or a contrivance to raise prices. Whilst not suggesting that teachers have engaged in an active conspiracy against the public (on most things the professional associations cannot even agree amongst themselves), it is arguable that for too long the teaching profession saw the running of schools, and in particular the content and development of the curriculum, as its own private garden. It became too 'holy' about its work.

Although the early stridency which accompanied moves to a marketplace in education has been toned down, there has clearly been a major shift in the balance of power between customers and providers. In theory, market forces mean production to meet consumer demand and competition between producers on price and quality. The predicted outcome is a better deal for the individual and more cost-effective production benefiting the whole community. The legislation of recent years has placed schools firmly in the marketplace, with parents perceived as consumers who have a right to know what is going on in schools and more freedom than ever before to influence schools by taking - or threatening to take - their children away. With schools dependent on pupil numbers for their ability to retain staff and plan their future, there are compelling arguments for examining how the management of schools should respond to this changed scene. Models which have served heads well in the past will no longer be as valid in the next decade. If we are to understand the forces at work better and cope effectively then new and hitherto possibly alien notions must be explored.

Pointers from the Health Service

In many ways the moves in schools have parallels in other areas of public service. The emphasis in the early eighties on management and management training as important elements in equipping schools for a new agenda was concurrent with new directions in the Health Service. There the cosy management team structure which had run hospitals and community services for the past ten years was swept away to be replaced by accountable General and Unit Managers on fixed-term contracts and performance-related pay. The central aims were extending patient choice; delegating responsibility to those best placed to respond to patients' needs and wishes; and securing the best value for money (DHSS, 1983). This was further emphasized in the early nineties with the government's insistence on a purchaser/provider split in which the providers had to earn their money in a health marketplace by the provision of high quality cost-effective services. Of course this was a Conservative government initiative; however, there is scarcely any difference between the major parties on the three notions of consumer choice, efficient and responsive management, and accountability.

These three features can now be seen as the signposts for those engaged in education. Indeed further legislation to promote these goals (from either major party) cannot be ruled out. Consumerism is the 'ism' of this decade. Under a Labour or Conservative administration, whichever Citizens' Charter the electorate chooses, parent power is set to be a feature of the educational scene of the present decade.

The changes

In mainstream schools the move to lessen professional dominance and create a marketplace in education has been pushed forward by a number of measures: the abolition of the Schools Council, an insistence on schools publishing more information about their philosophy and activities, and the placing of more buying power in the hands of parents by abolishing artificial entrance boundaries and increasing the role of governors at the expense of the power and patronage of local education authorities. The 1988 Education Act, with its thrust towards devolution of budgets and decisions which are taken at school level, together with the threat to local authorities of schools opting out, has continued the trend. The fall in the school population now affecting the secondary age group is accelerating the effects of these changes.

Tony Bowers (1989b) outlined the distinction between 'wild' and 'domesticated' organizations. The latter are protected from their environment whereas wild organizations struggle for survival, their existence is not guaranteed, and they can and do cease to exist. Support for them is closely tied to quality of performance, and a steady flow of clients is not assured. Wild organizations, unlike domesticated ones, are not protected at their vulnerable points. Under LMS, schools will increasingly have to stand on their own feet and live with the consequences of their own decisions. The prospect of 'no guaranteed breakfast tomorrow' can help wonderfully to concentrate the mind.

One secondary school in the North West, which in 1985/6 suffered badly due to teachers' action, in the two years after the passing of the 1988 Education Act lost half its potential sixth-form intake to a neighbouring authority's sixth-form college. Even earlier Glatter (1984) pointed out a general shift towards wildness throughout education, including the school sector. He saw closures being common, survival being problematic, and also institutions finding it necessary to supplement their income from non-traditional sources. Heads of mainstream schools are now very much aware of these pressures for survival.

Although the models for devolved budgets and management in special schools look like being less harsh, through funding the number of places and not simply the number of children, the need to design and deliver a service which meets the needs of children and parents will be no less important. The impact of losing pupils may be mitigated in any one year but will be reflected in the next. Special schools, too, will have to live with the consequences of their decisions.

Parental power in special education

Complete freedom of choice does not, and probably could not, exist for parents of children with special needs. However, factors such as the increase in supported places in mainstream schools, the opportunity to look outside LEA boundaries, new school designs allowing access by disabled students and statemented pupils likely to be worth a great deal under LMS, mean that parents now have more options. The balance of power has been tilted significantly in their direction compared with the position at the time of the publication of the Warnock Report (DES, 1978).

Parents now have the opportunity to contribute to statements (aided in a number of places by professional parent advocates), a right of appeal against the statement or the provision offered, rights to information about the school, representation on the governing body and a chance to monitor progress at the annual review or raise questions at the annual meeting of governors and parents. There is also a new complaints procedure for those who are not satisfied with the service they or their child are receiving. Parents now have more pressure groups to turn to and a greater awareness of their rights.

The important thing to realize here is that power is not only evidenced in overt conflicts. The threat of conflict may be just as effective in shaping the agenda. The effect of schools opting for grant maintained status has been much more far-reaching than the handful of schools which hit the headlines with massive votes in favour. The prospect of schools opting out and thus wrecking local plans for reorganization or rationalization of provision has meant that many LEA plans have been modified or shelved to avoid schools considering opting out. In the same way the threat of parent governors raising issues and finding sympathy and support in the governing body means that behind-the-scenes moves will be going on to head off the problem. Real power works to keep things from the agenda as often as to put them on it. Thus the shift in the balance of power may be more evidenced in a softer approach from the professionals than in open warfare with them.

Although the changes I have outlined may challenge existing professional notions, the task of managers is to work within the given framework to deliver the best achievable service to children with special needs and to their parents. Moreover, I consider that there is no fundamental incompatibility between moves to introduce an element of competition between schools in an educational marketplace and efforts to achieve the educational aims schools have always had for their pupils. Putting a price on pupils' heads can act as a spur to schools to clarify their aims, and weld together the team which has to deliver them. Peters and Waterman (1982) have shown that where commercial and service organizations value, listen to and respond to their customers there are advantages for all concerned. They set out a number of features they found in companies operating successfully in a market economy. These included a bias for action - for getting on with the job; fostering autonomy and entrepreneurship; treating those who work in them as the root source of quality and productivity - and thus respecting the individual. They go on: 'the excellent companies tap the inherent worth of the task as a source of intrinsic motivation for their employees' (p.72) and 'create environments in which people can blossom, develop self-esteem and otherwise be excited participants in the business and society as a whole' (p.86). These are surely laudable aims for any educational establishment and even more so for those working with children who have special educational needs.

One of the key features of these organizations and the one around which this chapter is woven is that of staying close to the customer. This means tailoring the activities to the needs of those who use the products and not getting too 'holy' about the products themselves or the processes by which they are made. The task of the educational manager in this new marketplace can be separated into:

> (1) An internal one involving welding together a team which recog-
> nizes the importance of the external dimension and which jointly

designs and delivers a customer-responsive service on which team members' livelihoods depend.

(2) An external one involving forming and handling opinion - a public relations function which will be new to many educational managers but no less important for that.

A policy which aims to stay close to the customer presents schools with both challenges and opportunities, and clearly has implications for every aspect of school management. These are examined in the following pages.

Clients and customers

As in other areas of the public service domain, the distinction between clients and customers is important in considering an approach to a market. The client is the person for whom the service is provided; the customer is the one who can determine whether or not the client goes to one source or another. The Disney Organization cited in the Peters and Waterman (1982) study might be seen as having parallels with schools, since the product is aimed to satisfy (largely) youngsters but the money is in the hands of their parents (or very often in this country charitable groups who take parties of children with special needs to Disneyland). Special schools are more complicated in that whilst they have the child as their client, they have to satisfy a number of customers - not all of whom share the same concerns as parents. The diagram on the next page illustrates this (Figure 6:1).

In the diagram I have tried to illustrate some of the individuals or groups that the school must seek to influence. They are either customers of, or people who influence the customers of, the special school.

The client

The child is at the heart of the operation because of its key position as both client and customer. In any business (except perhaps the public services ahead of the Citizens' Charter) it would be seen as self-evident that the provider should set out to ensure client satisfaction with the service. Which service industry would tolerate the dissatisfaction evident in the truancy rates of some schools - particularly among fourth and fifth year students? We know that children learn better if they are secure in school, if they know they are valued, and if they are set challenges which are beyond their grasp but within their reach.

This means an individually designed curriculum delivered in a manner sensitive to individual needs. Although, as the Warnock Report (DES, 1978)

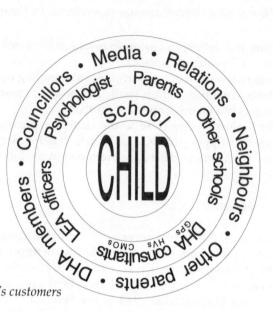

Figure 6:1

The special school's customers

argues, the aims of education are the same for all children, the content and philosophy of such a curriculum will vary from school to school. For the purposes of this chapter it is perhaps enough to say that the first aim of any school system - special or normal - must be to ensure that children make demonstrable progress (however small the steps) and set out happily and positively for school every day. The quality of the school experience, together with its balance and phasing throughout the day, should lead each day to an overall positive feeling about school. This philosophy, thought through in the context of terminally ill children (some of whom might not return the next day), has no less potency for any other child. Issues of pupil disaffection which are frequently evidenced in truancy should have no place in a special school.

Parents - the principal customers

Although the provision for the child should be the prime concern for professionals, however excellent that provision is, the winning of the prospective parent is the major factor in determining whether the child attends the special school or elsewhere. This is because it is increasingly unusual for a child to be placed in a special school against the wishes of the parents. Prospective parents may not have complete freedom of choice but their perceptions affect the perceptions of the other customers. Where they object to the choice of a particular school they can certainly make life difficult for an officer, with objections going to the Secretary of State or involving Judicial Review. Attracting prospective parents, then, is of vital importance; discovering what parents want and designing a service to meet their needs makes good commercial, as well as professional, sense.

The notion of parents as customers may appear to sit ill with the approach of many special schools which has been to involve parents as partners. Although schools can plan and work that way once the child is admitted, prospective parents are primarily customers and it is important first to understand what they want as customers. This may or may not include partnership.

The drawbacks of special schools

For prospective parents, any misgivings regarding special schools may these days loom even larger than the potential advantages, since so much has been made of their drawbacks in the media over the past two decades.

Between 1976 and 1986 I found no articles on the Guardian Education pages which had anything good to say about special schools. Pressure groups such as the Centre for Studies on Integration in Education have grown up arguing polemically for total integration of all youngsters with special needs, and colouring the views not only of parents but also their relatives and the professionals who may have to advise them. Some spokesmen seem to consider the very existence of special schools as an indictment of the whole education system. Rather than ignoring the drawbacks, let us examine some major ones and ways of overcoming them.

(i) *Living at a distance.* Most special schools are sited some distance from children's homes. Parents may want to be involved but fear they will not be able to reach school. If they do not come in (or see other parents) regularly, how will they know what is going on? By utilising existing school transport or the school vehicle, by arranging lifts or even paying for taxis it is possible to allay this concern and ensure that for all special occasions - the first day (or longer), the Review, Parents' Evening - and perhaps some less special ones, such as sports days, transport is offered. Is it money well spent? That is a decision for the school. Certainly it was one of the factors which was most consistently appreciated in our surveys - and the cost was not prohibitive.

Another factor in creating a sense of closeness is good written communication. From the school prospectus and welcoming notes to each class or department, through daily home/school books and regular newsletters, it is possible to keep parents well-informed and feeling they belong. One of the earliest outcomes of our dialogue with parents was a wider spread of home/school books (previously they had been thought of as a nursery service) and the establishment of a monthly newsletter. Although both require an investment of time, it is one which really pays dividends. The newsletter underlines the values of the school by celebrating the successes of children in every area, gently expounds policy, gives notice of school events and accounts of them for those who were not involved or could not make it, flags up impending changes and responds to local or national developments. When, for example, the film 'Stand up for Joey' appeared on television - with its tear-jerking pictures of the work of the Peto Institute in Budapest - the school was able to respond through the newsletter. With subsequent correspondence from parents it could carry debate on to a more rational level. The letter allows lobbies to be created or rumours stemmed. Parents are given information which they can use very effectively, such as the fact that the school has never had a waiting list.

One of the major worries of new parents in our survey was: could they get in touch if they had a problem? Parents who feel they can ring up and be assured of a friendly reception can feel very close to a school - even if they are two hours away by bus. An unanswered telephone is a most effective way to cripple contact.

(ii) *Stigma*. This may be one of the hardest for parents to cope with. If they are convinced that their child will be stigmatized for attending a special school, they need powerful reasons for sending him or her there. This view will be variously supported in the neighbourhood. In the past we have had requests for taxis rather than the school bus, which by its clientele marks the child out as very different. Countering this is something which has to be done on a wider scale since the arguments which parents encounter will often never come to the school's notice until late in the day. Others - neighbours, grandparents, relatives, the media - will have the chance to put their views forward while the school usually has no right of reply. Because of this the school's reputation for its provision is important. Its links with other professionals, and its education of them on what it has to offer, can only partially affect the outcome. However, a positive profile in the local media, as well as within the population of its own past or present parents, helps to provide a counter lobby.

In the case of children with a physical disability, impressions of the school are often gained in places where parents of young disabled children meet: hospitals, clinics, nurseries, support groups, parents' groups. Where existing parents are on the side of the school and pleased with its service they will speak up for it. Their own self respect is at stake and they like to feel they have made the right choice. Where they are kept well informed, they are potential allies at key strategic points who will correct misunderstandings, stem rumours and feed back to the school. Good news is shared with four people, bad news with sixteen, hence the importance of good lines of communication with existing parents and plenty of positive features for them to work on.

(iii) *Lack of normal peer group.* Great emphasis is laid these days on the importance of the child's peer group. A special school which has no contact with its mainstream counterparts exacerbates parental concerns. Most special schools are able to arrange joint projects with mainstream schools and a number, our own included, have been able to counter this by reverse integration at the nursery level whereby 'local' (i.e. non special need) children are admitted. Feedback on our scheme after the first year from both sets of parents was enthusiastic and at times ecstatic, and ensured that it was continued.

Other factors which parents told us were important in making their decisions were:

(i) Ease in making a preliminary visit (sometimes including the provision of transport). Having an 'open door' policy, even where parents may not take up a place, pays off in the long run. All members of staff, governors, advisers, officers and parents (through the newsletter) know that enquiries will be warmly received and that we are willing to show round interested parents. (ii) First impressions. An open door policy means that the school in always on show, and resources - human and financial - have to be deployed to ensure that a good welcome is there. Arrangements should also give a flavour of the school without undue disruption of what is going on (Farrar 1987).

Customers beyond the parents

Some of the means of gaining parental acceptance and satisfaction are also applicable to the wider group of customers outlined in Figure 6:1. The school newsletter can go into education offices, to key psychologists, to governors and to interested councillors and members. Prospective parents and some past parents may welcome being included on the mailing list. Thus the school can create and manage its own constituency, with informed lobbyists in strategic positions. The local media are always looking for copy and, whereas they may focus on controversy and bad news in other areas, find no difficulty in running 'good' stories about schools. The key to success here is to approach articles from a 'human interest' or 'special project' angle and make the reporter's work as easy as possible. For advisers, officers and psychologists the received wisdom about a school is often dependent on the quality of reports received, the school's co-operation in its agenda and the absence of complaints from parents. A cheerful 'rendering unto Caesar' is the minimum a school should aspire to (fortunately with LMS in mainstream schools there are less little Caesars about) but a cultivation of these people can also handsomely repay the investment.

The Community

The community in which the school is situated has a legitimate interest in its working and the amount of community chargepayers' money it consumes. There may be key people there whose support or understanding is needed. For some schools the health visitor or doctor may be the first person to whom the parent of a potential pupil talks about schooling. Where the child is of school age, other head teachers will be the point of contact. Through direct (e.g. invitation to Open Days) or indirect publicity (e.g. reports of achievements in the local press) these are potential allies to be won. All members of staff, if they are pleased to belong to the school, are ambassadors to the circles in which they move. Increasingly now special schools have a role as training institutions (Farrar, 1987) and the 'open' school will influence positively most of those who come through its doors. The days of the 'closed' community within schools are coming to an end and those schools which survive into the nineties will have to demonstrate their responsiveness to their environment. Good lines of communication - in both directions - help to keep schools in touch with their constituency.

Marketing

Encouraging direct contact by parents and having an open visiting policy helps to reach a wider audience, but for special schools it would be self-defeating in the long run to 'sell' a school place if that is not in the child's interests. Those special schools which have coped best with falling rolls do not appear to be the ones which have clung on to children at all costs, but rather those which have fostered integration projects. In a more open market, parents have seen admission to the former as a one-way ticket and have, where possible, steered clear. Integrity is a major feature of the best companies which survive and should be a fundamental element of the school's marketing approach.

There is, too , a difference between 'one-off' sales and long-term sales. Schools have to provide a service over many years. In this context you cannot , in an open climate, go on for long successfully selling a bad product. However, some good products fail because the ideas have been badly handled (i.e. marketed). As universities, polytechnics and colleges are finding, PR skills and a PR function will be necessary adjuncts in the schools of the nineties.

Given that 'all that glitters is not gold', there is no excuse for a school not putting its best endeavours into promoting the establishments's worth. There is a professional task here which is just as important as good lesson preparation. Tastefully done, videos, brochures, newsletters, newspaper articles, etc. express the value of the customer, existing as well as prospective, and can reflect and enhance the parental and staff sense of pride in 'their' institution.

Maintaining the satisfaction of clients once a selection has been made is a key part of any marketing strategy. Some of our children's medical conditions run in families, but even where they do not parents will turn to other parents in a similar position whenever they can. The endorsement of past or present parents then is vital. The long-term maintenance of parent support needs to be worked for. Because of the disruption where children are involved, parents will not change schools as easily as they will their supermarket. In the motor trade, however, manufacturers take the view that for every customer who complains to them, seven will criticize the product to others and a similar number will take future business elsewhere without raising a complaint. So it is not enough to assume that an absence of complaints indicates parent satisfaction.

The importance of market research

As a school which has for many years had to compete for 'extra-district' pupils we have always been aware of the importance of market research. Thus at regular intervals over the past eighteen years, and annually for the past six years, surveys have been conducted to find out what current and past parents think of our communications and services. Over seven hundred families have been surveyed, with response rates ranging from 40 - 70% and averaging 55%. From these responses we have been able to build up a picture not only of what they are satisfied with but also what they would like to see in an ideal situation. 'Are there any services we should be trying to improve and how?' 'What should we be most proud of?' and 'What do/did you as a parent most appreciate?' Of course perceptions are coloured by their experience of the service they have received but, since all pupils come from or go into other settings and many parents have children at other schools, their ideas are not bound by that and many of the suggestions which we have followed up originated elsewhere.

Our own research suggests that in general what parents want for themselves and their children are expressed in the 'soft' or affective areas: that children set out happily in the morning, that parents are welcome and can easily make contact and so on. None of these should be particularly threatening to professionals who are ready to consider individual needs, respect children, afford them dignity and take time to explain what they are doing. Over the years our service has been designed to ensure that those concerns are addressed but it is a dynamic, never ending task.

The interesting thing here, and probably the key insight from our own efforts and experience, is that if parents are satisfied with the 'soft' things then, in special education particularly, they are happy to leave the 'hard' areas to the professionals. Whilst they may want to know enough to help their child effectively, most do not what to become 'expert' in teaching techniques, in matters of organization or curriculum development. Thus it is possible to reconcile the apparently competing objectives of achieving one's professional aims for children at the same time as satisfying parents.

Checking out the satisfaction of existing parents is vital and this can be done through discussion at parents' evenings, School Association meetings, in the Parents' Support Group, on informal social occasions and in reviews so that the figures which show up in any surveys are not treated in isolation. 'How well do you feel we deal with your complaints or problems?' is a key question. The very fact of doing our own audit and following up the results demonstrates a willingness to take parents seriously.

One of the key aspects of staying close to the customer is learning from the people you serve, and the school has been able to demonstrate a responsiveness to the things which parents thought might be reconsidered. This has caused us to review the number of parent evenings, the arrangements at lunchtime, the quality of school meals, the extension of home/school books, the level of detail in reports, and the opportunities for children to win awards in school. Around 94% of replies regularly told us that parents did not want more events on the school calendar. There were also several suggestions on the format for conducting reviews. The disappointment of parents at the provision of speech therapy helped us first to take a case to the Health Authority and later determine that the School Association should put its funds into personnel as well as hardware. Eventually the school was able to agree a deal with the Health Authority to fund extra qualified sessions and a speech therapy aide.

Parents were asked if they felt they should have more say in the running of the school, and in the first survey 33% said they should. Over the years that number has gone down to 7% because it has been possible to demonstrate that their views are taken into account. However, it is no use making changes if people do not know about them. Hence the importance of the newsletter and the annually published survey results for underlining the fact that the school does listen and does care about how parents feel. At the annual meeting of parents and governors, the flavour of the meeting can be influenced by one parent who may have had a bad (or good) experience.

Whilst it is important to take that seriously it is equally important not to allow it to be seen out of proportion, and in this the evidence from the responses of fifty or more parents ensures that the full picture is painted.

Dealing with customer complaints

One question in our survey asks how well the school is perceived to be dealing with complaints or problems. The percentage score here is a reminder to all staff of the importance of treating all complaints seriously and being as helpful as possible when parents bring up problems. We have adopted a policy of actively seeking out potential problems, assuring parents that the school is interested in the quality of service, and handling complaints promptly and sensitively.

Quite a number of heads still see their role as defending indefensible member of staff, and will tend to close ranks professionally in the face of justified parental protest. This is wrong both practically and morally: practically because they misunderstand the present position and are storing up trouble for the future, and morally because the closing of ranks one occasionally finds in other professions, where serious negligence can sometimes go unremarked, ought to make heads stop and consider whether they are right to be involved in a similar conspiracy. The cost of maintaining the 'closed' climate in which such action can be sustained is arguably too great for a developing organization in a service industry. A good leader and a good team will offer support and some shelter for a colleague going through difficult times, but part of treating people as responsible adults is to recognize that responsibility cannot be evaded. Blemishes have to be openly addressed.

A planned approach

Our research shows the importance of a planned approach to parents which begins before they ever see the school. From the initial contact, through the advance information, the initial visit and the interview to the first day of admission and beyond, schools should have a clearly thought-out procedure to make parents and children feel welcome and at home. This procedure should be known to all staff. Investment of time here can save time later in dealing with problems.

Once the child is admitted, the parent is in daily contact with the school's service and in any year there are thousands of transactions which can go right or wrong. If the school demonstrates that it is always trying its best and succeeding for most of the time, which will be dependent on good communication to let people know, then when a problem does occur it will be seen in that context. In the best-run schools, clothes get lost or ruined with glue; acknowledging responsibility and putting it right is worth the cost. If something has gone wrong, ringing parents before they ring the school is a must. Everyone on the staff should know the school's policy on this. They should ensure that a note is sent home or a telephone call made as a means to get things on the best footing.

The information provided by keeping close to the customer should inform decision-making in the school and help the senior manager complete the feedback loop by checking that the vision enshrined in the school's mission statement and the policies whereby it is put into practice really are reaching the intended audience. In this context a school which sets out to involve parents but leaves it to them how they reach school is not practising what it preaches. It is legitimate to ask what attempts and what resources it puts into ensuring that parents can attend such events as reviews or parents' evenings. The provision of lifts or taxis may appear expensive but it can be a good investment in that it addresses a real problem.

Although schools may look on parents as their principal customers, they will always be in a system where there is an upward agenda to work to. Everyone can be seen as locked into a system where each is a supplier of services but also a receiver of services: a consumer. The classroom teacher depends on the caretaker to have the room ready, on the head of department to obtain the stock she needs, on the secretary to see that the photocopier works, on the head to plan a timetable for the swimming pool, and so on. Each of these service providers is dependent on someone else in the chain. Some transactions are dependent on efficient administration systems but there is human element in all of them; how the service is delivered may be as important as whether it is delivered. This applies from the education committee down to the child who receives the service. All must bear in mind the importance of the internal customer. The purpose of all these transactions is to give a good service, but how it is received and perceived will depend on the people through whom the policy is turned into practice.

Concern for staff

Although children are at the heart of the school community, in seeking to serve the needs of the customer, managers must sustain a golden thread of commitment to the needs of staff. Does the school offer them success, is it in tune with their hopes and their visions? Concern for employees extends beyond the physical environment and emotional climate, beyond security, social opportunities and achieving status. Growth, personal development and fulfilment are the highest of a person's needs and the good school can - indeed should - provide opportunities for these for its team. This points to the importance of a strong organizational culture - one in which all staff have an investment, and in which all play their part. Total quality management is about striving together for ever higher levels of achievement and excellence.

Many argue that market forces will have a malign effect on staff in schools, yet this is not inevitable. Excellent schools, like excellent commercial organizations, will be concerned both to attract and retain staff who can maintain their reputation. Those organizations with the best reputations for quality generally provide better than average conditions for their staff.

The more autonomous special school of the nineties has a particular opportunity and responsibility. An opportunity to influence its own agenda to a much greater degree; and a responsibility to ensure that staff are fully involved in that process and the whole enterprise. To grasp the former and to meet the latter will require skilful leadership on the part of senior managers in the coming years.

Chapter 7
Marketing a support service from a special school

Malcolm Clayton

In this chapter I shall seek to show that we can apply a marketing philosophy to the management of a special school and the support service that operates from it without detracting from the underlying principles of special education. I shall show that marketing can be conducted professionally, ethically and with consideration. I shall seek to present a model of marketing that enshrines those principles and yet firmly embraces the new philosophy of competition and accountability. I shall show that many of the activities upon which one needs to engage in order to have an effective marketing plan are already a feature of our work but that they are often applied in an unsystematic, reactive way with a keen lack of understanding for all the tools of marketing and how they can be combined into a total programme.

Misconceptions and ignorance

The concept of marketing a special school seems alien to many people and its very mention can produce some quite strong emotional responses when it is raised in a meeting of special educators. In many educational establishments there is a real fear among head teachers and governors of adopting what are seen as commercial practices. The belief is that to adopt the 'methods of commerce' will tarnish and devalue the very essence of a special school. It seems alien and somehow transatlantic, involving the foisting of worthless products on an unsuspecting public; it evokes the myth of the double glazing salesman and smacks of the immoral manipulation of people. Such attitudes are typified by statements such as 'We are not selling ice-cream'.

It is my contention that these fears are based upon misconceptions and ignorance and are usually groundless. As Krachenberg (1972) says, 'If anything is undesirable about marketing it is not the activity per se; but rather it is in the motives of the people guiding the activity and the manner in which it is carried out ' (p.380). If we are to give serious consideration to marketing as a management tool, it is necessary that we set aside such prejudices and give some serious thought to it as a concept.

Market forces

We need to acknowledge the climate within which all our schools, including special schools, are now required to operate. Collectively they have a poor public image because the predominant message from the media over the last few years has been that schools, and by implication teachers, are inefficient. It appears to have been given tacit approval by the political masters at the DES. This was a consistent message that in itself put anxiety into parents' minds and was then given further dimensions of disillusionment by teachers on strike, children being sent home when teachers refused to cover for absent colleagues, rotten school buildings, tales of violence and vandalism, and reports of under-achievement of pupils throughout the school sector. Lest we think that such criticism is not applicable to our situation it is worth noting the comments in 'A Curriculum For All' (NCC, 1990) which refer to HMI surveys highlighting deficiencies in the provision most special schools made for certain subject areas.

Within such a climate, the government was able to introduce the 1988 Education Reform Act. During this time the educational political scene was characterized by such statements as 'It is about competition, choice and freedom. It is part of the search for educational excellence. It is about quality and standards' (Secretary of State's Speech to The North of England Conference, Nottingham, 6 January 1988). We must be careful to recognize that the climate referred to is not just what has been termed 'Thatcherite'. It embraces more than one political party and focuses on all geographic and demographic regions. But we also need to recognize and accept that, even before the advent of 'Thatcherism' and the emphasis on market forces, schools were involved in promoting themselves. Those running the best schools have always been aware of the need not only to be successful but to be recognized within the community as being successful. A school perceived as successful is one to which parents are proud to send their children, be it a mainstream or a special school. A successful school is one in which staff are proud to work and one to which visitors are keen to come. These factors apply equally to the special school as to the mainstream school.

It is dangerous for those in special schools to think that because the focus of attention was mainstream schools and the raising of their standards, we are immune from the impact of the Education Reform Act. Indeed Bowers (1989b), among others, has drawn attention to the fact that with the introduction of Local Management of Schools and its financial implications there will be an increasingly large degree of autonomy over financial decisions at the mainstream school level. This will ultimately see schools paying directly for the services they use. It will also leave them free to excercise choice and decide what services they want to buy. It is likely to apply equally to services from a special school and to those coming from the LEA or elsewhere.

Why marketing?

There may be many reasons why you would wish to adopt a marketing approach, but if you are unclear about them then your marketing efforts will be wasted. As examples your reasons may come from a list such as: awareness raising about the role of special education within the overall provision available; a wish to increase numbers; a desire to increase resources available to the school; a wish to expand services currently offered; a wish to provide a service to a new client group; a need for better links with other professionals; a need for better links with mainstream schools.

There is no doubt that the development of special schools has left many of them inward-looking and badly placed to deal with an uncertain future in a changing environment. I believe that a strong attraction of the marketing approach is that it provides a framework within which to identify customer needs in a constantly changing environment. Marketing is concerned with the medium and long-term and it requires the school to look outwards from its own environment, causing it to make future-oriented decisions in the best interest of the *whole* school. Marketing creates the impetus for the clarification of goals and it provides a powerful set of tools for the selection of targets that fulfil school objectives. It can thus be said to promote the optimum use of resources because decisions which will determine the school's marketing portfolio are central to its continued success.

Marketing writers (e.g. Krachenberg, 1972; Frain, 1986) stress that their subject must not be seen as a series of isolated institutional activities but as a fully integrated plan of action. It is therefore evident that adopting a marketing approach to the total management of a school will contribute to the fulfilment of the overall aims of the school. The first step in marketing poses the question, 'What business are we in?' The product-oriented response is 'Education', but a marketing orientation draws attention to the global nature of the school and its activities.

What is marketing?

There is a lot said and written about marketing and one can now turn to an increasing number of articles on marketing and Further and Higher Education (e.g. Adams-Chapman,1986) but virtually none of it has schools in mind. There is much literature that refers to promotion and public relations (Bowman and Ellis, 1977; Coulson-Thomas, 1979) but little that helps with the marketing of schools, and in particular services that operate from schools.

Many head teachers have become more conscious of the part the picture others have of their school will play in the future health of their school. The 'image' that your school has is actually made up of a wide range of components, and the weight given to these differs between audiences. I shall draw out later the integral part a public relations exercise plays in a marketing plan looking more specially at the concept of the 'brand image'. The school's image may be one of the best arguments for promoting your school, but the mere act of promoting your school is not all that there is to marketing.

It is clear that we need to develop a definition and model of marketing that will fit the school situation. However, in order to do that we have first to draw upon the existing definitions and theories that are available to us from the business community before we can modify them for our own situation. Within the business world, marketing has been described as everything to do with focusing on client needs and their satisfaction. As Drucker (1973) shows, the aim of marketing is to know and understand the customer so well that the product or service fits him or her and sells itself. In order to distinguish marketing from public relations it is worth noting that Frain (1986) defines PR as being 'concerned with maintaining good communications between an organization and its various publics' (p.277). We will see that public relations is an important part of marketing but is not in itself sufficient to carry forward a marketing plan.

The cornerstone of marketing is recognizing the importance of the customer and it is evident that this has become as applicable to schools as to any business. In essence, therefore, marketing aims to identify customer needs and satisfy those needs. The marketing concept that I have adapted and developed for a special school with a school-based support service is one based upon the following activities:

(i) identifying the needs of your market;
(ii) identifying your resources;
(iii) developing appropriate services and resources to satisfy the needs;
(iv) promoting those goods and services you have to offer;
(v) offering these at the right place and time.

A whole school policy

If a marketing strategy is to be an integral part of the management of a school, it must be embraced wholeheartedly. It is evident from various discussions that many colleagues are still unsure about the place their institution occupies in the overall continuum of provision and even whether it has a right to occupy that place. This is particularly true of heads of MLD schools. It is absolutely essential to resolve this fundamental issue in order seriously to adopt a marketing plan for your special school.

It is also important to note that the application of a marketing plan to the delivery of a support service from a special school cannot be done as an isolated activity. It has to be treated as an integral part of the whole school.

Ambassadors

As I have already stressed, to develop a marketing plan it is necessary to have a clear understanding of why you wish to adopt a marketing approach to the management of the school and any associated support services. Having ascertained why, you have to identify to whom you will target your marketing. Remember that there are two audiences to consider in this exercise. The first is the school's own internal audience (Figure 7:1). In researching the marketing of schools it has become clear that often we pay little attention to our internal audience and we tend not to articulate our school development plan to this audience. We do not fully understand the role of such staff as effective ambassadors for our schools. Even when we as head teachers come to that understanding we still have to get them to appreciate it and therefore accept, in a conscious way, their role as ambassadors.

When a special school operates a support service it is all too easy for subgroups to develop and for one group to become isolated from the others, and yet they are all part of the total resource of the school. This issue is likely to become more apparent as special schools become involved in their own local management schemes. A s with the mainstream scheme, eventually a special school will receive a total budget to fulfil its agreed role. However, it will be up to the governors to decide how to allocate that resource to achieve and deliver the service. All members of the school work as ambassadors for all the other members and therefore any tensions that exist between the various sub-groups have to be resolved if each is to develop and grow. Failure to do so will ultimately result in a general loss of resources.

It has also become apparent in discussing this with heads of other special schools that, when we do think of our internal audience, we often have too narrow a view of who constitutes that audience. Obviously the most important members of staff are those in the front line, but how the front line is defined depends on what your needs are. For example, if school closure is the issue that you identify as your primary reason for adopting a marketing approach then your external target audience will include elected members of the local authority. In any event the front line will be made up of those members of your school who have initial contact with your external target group.

Internal Audience	
School All teachers All ancillary staff Students School meals Caretaker Parents	*Community* Governors Voluntary helpers Other professionals Contract services Traders Social services Medical services School library service

Figure 7:1 The school's internal audience

As management guides will tell you, the best way of communicating an aim or a programme is through the involvement of everyone in some way, but at the very least all in your internal audience should be aware of your overall aims. As an example, do the parents in your school know that you have a support service operating from your school and the role of that support service? They will almost certainly have other children in the family attending such schools. It was only when I looked at applying a marketing approach to the management of my school that I began to consider the implications of such a simple fact as this. Then when I began to delineate my internal audience I came to comprehend fully the extensive and complex network of contacts that exists to promote, or otherwise, the work of the school. Perhaps we can all think of times when we have treated cleaners, school meals staff, lunchtime assistants, as if they were invisible.

Developing a marketing plan

The process of marketing planning is aimed at producing something which can be described as:
a statement that specifies a systematic and integrated programme for achieving

certain marketing goals within a perscribed period of time.
The tasks that you will need to complete in order to draw up your marketing plan are:
  (i) Conducting an internal audit of the school's strengths and weaknesses.
 (ii) Conducting research into your external market.
(iii) Developing the service (s).
 (iv) Promoting those services.
  (v) Offering them at the right place and time.

Internal audit

Most schools will by now have conducted an internal audit in drawing up their school development plan. Such an audit may well have focused solely upon the school's plan to develop and deliver the National Curriculum. However, if one looks at school development planning as a whole school activity then one will have reached the same agenda that would apply to marketing. Marketing planning will require that a compete audit is completed in order that a full analysis of the school's strengths, weaknesses, opportunities and threats is arrived at. This exercise is a well known tool in marketing terms (Baker 1987) and is known by the acronym of a SWOT analysis.

SWOT analysis

Information will have come from conducting market research into the external audience. The internal audit and the external market research activity can initially be conducted at the same time but they will then become a part of a cycle of activities that are an integral part of your marketing planning and fulfil the requirements for schools to produce school development plans annually. I propose as an example to look at the case of my own school and how the conduct of a SWOT analysis led to the development of a market plan.

The decision to develop a marketing approach to the management of the school was taken at a time when the school was an all-age mixed day school for pupils with moderate learning difficulties; we had up to 120 pupils on roll, we had strong links with mainstream schools and we were running a small scale mainstream support network that had for some time been recognized by the LEA. Although the school was full, the overall position for MLD provision within the LEA was one of gross over-capacity. We were housed in buildings that were originally designed as an infant school, although modifications had been carried out to make the buildings 'suitable' for housing a special school. We share the same parcel of land as a local primary school and excellent relationships existed between the two schools. At this time the LEA was in the process of drawing up a series of policy statements covering all aspects of its SEN provision. Of interest to us were the options being considered by the LEA for its MLD schools. There were three main options under consideration: (i) no MLD provision; (ii) age-phased MLD provision; (iii) maintenance, in a reduced number of schools, of the all-age policy. A further area for scrutiny during this LEA review was the purpose and responsibility of support services.

Strengths and weaknesses

Our own internal audit revealed, after much heart-searching, that we felt unable to meet all the needs of the pupils in our all-age school to our own satisfaction. As part of our ongoing internal school review, now encompassed formally in the process of school development planning, we had for some time been asking for a wide range of changes to be made to the school to allow us better to meet the needs of our pupils.

We had attempted, in common with any all-age school, to maintain a sound primary curriculum and an equally sound secondary curriculum. However, an open frank internal assessment confirmed serious deficiencies in our ability to deliver a broad, balanced and differentiated curriculum to such a wide age range. In addition, the results of research into our external market had revealed that mainstream schools at that time perceived us as very different to them. The research took the form of questionnaires and personal interviews conducted amongst our local primary schools. The image others had of the school was one part of this information gathering exercise and in addition to this perception of difference there were many positive facts revealed about the school and the work we did. It was concluded that for the support service operating from the school to be perceived as an appropriate source of support by mainstream schools, it would first be necessary for mainstream colleagues to perceive a common purpose in our work. A closer analysis of this research revealed that the greatest disparity lay between ourselves and our local secondary schools.

Things were uncertain. Should the LEA adopt certain of the options open to it then radical changes were inevitable. It became necessary during this period to direct marketing efforts to several audiences, not least among them the members of the Education Committee. With the information gathered from the internal audit and the external market research it was possible to identify what was likely to be the best option for the school. It was clear which of the options facing the LEA was best suited to our situation and for which support would be forthcoming from the local mainstream schools. We therefore backed the proposal that the school become a primary school rather than remain as an all-age school. In order to secure that the LEA took up the option most suited to our situation, a marketing effort was made to the various audiences necessary to secure its success. It was also possible by this means to ensure that the support service that we had operated for many years, outlined by Casteel (1984), would feature as an integral part of LEA policy.

We identified a range of activities within which it was perceived we had particular strengths, among them assessment and record keeping, good curriculum for pupils with SEN, resources and teaching materials adapted for pupils with SEN, specialist resources, extensive knowledge of information technology (IT), experience of providing support within other schools, classroom organization and management, an appropriately experienced and committed staff, a good professional base for other teachers of SEN pupils, and established links with mainstream schools.

From this list it was possible, in conjunction with the information revealed by our market research, to identify certain features unique to ourselves. In marketing terms these would be known as our unique selling points (USPs). It is an important part of a marketing approach that you clearly identify the USPs that apply to your school. If you have difficulty in arriving at this understanding it may be worth imagining that your school is due to close and then to itemize what in particular would be lost to the community.

I have mentioned that as a part of a SWOT exercise it is necessary to be aware of the school's perceived weaknesses, both from internal and external market research information. Since negative images are too easily retained, it would not be sensible to reveal here all our perceived weaknesses. However, there are certain general issues that are relevant to a wider audience.

High on such a list is the label of 'special school' and the in-built prejudices that still exist in the wider school community. In order to counteract these prejudices and preconceived notions it is necessary to maintain a high positive profile. Other areas that were identified in our particular situation as having the potential for imparting a negative rather than a positive image were the lack of car parking and limited INSET facilities. The school had inadequate parking and we knew from information gathered at other schools' INSET activities that frustration with parking led to a wide range of negative outcomes for the providers. This factor was also linked to concerns we had over geographical location: we are very close to some schools but quite some distance from many with which we need to work. We did not have any areas that could suitably be used for INSET activities nor adequate staff facilities to accommodate visiting teachers.

All of these deficiencies are in the process of being overcome through a large building programme. We are having an INSET/resource base built and are undertaking a total refurbishment of the staff room to make it both an integral part of the learning support base and of the whole school. Substantial car parking extensions are included, as is an element for equipment and resource enhancement.

Opportunities

The third element of a SWOT analysis is that of identifying opportunities. Of several that were identified, some were seen as opportunities for developing an existing resource. This would be done to a point where it could be made available to the outside educational community. We had, as I mentioned, offered for many years a limited support service to local mainstream schools. This was obviously a canditate for development as a market opportunity, particularly as our research revealed that the service was perceived as a highly beneficial resource by our local mainstream schools.

A further analysis of the research revealed several areas in which we perceived we had opportunities for new developments. One of these was making ourselves and our resources available to mainstream schools for school-focused INSET. A second area was making additional provision in mainstream schools for pupils with SEN who had been identified through a statement as needing additional teaching support. Our local mainstream schools had some time before asked the LEA if they could pool additional staffing that they had been allocated through the statementing process, using us as the resource. They had commented in writing to the LEA that such a process would provide them with a better supported and trained additional teaching resource. We were then able to link this to an issue raised by the part-time teachers who were at that time doing the additional teaching within the mainstream schools. They wanted to be part of a properly resourced and supported professional service with a professional base from which to operate; we could be that base.

Through our market research we had also identified a gap locally in support of IT across the curriculum. We could see that we had extensive facilities that could be made available to visiting teachers after school and we had already secured a small amount of staffing as the SEMERC (Special Education and Micro Electronic Resource Centre) link school for the LEA's area. We provided a resource for other schools and so we were responsible for the dissemination of information to schools throughout the LEA.

As an outcome of this we decided to offer INSET for IT to mainstream schools. We had a resource advantage in that teachers could have access to training on an individual machine, something denied them if they attended an INSET activity elsewhere. We also had a very wide range of peripherals and software available for visiting teachers to view and try out.

Threats

While this was going on, the LEA had embarked upon a major reorgani-zation plan and if we were to do more than merely await the outcome of their deliberations then it was necessary to influence that process. This was achieved by ensuring that those involved in decision-making were clear about the options available to them and the possible outcomes of adopting particular choices. One of the most effective ways of achieving this was to make a personal presentation, along with like-minded colleagues, to the elected members at a crucial stage in their decision making.

LMS in mainstream schools may also be perceived by many in special schools as a threat. This is particularly true when one considers that they may have to buy in the services they use. I believed that the only way to deal with this was to treat it as an opportunity; to treat it as a threat could produce defensive attitudes and activities, whereas treating it as an oppor-tunity can lead one into a range of proactive ventures.

External market profile

What becomes clear when one develops a marketing approach is how easily a negative image is created and how hard it can be to overcome it. It is significant that the creation of a negative image for education at a national level has been achieved at the same time that opinion polls have consistently revealed, at individual school level, parental satisfaction with schools. When considering marketing a service, this is worth noting since parallels may be drawn. It is possible that within your marketplace other support services have been perceived in a negative way, and this then becomes the prevailing attitude to support services as a whole. At the same time your own support service may be well received and respected at the individual school level. It is important to be aware of this disparity in order to take steps to deal with it.

To draw up your external market profile there is a series of activities in which to engage. These are: identifying your clients, developing your brand image and enhancing public relations. They are examined more fully in the next sections.

Identifying your clients (the external market)

This is not as simple as it may seem. It requires questions to be asked. Is it the mainstream school? Is it the head teacher? Is it the class teacher? Is it the child? Is it the child's parents? Is it the educational psychologist? The answer may be that it is some, all or others, depending on what you have to offer. What is certain is that you have to be clear about who your clients are and upon whom you will target your efforts. In Chapter 9 Tony Bowers explores this notion of market segmentation in more detail.

Your brand image

In marketing terms a brand is a product or service which has been given an identity and the image is the attitude that people hold towards that brand. It is crucial to remember that any service operating from your school will carry the image of your school and any service operating from your school will also influence the brand image of the school. In order to ascertain your brand image it is necessary to conduct a survey of your external market and your internal audience. The purpose is to identify the perceptions and attitudes that prevail towards your school and its service. A school's image and that of its learning support service are, however, made up of a wide range of parts and you will on occasions be interested in the image attaching to one of these constituents rather than the overall image. For example, if you intend to run INSET you will need to receive comment on such items as: the content of the course; the audience's perception of the providers; reaction to the facilities, etc. If the providers are perceived to be weak, does this carry over into creating a negative perception of the quality of the teaching within the school? In conducting research into our proposed target groups, many interesting perceptions and misconceptions emerged.

We all carry with us the label of being a special school and we will have our own internalized image for that, but are we aware of the attitudes that individual mainstream schools have towards special education? Where there has been contact between your school and a mainstream school, are you aware of the impression that was created? It will be necessary for you to be able to answer with clarity these questions and many others.

Earlier in this chapter I drew attention to the fact that everyone in your internal audience is an ambassador for your school. The issue is deeper than merely saying the right things about your school. If, for example, you have a nursery teacher visiting your nursery, will they find themselves talking to staff who have experience of early years education and will they observe facilities and practice that are in accord with their expectations?

Public relations

The application of public relations (PR) provides a tool for supporting the marketing plans that you have developed for your school. It is worth reiterating that public relations involves a deliberate, planned and sustained effort to establish and maintain mutual understanding between an organization and its public. PR is also likely to be the area which is open to abuse and within which people may find others engaged in a less than ethical manner. PR must be treated in the same way as any other aspect of school management. It needs to be operated professionally, ethically and with consideration. The National Association of Head Teachers has produced a useful set of guidelines for schools engaged in this kind of activity. A public relations exercise will itself have a cycle of activities: Aims, Targets, Message, Methods, Programme, Implementation, Monitoring.

Aims: The first and crucial question is: Why are you undertaking a public relations exercise?

Targets: Who are your most important targets?

Message: What are you going to tell them when you have identified them and you have reached them?

Methods: How are you intending to deliver your message?

Programme: When is the programme to be implemented?

Implementation: What is needed in terms of time, resources and manpower?

Monitoring: How will you evaluate the success or otherwise of the programme?

When all of the other parts of your marketing plan have been implemented it is through the quality of the public relations exercise that the plan will ultimately succeed or fail. It is the vehicle for the planned and coordinated articulation of your marketing efforts.

Outcomes

Major changes have taken place at our school and the most important, change to primary school only, was clearly not in itself a direct outcome of our marketing plan. However, it would be fair to say that the application of a marketing plan to the management of the school has produced significant benefits to the school and it has confirmed its position within the overall education serivce. Facets of the school's work have been enhanced as a result of our marketing efforts and many additional resources have accrued.

Part III

Clients, customers and the marketplace

Chapter 8
Issues in marketing

Tony Bowers

Marketing in context

Any writer who tries in a book to provide an up-to-date commentary on the precise regulatory scene within the field of special educational needs is probably doomed to failure. New circulars alter situations very quickly, as well as moving terminology on apace. Speeches by government ministers or senior civil servants can quickly cause consternation and the changing of courses, while the uncertainties caused by such factors as charge-capping in some LEAs, schools opting for grant-maintained status and radical shifts in the way that education is financed, are overlain by the possibility of major governmental change. Even contemporary reports, such as that of Lunt (1991), who refers to the now irrelevant reduction of discretionary exceptions from 10 per cent to 7 per cent, can seem dated due to the delay between writing and publication.

The reader is therefore asked to forgive any technical shifts which may have occurred between the writing of this chapter and the time it is read. Such shifts, however, occur within a climate which is more difficult to change. Like any climate, it may be unpredictable in the short-term; taking a longer view, its general nature and course is easier to forecast. This climate can be linked, not to the whim of party politics or to the vagaries of individual politicians, but to a general acceptance of financial accountability and the discrediting of collectivism, centralization and economic protectionism which have become associated with the failed and overturned systems of Eastern Europe. It is one which emphasizes consumer choice and the notion of 'getting what one pays for'. It is about, however uncomfortable the term to some of those in professions with a strong ethos of caring, the functioning of services within the framework of a market economy.

The idea of associating marketing with children's special educational needs can at first be received with abhorrence. These are by definition the most vulnerable members of the education community; in many cases the established system has failed to accommodate them or to meet their needs effectively. The term 'special needs' encompasses children who usually are not 'marketable' and who cannot make informed choices as 'consumers', so how can we possibly expose them to the vagaries of market forces? What such responses fail to recognize is that it is not the children themselves who are in the front line when these forces start to operate. It is the services which have been set up specifically to meet their needs. I use the term 'services' generically to encompass special schools and units, the various SEN support and advisory services run by LEAs, as well as school psychological services and educational welfare services; it also includes services internal to mainstream schools, which may go under the banner of a special educational needs 'department', 'support team' or other structure which usually works under the direction of a special needs co-ordinator.

It may seem to be splitting hairs to distinguish between the forces operating on these services and the quality and nature of what is received by the children they exist to serve. Surely, if some of them suffer contraction or extinction because of economic factors, their clients will also suffer. Underlying such an assertion, however, is the assumption that separate services are a prerequisite for meeting needs. This assumption is now being called into question.

During the ten years following the Warnock Report (DES, 1978) we grew used to seeing proportionately more money spent on special educational needs than on other areas of education. One way or another, whether as part of national initiatives or as LEA-inspired priorities, spending on this area of the education system was expanded or at least protected. Some special schools and units may have closed as a matter of local policy, but the money saved was redirected to other forms of educational support. Effectively it was 'earmarked' for individual pupils or for initiatives aimed at sectors of the school population which were seen to have special educational needs. Now, as the recent GEST figures make abundantly clear, special educational needs can no longer benefit from major national initiatives; there is something set aside for sensory impairment and for severe learning difficulties, but very little else. The logic, of course, is that we now have a *National* Curriculum which is intended to include all children, not just those outside the apocryphal 20 percent of Warnock. By differentiating within the delivery of the programmes of study for that curriculum, there is no basic requirement for the underlying specialist knowledge which has tended to be the stock in trade of SEN staff. It is therefore no longer enough simply to assume that the notion of special educational needs will be given prominence by planners and decision-makers.

Market awareness

We have become used to what I have termed (Bowers, 1989b) a 'service-led' economy within special educational provision. This is one in which centrally-provided resources are made available and, if they are not liked or do not fit what the receiver requires, they are still offered in a relatively unaltered form or are simply withdrawn. 'Market-led' services, on the other hand, are more responsive to the needs of their recipients. If they are not, the recipient has the freedom to go elsewhere. Outside the field of special education this notion underpins the 1988 Education Act and is what LMS was constructed to sustain. It becomes uncomfortable when applied to special educational needs because the recipients are often seen to be disadvantaged children. What choices do they have? How can they go elsewhere?

However, if we reframe the recipient structure, a different picture emerges. To do it we need to look at a form of differentiation commonly used by those responsible for marketing services. Within this it is not sufficient to talk of recipients, but to try to identify the nature of :

(a) those whom a service sets out to benefit, or its *end-users;*

(b) the *deciders* who take the decision that a service is necessary or desirable;

(c) those who have the capacity to encourage, modify or discourage such a decision, or *influencers;*

(d) the *purchaser* or budget-holder who actually funds the results of any decisions;

(e) the *gatekeeper* who can grant or deny access to any or all of the above.

Each element is important, but the marketing process is directed not towards the 'end-users', or children, but at the deciders and purchasers. Meanwhile, a less direct process of establishing effective relationships and positive views of a service - what Malcolm Clayton calls public relations in Chapter 7 - also has to be implemented to deal with the influencers. Using this framework it quickly becomes apparent that marketing and special educational needs provision are already no strangers to one another. The efforts that preceded the 1970 Education Act, which established schooling for those previously considered ineducable, were directed primarily at deciders - in this case Members of Parliament - with the additional lobbying of a wide range of influencers, who included educationists and medical practitioners as well as many others who could bring pressure to bear on the deciders. On a much smaller level, anybody involved in a project to integrate a child with significant special needs into a mainstream school will be aware of the impact that influencers - often teachers and other pupils - can have upon the decider, who is usually a head teacher. In both cases, 'marketing' approaches have been used to present an effective case and to benefit the eventual 'end-users'.

It is easy to see how a similar analysis can be applied to such developments as 'whole-school' approaches to special educational needs in mainstream schools, or to the introduction of a variety of curricular innovations such as Derbyshire Language (Masidlover, 1979) or multisensory approaches (Longhorn, 1988) in special schools. Marketing efforts have always been with us. Somebody has had to take decisions and somebody has had to make resources available. The two critical issues at present appear to be that the introduction of delegated management to schools has sharpened our awareness of who pays and how much it costs, and has generated a natural fear that under these circumstances special educational needs will not receive the priority they require or deserve.

There is certainly evidence to support this fear. In some LEAs, major reductions in SEN support teams have been witnessed in recent times, with redeployment to schools as the first option and redundancy as the second. Tales abound of posts for special educational needs in mainstream secondary schools, particularly when they involve in-class support for non-statemented pupils, being redesignated for subject teaching. In some cases special needs co-ordinators have been made redundant. Dyson (1990) has pointed out that 'A special needs co-ordinator operating a whole-school approach accounts on his/her own for the education of not a single one of the pupils in the school, and is eminently dispensable' (p.119); whilst this is not necessarily predictive of what will take place in all our schools, its economic message has to be borne in mind. The whole matter was brought sharply into focus in the Spring of 1991, when the Secretary of State for Education announced that grant-maintained schools would be free to exercise criteria for selection among would-be entrants. The 'market', it was felt by many, did not favour special educational needs.

Perhaps not. Certainly it has changed. However, it is precisely at such times that any organization needs an effective marketing analysis and a focused strategy is called for. When the old ways of doing things aren't working, aren't wanted or when new clients enter the arena, marketing - under whatever guise - has to take place. The alternative is decline or extinction.

Schools, LEAs and responsibilities

For those who had grown used to things as they were, the 1988 Education Act contained profound implications. Local Education Authorities in particular, whose officers had become accustomed to guiding decisions and deploying resources, have lost many of their powers. To replace them, the Audit Commission (1989) has identified (p.1) the following roles for LEAs:

(i) *leader,* setting out a vision of what the education service is trying to achieve;

(ii) *partner,* supporting schools in fulfilling this vision;

(iii) *planner* of future facilities;

(iv) *provider of information* to the education market to assist people in making choices;

(v) *regulator* of quality of educational provision made by schools; and

(vi) *banker,* channelling the funds which enable to schools to make that provision.

The strategic distribution of resources is not included. The notion of a banker implies neutrality in terms of what money is spent where; indeed Circular 7/91 (paragraph 55) is critical of even this limited role for LEAs, suggesting that actual bank accounts be made available for schools non-salary expenditure and requiring it for secondary schools.

More recently, an even shorter list has been provided by Geoffrey Morris (1991), ex-Chief Education Officer of Cambridgeshire. He sees the LEA of the future:

(i) determining the strategic pattern of the education service in response to the views of those who use and pay for it and who manage it at school level;

(ii) securing high standards; and

(iii) distributing resources, 'including those used for providing support to schools so that the schools themselves can decide whether or not to buy these services back' (p.20).

This last item offers a more radical view than that currently articulated by many LEAs. It is worth remembering, however, that Morris represents the local authority which delegated budgetary management to many of its schools long before the 1988 Education Act. He continues: 'The LEA of the future will be that which heads and governors will collectively invent. Support will cease to be provider-led and become buyer-led.'

From these two lists, the shift of power from LEA to school governing body and its managing executive, the head teacher, is quite apparent. But it is power that should - and does - carry responsibilities. There is a confusion, caused in part because the 1981 Education Act was not drafted with any foresight of the intent of the 1988 Act, which centres around the respective roles of schools and LEAs. We have become used to children seen to have special educational needs, whether statemented or not, being regarded as the LEA's responsibility. Where a child has been placed in a special school or unit such responsibility has been unequivocally stated, as it has been when extra staffing or material resources have been provided for statemented pupils in mainstream schools. However, many LEAs have also sought as a matter of policy to sustain special educational needs awareness and provision in mainstream schools through a number of mechanisms, among them making extra teaching posts available within a school's staffing complement, funding the costs of posts of responsibility for SEN, or sustaining centrally-managed but permanently-placed teachers within one school. In the case of primary schools in particular, centrally - or regionally - located support teams have been developed, whose ways of working have often varied but whose purpose has been to improve the educational lot of children experiencing difficulties in coping with the curricular or organizational expectations of those schools.

Such additional facilities have had the effect of increasing the substance of what is available as a part of the school's general provision. However, there has also been criticism that the very presence of special needs 'specialists' is inclined to reduce teachers' and head teachers' acceptance of responsibility for examining their own practice and accommodating children's needs within the ordinary framework of the school (Dessent, 1987; Gray and Freeman, 1989). This may not be for the want of trying: a recent HMI survey (1991) found that 'Some head teachers prevented whole-school issues from being adequately addressed' (p.2), and marginalization is a problem that SEN support services as well as designated specialists within schools have often been at pains to overcome. There is, though, a potential tension between dealing with individual pupils and their problems, which forms a substantial part of a special needs co-ordinator's role and - because of their place in a staged LEA assessment process - is often built into the function of advisory and support staff, and taking on more global issues of change through consultancy, INSET and related processes.

The legal framework

The problem with the bulk of special educational needs is that they do not reside in the child. The needs themselves stem from the educational experience which the child encounters. It is therefore in the hands of schools to exacerbate or diminish them. LEA special needs policies in recent years have recognized this, seeking to influence curricular practice, school organization and teacher attitudes. Basically, local authorities have come to regard themselves - operating through the agencies of SEN co-ordinator, advisory and support teachers, educational psychologists, etc. - as central in influencing or determining the provision made for special educational needs. We need, though, to look at recent case law on the legislation to determine where the 1981 Education Act places the emphasis of responsibility. To do this it is relevant to look at recent judicial pronouncements; otherwise we can only rely on established practice and our own interpretation of the Act.

In 1987, Lord Justice Dillon in *Regina versus the Secretary of State for Education and Science, Ex parte L*, said (p.24) 'I conclude that the local education authority has discretion whether or not they will themselves determine the special educational provision required for any particular child which has special educational needs, or will leave the determination of that provision to others, e.g. the ordinary school which the child attends.' In the same judgement, Lord Justice Nicholls (p.30) pronounced that 'The authority's obligation to make a statement arises only if the authority are of the opinion that they (as distinct, for instance, from the child's school) should determine the special educational provision that should be made for a child who has special educational needs.' More recently, in the 1991 dismissal of the DES's appeal in *Regina versus the Secretary of State for Education and Science Ex parte E*, Lord Justice Woolf said (p.19) 'It appears to me that there may be cases where the school is not already providing the special educational provision (which ex hypothesi is additional to, or otherwise different from, the provision made generally for children) but is capable of doing so once the need is demonstrated.' The significance of this judgement is that it distinguishes between the responsibility for statemented pupils (the LEA's) and 'the special educational needs of the remaining 18% (which) are, it is to be presumed, being met by the schools themselves' (p.14). Once a child is statemented under section 7 of the 1981 Act, the LEA is responsible for ensuring effective provision for any identified needs in a child; however, it endorses the judgement of Lord Justice Nicholls, in the first case cited, that by simply carrying out an assessment of 'the nature and severity of the child's learning difficulty' (p.30), the LEA cannot be regarded as having committed themselves to make special educational provision for the child.

There is a predominantly medical flavour to the model presented, which is sharpest in Lord Justice Dillon's pronouncement in *Ex parte L* (p.13) that 'The statement is no ordinary form. Part II may be compared to a medical diagnosis and Part III to a prescription for the needs diagnosed'. The notion, widely accepted in educational circles, that the need to statement will often arise from the interaction between the child and the environment of the school is not something yet explored by the courts. Responsibility, it seems, is sharply defined. Statemented pupils are the LEA's concern, non-statemented special educational needs fall squarely within the school's domain. This distinction is reinforced in Circular 7/91, although paragraph 59 blurs the edges with the observation that 'The LEA must ensure that pupils with special educational needs receive appropriate provision, where possible in ordinary schools. In particular, the LEA has a duty to identify pupils who may require a statement of SEN, and to ensure that appropriate provision is made for such pupils.' The Circular (paragraphs 103-106) goes on to provide an incentive for LEAs to vary their LMS schemes to allocate additional weightings within their formulae to account for non-statemented SEN pupils: such provision will now count towards the 80 per cent of the Aggregated Schools Budget (ASB) which is pupil-weighted and not (as before) towards the limited non-pupil-weighted element. The message seems clear: where statements are not made, schools' financial allocations incorporate pupils with SEN and it is they who make the decisions. Paragraph 107 of the Circular emphasizes this by stating unequivocally that money cannot be 'earmarked' or set aside for particular pupils in the absence of a statement. 'In planning to meet the needs of such pupils, and its other pupils', it concludes, 'a school will have at its disposal the whole delegated budget'.

The position for pupils with statements is expressed differently in Circular 7/91. It declares 'a strong case for' (paragraph 100) delegating provision for statemented pupils to mainstream schools, but does not go so far as to require it. In such a case, the relationship between the LEA and the school is summarized in the same paragraph: 'The school will be bound to make provision in accordance with pupils' statements, and the LEA will monitor that provision'. This may create problems in the future for LEAs: the courts appear to see statemented pupils as their responsibility, but they are being asked by the DES to pass that over to schools. The notion of 'monitoring' is an interesting one, in that it implies a contractual relationship which carries potential sanctions against the contractor, rather like a cleaning or a maintenance contract. The reality, where people are concerned, is not as simple or cut and dried. However, such an arrangement only replicates the situation which does - or should - exist in relation to statemented pupils whom the LEA places in independent or non-maintained schools: the authority remains responsible for ensuring the effectiveness and appropriateness of the provision made. The fact that we can cite examples of this not working does not mean that it cannot or should not do so. LEAs, in all probability, may be able to delegate executive actions relating to statemented pupils, provided that they can arrive at adequate incentives within the formulae. The problem lies in whether they can delegate accountability.

It is not my intention to continue this legalistic analysis. This chapter is about marketing. However, it is necessary to understand the systems in which any marketing is to take place, and these inevitably include financial and legislative elements. I shall shortly look at these systems in more detail in relation to special schools, and those offering support and advisory services, in particular those which have operated on an external basis (Bowers, 1987). What is apparent is that it will become less possible for schools to rely on direct LEA services and assistance for children with special educational needs; they may choose to reduce the provision they make, but in doing so they risk contravening section 2(5) of the 1981 Education Act; they may opt to make adequate internal provision; they may choose to use the services of outside agencies, bearing in mind that these have in one way or another to be paid for; and they are still likely to have some services provided centrally, though the level of these will depend upon the political will and overall strategy of the LEA, and indeed upon the continuance of LEAs as we know them.

The components of marketing

For many people the term 'marketing' implies selling something. It is often linked with attempting to dress a product up, to package it, and to trap the unwary buyer into purchasing it. Effective marketing, however, requires integrity: few of us would return to a shop where we felt we had been cheated, or use a garage to service our car which manifestly had failed to do so in the past. It is necessary also to emphasize that marketing is not necessarily about 'selling a product'. It is about identifying the nature of what is required, ensuring that it is delivered and seeing that every facet of the organization contributes to its quality.

Marketing as a separate, identifiable component of management has grown out of the philosophy which recognizes the importance of the 'customer' to any enterprise. The assumption is that without clients or customers no undertaking can exist for long. It is sometimes simplistically assumed that marketing for schools or services implies a one-way relationship in which they try to sell what they have to offer to whoever they perceive to be the consumers. It is more complex than that, however. It involves a subtle interactive relationship between a variety of clients, who will occupy differing roles within the marketing structure outlined earlier. Each will offer the other something; each will have something to give and something to gain from the association. In many cases, the clients themselves will interact: parents interact with LEA officers, officers interact with elected members, elected members interact with parents and so on. One of the assumptions that I often find both in special schools and support services, even where there is an acknowledgement that some level of energy has to be applied to the marketing process, is that this is really the role of management. 'Our head teacher does that.' 'That's what our Head of Service is for.' We are all aware of the complacency that can stem from assuming that somebody else is dealing with an issue and that it is not our concern: plenty of books and articles have been written on whole-school approaches, not only to special needs, but to PSE, health education and so on. Far less has been produced on whole-school or whole-service approaches to marketing, but the notion is just as important. It is actually an axiom of effective marketing that *everyone* in an organization is responsible for selling the service or product that it offers.

The belief that the task of marketing can be delegated to a particular person often stems from the assumption that marketing is about advertising, producing attractive brochures and such peripheral issues as gaining sponsorship from local firms or designing logos and tee-shirts. These may be components of the process but they are superficial. At a far more funda-mental level, marketing involves systematic *impression management*. The term does not imply any form of deception: what it means is that the school or service takes careful steps to ensure that each segment of its potential market has an optimally favourable view of its functioning. I will look at the notion of segments and segmentation in the next chapter, but deal with impressions here.

Impression management is something that any successful organization which relies on its customers' support has to address. When we walk into a restaurant we have already made a decision to do so based on certain aspects of its exterior presentation. We will subsequently make judgements which are founded not just on the nature of the food but on the interior cleanliness and decor and - importantly - on the friendliness and efficiency of the service we receive. If the non-food elements are of a low standard, we probably won't return, even if the food is good. If that too is mediocre, we have almost certainly visited for the first and last time. The same issues arise for special schools and services. Many have of course already come to grips with these. It is by now well established that the first impressions given to a visitor to a school significantly influence the way he or she perceives it. Bright displays of work, well set-out notice boards and so on are generally acknowledged to be important. Unfortunately, it is not uncommon for the visitor to some special schools to have trouble even finding the entrance; or when they do find it to have to walk around corridors looking for 'the office'. Simple first impressions can also make a major difference to the way members of services are perceived. Small things like arriving punctually, dressing in a businesslike way, and coming well-briefed on the school and the reasons for the visit are, whilst obvious, not always acted on. I have pointed (Bowers, 1991a) to some of the negative ways in which support services can be perceived by teachers without realizing it. It is easy to miss lunch through extending a previous appointment and to arrive in a hurry from a hot car and a traffic jam; it is not so easy to appear calm, efficient and to give a full attention to new people, new children and a new situation under these circumstances. If this notion of early impressions seems super-ficial or over-emphasized, bear in mind that one of this country's major educational research establishments has recently invested in 'style consultation' for many of its staff whose job involves them in working with other organizations.

The essence of impression management is that it is everybody's responsibility to ensure that it is carried out efficiently. That doesn't mean that a designated group of staff shouldn't consider the issues in some detail and develop possible strategies to put before all members of the team. Essentially it relies on a team effort. We are all aware of the harm that can be done by such things as a thoughtless letter to a parent, a casually answered telephone call, a poorly prepared report or non-attendance at a meeting that others consider important. One person's actions - or inactivity - can undo the positive work done by everybody else.

The purpose of impression management is to create positive attitudes within the spectrum of clients or customers. Attitudes can be broken down into three basic components: informational, emotional and behavioural. In marketing we seek to influence the last of these through ensuring that the first two are dealt with in an effective manner. The informational component consists of not only factual knowledge but also the beliefs which the individual possesses about what a school or service can achieve or can provide. If these were rationally based, they would be relatively easy to deal with; unfortunately, it makes no difference to the attitude whether or not the informational component is empirically real or correct (Luthans,1989). This is why misperceptions so often occur in the community over what kinds of population a special school serves or what curriculum it offers, or among teachers and officers over what a support service should try to achieve and how it should work in order to do so. Simplistically, some managers think that the response to this is to put forward any image, however unfounded in reality, and people will believe it. If they advertise a school as 'dynamic' or a service as responsive and effective, this information will become embedded in belief. Theoretically this is possible, but if other information based on observation and direct experience is inconsistent with the overt information, then the dissonance created is likely to lead to the rejection of the first message and subsequent rejection of further messages. The safest approach is to aim to provide high quality in what you do and at the the same time ensure that it is widely appreciated that you are doing so.

Identifying clients

Special schools

I shall not dwell too much in this chapter on marketing issues for special schools. They are addressed directly by Malcolm Clayton in Chapter 7 and by Mel Farrar in Chapter 6. At first glance it looks as though LMSS will have made little difference to special schools in general, though of course individual schools may gain or lose in terms of the budgets they have been used to when formula funding becomes a reality. Because an LEA's formula is not to be pupil-led but place-led, there will not be the pressure to recruit pupils which mainstream schools experience. Their pupils, unless there for assessment, should be the subject of statements and therefore the LEA's responsibility. In terms of marketing, nothing much has changed: the LEA makes decisions on placement and pays the bills. With the cushion of the 'place factor' there is no imperative even to run close to the notional figure indicated by that element of the formula.

Some of this may be true. The LEA is, in terms of the system outlined earlier, the decider. However, there are likely to powerful influencers, not least of them a child's parents and teachers in his or her existing school, not to mention a variety of gatekeepers who control the effective flow of information to such influencers. The term 'LEA' usually implies one person who eventually makes the decision about what provision is required within Section IV of the statement. But before that a wide range of advice may have been received from a number of professionals who will have given it in the knowledge of the nature and quality of available resources within the LEA and outside it. Their knowledge of the school and their beliefs about it may be crucial in determining the final recommendation.

Special schools also have two key areas of vulnerability. One is a current one, in that the LEA's policy statement, which must accompany its LMSS proposals, has to identify the role which special schools play in that policy. In some cases certain special schools may no longer be seen to have the role which they have become used to, or indeed to have a role at all. Beyond that, however, lies the freedom that LEAs have to alter the basis on which their formula share is calculated from year to year. Circular 7/91 makes it clear that 'It will not be necessary in the scheme to state how many places are to be funded at each school' and continues: 'The LEA may determine annually the types and numbers of places to be provided at each of its schools' (paragraph 84). From this it seems that unlike a mainstream school, which has its actual pupils on roll to substantiate its financial allocations and very existence, a special school will be subject to an annual review by the LEA which could easily decrease or alter the nature of its allocated place factor or factors. The case for a marketing plan which directs itself to key individuals and groupings who are part of this review appears to be strong, a point emphasized by Judith Charlesworth in Chapter 5.

There is also the issue of outreach services. Many special schools have over recent years built up their own support services which offer a variety of services to individual children, to parents or to teachers. In some cases this has been done at the same time as the LEA has developed centrally-resourced support services and there has at times been confusion or even competition over their respective roles. In principle the preparation of an up-to-date policy statement should remove such confusions, though only time will tell whether it has been achieved in practice. The funding for special school outreach has not often been formalized by LEAs, frequently being left to goodwill, the stretching of resources (Dessent, 1984) and to individual school initiatives. Now, however, Circular 7/91 provides (paragraph 88) the opportunity for LEAs to designate a component of the place factor for outreach work from some or all of its special schools. At first sight this seems simple. The LEA will be the client, and the special school will provide some form of support for pupils retained in the mainstream who might otherwise have been on its roll. In many cases, however,this is an oversimplification of the outreach function which may not primarily be child-centred, concentrating instead on teacher support through such mechanisms as advice, the provision of materials and INSET. Although the service will be 'free' to the mainstream schools, when centrally-retained support services also operate on a similar basis there may be a tendency for those schools to begin to makes choices.

A further complication arises. Where the LEA has a policy delegating funds for statemented pupils yet has an outreach place element for one or more of its special schools to enable it to support some pupils with statements, how is funding allocated? If the school's service is named in the provision to be made, then presumably the funding will not be made available to the mainstream school, otherwise the statement would be 'double-funded'. Yet this runs counter to the notion of choice which underpins delegation, and may later lie open to contest by the school. In such circumstances the special school will be operating in an uncertain market which has yet to be tested.

Support services for children with special educational needs

When the draft circular on LMSS was issued at the end of 1990, there was considerable consternation over the possible demise of support services. The term 'service agreement' became introduced to those in special educational needs, although it was already part of the parlance for mainstream schools. There was a widely-expressed fear that such agreements, made 'so that schools can set their own priorities for expenditure and choose what use to make of the LEA's service' (Circular 7/91, paragraph 37), would never be made because of the high unit cost of a support service member. Subsequent pronouncements by a senior civil servant at the DES that 'Hardly a day goes by now without a plea from one group or another for protected species status' (David Miller, CEA Harrow Conference, February 1991), did little to allay fears which were founded on an identify crisis. Did the criticism of 'unspecialized teams which are occasionally directed to schools instead of allowing them to enhance their own staffing' apply to them? Some said it was really directed at those offering 'curriculum support' in schools. But for many SEN support teams the model of assisting teachers to make differentiated provision within the National Curriculum was one they had begun to adopt.

The tone of Circular 7/91 is more muted, possibly as a result of representations received during the consultation period following the draft circular. It still expresses the belief 'that there is scope for the delegation of the costs of centrally-managed SEN support teams' (paragraph 198), but adds that LEAs will wish to consider carefully the impact of such delegation. The concern that the widely-reported rise in requests for assessments under Section 5 of the 1981 Education Act would be further exacerbated if LEAs could not offer flexible resources to schools was undoubtedly behind the more guarded tone of the circular. However, implicit in this permission to LEAs to retain central services is the assumption that SEN support services will need to be child-focused in order to counter schools' requests to secure resources which have formal - and legal - backing.

With the less strident tone of the substantive circular, there has been a perceptible release of tension within many support services. However, a number of points need to be borne in mind. These are:

(i) The continuing need for LEAs to ensure that centrally-funded services do not exceed 15 per cent of the PSB.

(ii) The political intention in some LEAs to delegate as much funding as possible to schools.

(iii) The pressure from school governing bodies, coupled with the new-found power on the part of head teachers, on LEAs to delegate centrally-funded resources to allow schools to choose the type and level of services they receive.

(iv) For some LEAs, the lack of ability to remove some of the budgetary costs of their support services from the GSB by notionally ascribing them to special schools. When special schools enter the GSB this will no longer be possible, as the Touche Ross Report (1990, p.48) points out.

(v) The potential movement of many mainstream schools towards grant-maintained status. At the time of writing this has been almost exclusively confined to secondary schools, but primary schools and consortia of schools of all ages are being encouraged to do this. The present government policy appears to discourage schools from remaining within the aegis of their LEAS. As less schools remain within the LEA, the amount of money which can be held back within the GSB naturally decreases. Even an LEA which is committed to the central retention of support services could find itself unable to sustain current provision within the dwindling pool of money which would result from schools opting out of its control.

Most LEAs do not at present seem to be looking to the future in an imaginative way by creating a phased programme of delegation of support services. There appears to be a defensive strategy in which the numbers of personnel are trimmed down or new appointments are made on a temporary basis, but funding is retained centrally. As a result marketing is not seen to be a necessary component of service management, potentially perpetuating the notion that if something is 'free' it does not have to be attractive to its recipients.

In fact market responsiveness remains a key component of support service delivery. In one LEA which is committed to delegating as much as possible to its schools, head teachers have still voted for the central retention of SEN services simply because those services have been aware of the importance of marketing themselves to key deciders. In another nearby LEA, the response has been more equivocal. Of twenty five head teachers of first and middle schools polled, nineteen said they would prefer to have control of the budget currently retained for SEN support. A variety of reasons were advanced, but two representative comments were 'We could choose the support and expertise to suit the pupils' needs and ensure continuity and reliability' and 'It would give me some ability to provide services that I am without at present as I have minimal LEA support.' What this points to is that marketing is not something that has to be reluntactly tackled by support services only when funds are delegated to schools. It is something which can and should be a part of any service's operational strategy. In an insightful analysis, Watts (1990) has singled out some entitlements that support services should ensure their clients receive. Even where the funding of services remains centralized, meeting the demands of the recipient organizations - the schools - must be high on the agenda of any service.

Educational psychology (EP) services

An early response to the delegation of support services was that it threatened educational psychology services. These were seen as vulnerable to the new purchasing power of schools. Their role as assessors under Section 5 of the 1981 Education Act would be compromised if their new paying client - the school, represented by its head teacher - could now call the tune. Their other work, as consultants to schools, providers of INSET, interventionists with parents, and so on, would no longer be seen as a priority and so simply not purchased.

A report published by HMI in 1990 acknowledged the variety and complexity of work undertaken by educational psychology services. The marketing of EP services, however, was already under way in some LEAs. 'Several services,' the report noted (p.6) 'are beginning to consider the variety of strategies that might best be used to promote psychology services and inform LEAs, other professionals and the public at large of the nature of their work.' This proactivity is a notable feature of many educational psychology services. They have the advantage also of starting from a good baseline in many LEAs. Whilst it is not uncommon to encounter the complaint that they are hard to contact, a recent survey of primary schools in a large county LEA revealed that they represented the support service that would be most in demand if the delegation of funds took place. It could be cynically suggested that this response indicated a desire to obtain more statements of special needs, with the resultant resources that accompany them. This may be true, but many schools' experiences of EP involvement will include assessments which never reach the formal procedures set out by the 1981 Education Act.

It is in fact highly unlikely that LEAs will delegate formal assessment procedures under Section 5 of the 1981 Act. It is theoretically possible through, for instance, the establishment of long-term service agreements consented to by all schools within the LEA, but this would merely be an accountancy device to reduce the exceptions to delegation within the Section 42 statement. It might be attempted, however, by LEAs faced with significant numbers of schools opting for grant-maintained status. This is because the LEA retains a duty (Circular 10/88, paragraph 64) to treat pupils with special educational needs in grant-maintained schools 'no less favourably than those in those schools which they maintain'. This should mean that a full range of advisory and support services is available to grant-maintained schools, but in practice they tend only to retain links with EP services. A charge-back arrangement for the LEA schools would mean that grant-maintained schools could then be invoiced for similar sums; otherwise the LEA would be obliged to provide the same level of services from a dwindling pool of financial resources.

Even when special schools are included within the LEA's GSB, not all EP services will necessarily be attributable to it. An allocation for work in FE, with pre-school children or in social services establishments, for example, can be held back from the sum set out in the Section 42 statement. This does not reduce the actual cost, but can have an impact in reducing the exceptions to delegation. One difficulty for a service is that the range of activities of its members is not always clear even to those within it. The 1990 HMI report recommended that EP services should not merely review and declare what they can offer, but also make clear the limits of what is available. This is one of the first principles of effective consultancy, whether or not services are 'sold' (Bowers, 1989a); the fear that doing so will cause an impoverishment of the variety of experience which the job can offer is a real one, but it may not be substantiated by events.

As mentioned earlier, the prospect of an entirely delegated EP service is unlikely in the short term. Many LEAs will probably retain their entire services as centrally-funded exceptions to delegation. Even when delegation does occur, it will probably be partial, holding back elements designated for 'statutory' work under the 1981 Education Act and for monitoring state-mented pupils and the provision made for them in mainstream and special schools. It would be a pity if concentration on these aspects were allowed to delimit the work of services. We already hear of moves to delegate EP costs to special schools but to charge them for attendance at annual reviews of statements,which would become standard as part of the LEA's SEN policy. By doing this, compulsory service agreements would effectively be estab-lished. Such activity may be necessary; if not, it constitutes a protectionism which is unwarranted and which will deprive other schools of potentially valuable consultancy and advice.

It is likely that many EPs will start to explore the potential for marketing their services to schools, whether or not those services are delegated. Some have already done so. The alternative is to risk being reduced to offering a range of services restricted by the LEA's notion of its statutory responsibil-ities. If the role of the EP becomes limited in this way, there is of course potential for private psychology services to offer a greater range of consul-tancy to schools. For them the market would be open.

In conclusion

I have spent some time exploring the issues presented to special schools and services by exposure to the notion of market forces. They may not be comfortable. They are not always easy to define, and they may vary depending on the type of organization addressed, present practice and the LEA's policy and intent. What is easier to establish, however, is that successful schools and services will have to operate with the customer or client uppermost in their mind. Handy (1989) has succinctly set down the necessary actions in relation to these. We need to establish who they are, what they need, what they want and how we can gain knowledge about all of them. In the next chapter we will look further at the processes of marketing and examine the acquisition of knowledge relevant to these points.

Chapter 9

Key components of marketing services

Tony Bowers

By now, the notions underlying the marketing of schools have been well explored in the literature (e.g. Bowles, 1989; Davies and West-Burnham, 1990). The basic principles and procedures are the same for special schools and for external services working with children with special educational needs, such as designated SEN support services, EP services and Educational Social Work (ESW or EWO) services. However, an LEA special school will on the whole serve a single purchasing client - the LEA itself - which, as we have seen, will remain responsible for statemented pupils. Most children attending special schools already have statements of special educational need or are undergoing assessment which may lead to such a statement. This was certainly the assumption made in the statistics provided to Parliament on 17th December, 1990 (*Education*, February 15th, 1991 p.143), although the reality is that in some LEAs a substantial proportion of special school pupils have no statements of special educational needs. Most support services also have one purchasing client - the LEA. For some that may change: the creation of an 'agency' or 'service agreement' structure by definition implies a variety of purchasing clients. Even where the service is entirely retained centrally, however, it would be unwise to ignore the process of marketing. Without its acceptance as important throughout a service, user/client disenchantment is likely to lead to pressure to delegate financial decision-making to schools.

In this book, two chapters written by special school head teachers look at some of the issues that confront such schools in relation to marketing their services. I shall therefore concentrate in this chapter on those offering external services. Many of the components of the chapter, however, will be of equal significance to special schools, whether or not they themselves seek to provide support or 'outreach' services for children with special needs in mainstream schools. It is worth bearing in mind that the financial position of such outreach activities remains unclear. The Touche Ross Report suggested that the school on whose roll a pupil appeared should be the one which bore responsibility for payment, whether this was a direct transfer of cash or a reciprocal agreement which would be settled in kind. Circular 7/91 , on the other hand, uses the term 'collaboration with neighbouring schools' (paragraph 87), and leaves it open to LEAs in determining their place elements under LMSS to offer enhanced funding for 'specified outreach work' (paragraph 88). In principle this should mean that the LEA remains the client when outreach services operate. The practice is more open to question; some education officers charged with implementing LMSS have suggested that significant funding for outreach within the special schools' budget would prove expensive and potentially unworkable. If that turns out to be so, outreach work will either have to be funded centrally and controlled by the LEA like any other support services the LEA may offer or, where funds for statemented pupils are delegated to mainstream schools, be a service which tenders competitively for opportunities to work with those schools. In such a case, support services offered by special schools will have exactly the same marketing issues as those which operate on an 'agency' or 'service agreement' basis.

Researching a market

Most commercial concerns put significant resources into finding out just what market there is for what they offer. Very few would try a 'suck it and see' approach. Market research reduces risk because it ensures that resources are not committed without some knowledge of whether they will be required. For SEN support services, EP services and EWO services there is very little problem in researching the market. They know it is there. It consists of all the schools in their LEA, and of a wide variety of other agencies, not to mention the parents who frequently make direct contact with their services. For them, as for special schools without delegated budgets, the purchasing client - or 'customer' - is the LEA. They may talk of other clients and, indeed, may sometimes not even view the LEA as lying within their client system, but if their services are 'free' to their users, somebody still pays. This 'somebody' is the LEA. Without the LEA as sponsoring client, centrally retained services would be unresourced and so unable to function. Managers of successful services have always acknowledged this and have 'marketed' the importance of their services to their sponsoring client.

Of course, responsiveness to other elements in the client system has often been a hallmark of SEN support services. It is therefore easy to believe that we know what schools and parents want, without asking a critical question: would they want it if they had to pay for it? This question is necessary even if there is no expectation that funds will actually pass from the school to the service or, in the case of statemented children, from the LEA to the service. It is probably no less important than when such a transfer takes place, whether directly or through notional attributions arrived at through a service agreement, because it acknowledges that the recipients of a service will increasingly question whether they are receiving value for money; even where funds for those services are retained centrally, they are still effectively provided by those to whom they are not delegated.

The trouble with this question is that it is usually hypothetical. A number of services have used questionnaires with items based on it. Unfortunately 'What if . . . ?' questions do not usually yield answers that allow a great deal of planning to be centred around their answers, certainly when those answers are quantified but no firm obligations are entered into. Despite this, questionnaires are likely to be used because of their ease of administration. They can have value, particularly where they allow comment which is analyzed qualitatively to produce a profile of perceptions of what a service offers at present and the responses which its users and potential deciders have to that service.

Questionnaires provide just one example of data-gathering in *field research*. In its turn, field research is just one approach to market research, the others being desk research and research through internal audit. Where a service is in close touch with its potential market or markets, such as schools or parents, the informal interview can provide an effective means of data-gathering, as can simple and sustained observation. Where a market is so far relatively inaccessible, telephone interviews and carefully-worded letters inviting specific responses can also be useful. Field research contains a number of components, however it is carried out, which can be summarized as:

(i) *Distribution research*, looking at ways in which services are organized and how they reach their users.
(ii) *Service research*, examining client and potential client perceptions of the service and the benefits it can bring, providing profiles of clients and considering ways in which client loyalty can be sustained.
(iii) *Pricing research*, which looks at the effect of different forms of charging and differential pricing on the demand for the use of a service, and compares costs with those of other similar service providers.

Desk research is a generic term which encompasses all other research that seeks out new information. It includes such things as the scrutiny of DES circulars, reading LEA policy statements, the minutes of education committee meetings, and books and journals relevant to the activities of the service. It can use time, and the diverse data collected need effective collation for trends to become clear. However, without desk research the information generated by field research cannot be set effectively in context.

The *internal audit* is something that every service and school will do as a part of its institutional development planning. An internal marketing audit involves looking in as objective a fashion as possible at present activities: what a team or service does well, what it is currently doing but without full effect, what it has done in the past with success but does not do now, and so on. It needs to consider who are its satisfied clients and to examine the reasons for their satisfaction, and to acknowledge that there are also likely to be dissatisfied clients - or ex-clients - and to look self-critically at the reasons for any disenchantment.

An internal audit also needs to look at staff skills, their current relevance and the demands that clients are likely to place upon them. This is essentially research into the existing capacity of the organization. The development of service agreements with individual schools may not always lead to an acceptance of anyone the service chooses to send; the experience of higher education within the INSET and consultancy market indicates that often a particular individual is asked for because it is believed that he or she has specific skills or approaches which are attractive to the purchasing organization. An internal audit needs to look frankly at the likely demand for individuals within a service, at ways of developing agreements which provide sufficient flexibility for each member of the service to be able to contribute equitably, and at ways of appropriately enskilling particular people.

Market segmentation

When schools develop marketing strategies they have just one broad set of 'purchasers' in mind. These are the parents who, by the act of enrolling their child, increase the school's income through the LEA's system of age-weighted pupil units (AWPU), or through its equivalent grant element in the case of grant-maintained schools. However, as Hill et al (1990) have pointed out, by secondary age the pupils themselves begin to be instrumental in decision-making over their place of education. A wise marketing plan for a secondary school will identify at least two sets of targets: parents and pupils. In doing so it acknowledges that each set will have particular motivations and purposes which are often different; it has created two *segments* of its market. Of course, most of us know that not all parents have similar aspirations: we can often broadly differentiate between expectations and preferences on the basis of various factors which may include occupation, ethnic origin, religious belief, social class and so on. If the school then seeks to address particular groups of parents, it has segmented or subdivided its market still further.

A wide variety of segmentation principles appear in the marketing literature (c.f. Chisnall, 1985), many of which are linked to sales of consumer goods. All, however, are based on the assumption that decisions to purchase anything within a market economy are influenced by factors which involve different perceptions of products or services, different ways of learning about them, particular motivations to use them, and membership of specific social or professional groups. It is not difficult to see how these differentiating features can be identified in those with whom schools and services for children with special educational needs come into contact, particularly since the influencers within their client systems are spread so widely even if the deciders and purchasers are more clearly defined.

Some years ago, before marketing assumed the profile it has today, I explored the notion of 'power dependency', comparing the complexity of the special school head's task with that of a head teacher in a primary school (Bowers, 1984). The nexus of individuals upon whom the head is dependent can be reframed as potential influencers, deciders or purchasers, all of whom may require differing approaches in any marketing plan. Similarly, a head of service for children with special educational needs may need to segment the service's market to contain separate elements who can then be targeted using approaches which are specifically relevant to them. The segments might be broadly categorized as 'community' and 'professional'; within the first we could find parents, school governors, elected members, media representatives and so on; within the second group might be such segments headings as head teachers, class teachers, education officers and educational psychologists. The creation of effective segments for both SEN services and special schools is explored more fully in Bowers (1991b and 1991c), but it is not difficult for a manager to understand his or her potential market to draw up and prioritize target segments. Without doing this, much of the energy devoted to planning and promotion is likely to be misdirected.

The marketing plan

A good marketing plan will follow the classic stages of:
  (i) Specifying objectives.
  (ii) Setting out a programme of activities.
  (iii) Identifying responsibilities.
  (iv) Timetabling what is to be done.

(v) Budgeting the resources required (money, equipment, staff time, etc.).
(vi) Setting standards of performance.
(vii) Estimating the risks of objectives not being met; and taking steps to keep these at a minimum.
(viii) Monitoring results.
(ix) Making appropriate modifications.

This is the kind of process with which many people working with children with special educational needs will be familiar. It closely resembles many curriculum development models which have been presented in the past. There is an additional element, however, which is necessary to shape a marketing plan, and this is a *mission statement*. This transatlantic term is one which some people find hard to integrate within their own thinking; some service managers, when pressed to create one, come out with a trite mission statement which incorporates phrases such as 'help all pupils to fulfil their potential', or 'assist schools in meeting pupils' special needs'. These are of little use. A mission statement is a shared and agreed affirmation of what a service is there to do. One of the problems which managers encounter is that they know what their service is trying to achieve, but some members of the service are equally sure that they are there to do different things or, perhaps worse, aren't at all clear what the service is setting out to do.

There are at least five elements which a mission statement needs to encompass:

(i) The type of services which are provided by the team or organization.
(ii) The client or 'customer' groups that it exists to serve.
(iii) The particular features of the service which provide it with its basis for success (e.g. specialist skills, access to resources, promptness of response).
(iv) The values inherent in the service: what service members consider important, believe in and try to sustain.
(v) What the service strives for and how it evaluates its performance.

Despite endeavouring to meet these requirements, it should also be brief. A single paragraph should suffice. However, it is not something that can be done by a single manager or a management group. To be effective, a mission statement must be created and agreed by all members of the team; if not, it will become words on a meaningless piece of paper. As Henry (1991) has reminded us, we cannot rely on statements of intent to guarantee behaviour.

Done properly, a mission statement does not only allow a commonality of approach. It also enables new entrants to a service to understand the kind of organization they have joined and the ways in which they can expect to work. It has a fundamental purpose in coping with changing circumstances: new developments in the service are testable against the mission statement. If they fit with it, they can more easily be adapted. If they lie outside it, either they can be rejected or they signal the need to reappraise the existence and purpose of the service.

A marketing plan must obviously take account of the external environment in which any service will operate. The difficulty here is that the way things are when the plan is drawn up may not reflect the situation when it comes to be implemented. There are clear pointers which desk research as described above can help to identify. One current indicator is the widely-reported intention of the present government to encourage as many schools as possible to acquire grant-maintained status (e.g. *Times Educational Supplement*, 26.7.91). Other augurs of developments occur from time to time. As this chapter is written the announcement has been made that schools may be able to 'buy in' inspections from DES-licensed inspection services. Such developments presage clear marketing opportunities, but the mechanisms for realizing them may not always be in place when they are first encountered. A marketing plan must take account of the need to generate those mechanisms within the overall framework of the service's mission.

Another external element for analysis is, of course, the client groups with whom service will work. What resources do those clients have themselves? What are they likely to use the service for and why? Are there competing services operating with any of them? What do they offer? Do they work in ways different to your own? In what ways can you present your own service as better or more suitable? A marketing plan will need to address all these issues and many others which are specific to the service itself.

A major part of the marketing plan will consist of the *promotional strategies* which the service will adopt, together with the key people who will ensure that appropriate actions are taken at the appropriate times. Example structures of such plans for special schools and SEN services are provided by Bowers (1991b and 1991c). A plan needs to encompass the results which are to be achieved, the methods to be used to achieve them and the key people who will be involved - including the person responsible for steering and co-ordinating the action. A critical feature of such a plan is its time schedule. The school year inexorably imposes limits on what can be done, when people have their attention taken up by internal issues, when they are planning their own development programmes, when they have to make decisions over staffing and resourcing, and so on. Your own schedule needs to take account of these; your contacts with clients and potential clients should be neither too early nor too late.

Another important feature of any marketing plan is the budget that has been set aside for its implementation. Until now many services with centrally-retained funding have attempted to market themselves with little or no budget allocation for the activity. Not all marketing has to cost money, as we shall see, but even where it is financially inexpensive it may use up a lot of personnel time. That has a cost, although it may be one which nobody has so far attempted to quantify. A budget should include financial estimates and time estimates, and should make appropriate allocations of these.

Promotional strategies

By now it will be clear that effective promotion of any service or school entails more than producing a glossy brochure. If we accept the idea of segmentation of the client structure, one brochure will probably not suffice anyway. What is relevant and attractive to members of one segment may very well not be on target with another. Advertising in appropriate journals is, of course, more likely to reach a specific audience. The jobs pages of the Times Educational Supplement provide a good example of copy directed specifically at one major segment: teachers and related professionals. Study of the Special Education section reveals a growing trend towards the use of hollow descriptors for schools - 'dynamic', 'forward-looking' - and of potted biographies which involve the self-promotion of the head teachers. Unless backed up by a reality which can support it, such rhetoric can easily prove counter-productive. The most effective form of marketing, as I pointed out in the foregoing chapter, entails ensuring that your school or service does a good job and that this is recognized by all concerned. This intention should underlie all or any of the strategies which follow.

I have already looked (Bowers, 1989b) at some promotional methods available to schools and services. There is a wide variety of options open, some of them involving considerable cost and others very little. The most obvious one, direct advertising through such media as local newspapers or local radio, is unlikely to be cost-effective for special schools or special needs services. It should not be entirely ignored, however: there may be times where editorial material provided for, say, a local paper can be backed up with a small and focused advertisement. If we leave this costly option out, we are left with several broad areas which need to be considered in relation to the segments targeted. These are:
 (i) Promotional material preparation.
 (ii) Media usage.
(iii) Direct contact.

(i) Promotional material preparation

This includes such routine items as letterheads, visiting cards, leaflets and printed envelopes. It can also encompass newsletters and video films. The

main purposes which usually underlie their use are to:
  (i) build an awareness of what is offered;
 (ii) differentiate your service from that of competitors;
(iii) create a favourable image;
 (iv) communicate the benefits of the service you offer;
  (v) eliminate any misperceptions of what you do or what you offer;
 (vi) persuade potential clients to use or support your service;
(vii) advise existing and potential clients of new offerings and new resources.

By now, most special schools and SEN services have brochures. They are important documents. They speak on behalf of the organization and, if done properly, seek to meet most of the above criteria. Unfortunately, budgetary restrictions have meant that some brochures are visually unappealing; moreover, the copy is not always well constructed. It must be remembered that before the first words of any copy are read, an 'image message' is given. A service therefore needs to know who it is trying to reach and what it is trying to say with its format and cover presentation. When it comes to the message contained within it, one ground rule is basic: it should emphasize the *benefits* available to clients. Readers want to know first and foremost what any service can do to satisfy their needs, allay their anxieties or reduce the pressure which they experience. Of secondary, though relevant, importance are just who provides the professional skills. Here potted histories of key members of the service, together with their qualifications, can prove useful.

Newsletters can provide an important means of promotion, provided that they are planned carefully with the intention of achieving that function. They can easily assume an 'in-house' air which tells a lot about a service's - or a school's - activities and its members' movements, but which is of little relevance to readers who do not know it well or are not already part of its activities. If that problem is avoided, a regular newsletter which updates schools on matters concerning special educational needs, relevant issues relating to curricular provision, and on recent and pending legislation which affects their operation, is likely to be read and circulated among teachers. Service-related news can, of course, be included, looking in some detail at the activities of the service in endeavouring to assist schools in dealing with the issues confronting them. Some mainstream schools are now using video films to promote themselves to parents. For a service these can also be useful, provided once again that they are targeted at appropriately identified segments. In today's sophisticated environment there is need to produce something which is of high quality and which does not have a strong 'home movie' flavour. This costs money and will probably involve professional assistance. Another difficulty for a service is ensuring an appropriate distribution take-up and return. However, a high level of impact can be achieved by the use of well-presented and focused video presentations, and the time and money spent may prove worthwhile. They can often be a useful component of 'showcase' sessions, and may be worth producing simply for these.

(ii) Media usage.

Local newspapers have for a long time provided a ready source of publicity - most of it welcome - for schools. Many head teachers have established effective contacts with journalists in which they have the opportunity to check material before it is printed, but others have found that what is written does not always correspond with the information they gave or their perceptions of the facts. Most local newspapers are constantly looking for editorial material, and it is often better to study the style and format used and create your own article or news story.

Until now, SEN support services have not usually seen local publicity as necessary. Their roles and functions often are not widely understood by teachers; the broader public knows far less. With the advent of greater market awareness, and bearing in mind the power of influencers in their client systems, they may find it useful to adopt a higher public profile. One means of getting directly to the media is provided by press releases. These can be generally issued or offered exclusively; either way they should be brief. They clearly need to be topical and of potential relevance to the readership or audience (local radio and TV can of course be sent releases) and should contain the following elements: the subject of the story; the name and address of the service; a description of the project/activity/innovation with the features that make it of interest; the benefits to the community; contact names and numbers for further information.

Publication in professional journals has always been a way of becoming noticed - but only by other professionals. Among peers, kudos has tended to attach to the publication of an article in a journal which is read by all. There is nothing wrong with this; it aids dissemination of ideas and enhances professional networks. However, the writing of such articles can only be classified as marketing when the readers are potential clients, or may influence such clients, or where they may provide future referrals. Where these criteria are not met, energy devoted to the writing of such articles may at times need to be directed to more locally-based but potentially productive projects.

(iii) Direct contact

It is a general rule in marketing consultancy services that existing clients provide the best route to developing the service and generating new business. It is therefore important to devote time to ensuring that clients are satisfied with their relationship with the service. Two main advantages can be expected to accrue from this: existing clients will continue to use the service and increase their use; and referrals to others will be stimulated by those clients.

The process of *networking* is necessary for any service to examine closely and develop strategies to ensure that it is carried out effectively. Networking refers to developing and extending contacts, keeping in touch with people and through them meeting and creating working relationships with others. It can be broadly broken down into *client networking* and *professional networking*. In the first, existing clients may sometimes need reminding that your service might be put in touch with others that they know. This has to be done delicately, but not so unobtrusively that they don't respond. Some services have used a satisfied client school to 'host' an event at which their own service can play a leading role. An open invitation to an INSET session on a focused topic such as 'Spelling' or 'Bullying' can provide the means by which a service can underline the contribution which it has to make in assisting schools' responses.

Professional networking is something that goes on at the moment for most readers of this book. It is very useful for people to want to talk to others who do jobs which are similar to their own, to exchange ideas and to discuss common problems. Learning support teachers like to meet other learning support teachers, heads of special schools of a certain kind usually enjoy meeting heads of similar schools in other LEAs, educational psychologists like to exchange experiences with other EPs, and so on. Annual conferences and other get-togethers of professional associations are prefaced on this assumption.

In a marketing context, however, professional networking often involves crossing the boundaries set by specific training and interest and creating links with people who deal with those who are clients of the service or who could become its clients. The possibilities in the field of special educational need are very broad and will depend on the identities of the users and deciders in the system within which a service operates. A learning support service could, for example, take referrals from members of a behaviour support service or from educational psychologists. Beyond this, relationships with clinical psychologists or with general practitioners might yield potential users within the client system who would otherwise have been missed.

Extending a network can be done in a variety of ways. One which is becoming widely used by organizations providing consultancy services is the *showcase*. A showcase is a gathering of invited people, usually deciders within an organization, which takes place over two or three hours in pleasant surroundings. Typically a hotel is chosen, although any venue will do as long as it is attractive to potentially different invitees. Members of a support service holding a showcase would decide on the topic which was relevant to their activities. If the likely deciders were head teachers or, because of the topic's emphasis on a particular aspect of the National Curriculum, subject heads of department, they would be personally invited by letter. A follow-up telephone call would be made to those who did not respond, both as a reminder and as a means of finding out why they were not coming.

The structure of the showcase will depend on its topic and the time available. Typically it should start with a brief presentation, and then centre around one or more sessions which involve participants in some way. Support services are usually well experienced in workshop and other 'involvement' activities. The nature of the audience, who may not be the eventual users of the service, needs to kept in mind, however, in planning these. What has to be built in, particularly as the event unfolds, is what the service can offer, what people's problems are, how the service works and how it can assist in dealing with those problems.

A further component of the showcase format is the post-event follow-up. In this, one member of the service is allocated to telephone and if possible call on each participant to discuss their needs in more detail. This is the point where commitment to use the service is sought, and where firm agreements on working relationships are made. For some people this is uncomfortable because it appears that they are putting pressure on people. To some extent they are. The end point of any marketing strategy is making a sale.

Selling

Many people opted for a career in education because they did not want to involve themselves in commercial activity. The idea of having to sell their skills and services to others can therefore be unattractive to them. However, some years ago I suggested (Bowers, 1987) that the central components of effective selling, revealed by earlier research, were likely to transfer easily to the consultancy role which many support teachers and educational psychologists fill. These include:

  (i) showing and generating enthusiasm for what is offered;

  (ii) paying attention to customers' needs, feelings and requirements;

  (iii) showing integrity and professionalism;

  (iv) planning and organizing ahead;

(v) working steadily with little supervision;
(vi) devoting time and energy above the minimum requirements;
(vii) making effective contacts with new and prospective customers;
(viii) showing mood control.

A quick inspection of this list will demonstrate that these qualities are desirable in most support service members, whether or not they have been concerned with 'selling' their service to others. There is a well-established myth, emphasized by consumer programmes on television, that the process of selling is associated with lack of integrity, falsification and deceit. In a few cases it is, but where customer satisfaction and continued use of a service are essential it is obvious that such qualities would quickly become self-defeating.

The processes involved in selling have been the subject of very many 'how to do it' books. For anyone wishing to look at ethnographic research on the topic, Prus (1989) has produced a scholarly analysis of the relationship between seller and buyer. Although not particularly concerned with services, it provides a useful guide to the essential strategies in making sales.

It is significant that when many companies cut back their training programmes in response to recession, their sales training is usually retained. They place a high value on such training; services which are to be successful within a structure where they have to woo clients may have to give similar attention to this new element of INSET in the future. There are a number of steps in selling, each of which needs particular skills to maximize success. They can be summarized as:

   (i) identifying the customer;
   (ii) making plans before meeting;
  (iii) meeting and opening the interaction;
  (iv) getting information;
   (v) establishing what the customer wants;
  (vi) handling objections before they arise;
 (vii) summarizing for agreement;
(viii) putting forward benefits;
  (ix) overcoming objections;
   (x) closing: getting a commitment to use the service;
  (xi) keeping the customer.

These areas are expanded in Bowers (1991c). There is obviously insufficient space to deal with the processes involved in more detail within this chapter. What is clear is that in an environment where clients can make choices it is not enough to leave these elements to chance. Selling cannot be seen as something that one or two people are good at. In the future, if we are presented with an environment in which members of a service's client system - both real and potential - have the ability to choose, it may prove costly for a service not to ensure that its members are appropriately enskilled.

Chapter 10
The views of parents

Peter Caldwell and Michael Hunt

Introduction

There is no doubt that there has been an increasing emphasis within LEAs on a careful consideration of the services offered and on trying to determine what services are truly required. Clearly the Education Reform Act 1988 has provoked much of this examination and the pressure is now on all parts of the education service to ask what we are doing, whether we should be doing it, whether it could be done better, what the client wants, and just who the client is.

We have entered an era of market awareness and the primacy of the needs of the client. The assumption is that these underpin a successful business and that such a business will have researched what its clients want and then produce the goods accordingly. Some businesses have, no doubt, done their research and adjusted their range of products to meet the apparent needs of the customer. Others may not have done. We remember being asked questions about beer some years ago but the only subsequent change we noticed was the price. However, whether businesses actually do establish the true needs of the customer or not, the myth predominates and the pressure is on those in the public education service to establish needs and them deliver.

The notion of determining the needs of the client and then meeting them is actually not at all new. It is arguable that many parts of the education service have always done this. Certainly the 1981 Education Act had a lot to say about the client, despite being drafted at a time of centralized services. It also had a lot to say about the provision of evidence for the benefit of the client.

First, who is the client? Secondly, what do we mean by evidence? Our view is that we must always keep thing as simple as possible so we are quite clear in identifying the parent as the client in the context of the 1981 Act. It is the parent who has particular rights and responsibilities and this has been emphasized in later legislation such as the 1989 Children Act. 'Evidence' includes all the reports produced within an assessment and subsequent reviews or re-assessments. So in simple terms, an education service has had nearly a decade (the 1981 Act was brought into force in April 1983) of assessing the needs of pupils, taking into account the views of the clients and, in the majority of cases, 'producing the goods'. The emphasis on working with parents, of course, arose from the Warnock Report (DES, 1978) and has been subsequently stressed in relation to special educational needs in both mainstream and special schools (e.g. Wolfendale, 1987; Buckton, 1989; Rab, 1989).

In the LEA in which we work, the views of the parents were being taken into account and responded to in a customer-orientated way. What we didn't know about in a systematic way was customers' satisfaction with what they received. What were the perceptions of parents? Were we providing the right services? It seemed reasonable, therefore, to ask them. 'Quality assurance' is now a term beginning to be used in education, but one which has been with our National Health Service for some years. Vuori (1989) sees patient satisfaction as both an indicator and a prerequisite for quality health care. The same criteria can easily be applied to educational provision, simply substituting the work 'client' for 'patient'. Parents' views can therefore be seen as the foundation of quality assurance in special education.

A questionnaire for parents

Having made a decision to ask the clients what they thought about our services, a list of questions arose. Who exactly should we ask? What should we ask? How should we ask it? Having discarded interviews as too time-consuming, we chose to send out a questionnaire. This led in turn to further questions of structure, administration and scoring.

Decisions were taken and taken quickly. Staff were identified who were going to give this project the necessary priority. It was decided to design a questionnaire to send by post to all parents of children who had been assessed fully and were currently the subjects of statements of special educational need. These parents had therefore had the full services under the 1981 Act. Our computer produced the list: a total of 1438 would be sent a questionnaire. The 1438 included parents of children in both special and mainstream schools. The questionnaire had been designed to be analyzed by a suitable computer programme. A very speedy pilot was undertaken by writing directly to a small number of parent governors who responded positively. So the questionnaires, with a few amendments, could now be sent by post with pre-paid envelopes and a letter encouraging parents to respond.

The questionnaire was not perfect and the language used was not perfect. We comforted ourselves by reflecting that this was social research not academic research: we needed speedy results and our questionnaire was hopefully adequate for the job. All we could do now was sit back and wait. Clearly there was danger of a poor response. The story about the person who did research on apathy is well known: out of 100 questionnaires sent out none were returned. Would this happen to us? We had been well aware that some parents would find the questionnaire difficult to answer, and so had kept the design and language as simple as possible. We had set up the questionnaire in such a way that parents could respond and preserve anonymity. Would that lead to problems? Would anyone photocopy some of them and complete more than one, so distorting the results?

In the event, we were well pleased with the response. We received 684 returns which were completed fully enough to enable their analysis.

Consistency of returns

The proportions of returns from parents with children at residential special school or college (15%), special school or college attended daily (48%), special unit (7%) and extra support within mainstream (27%) were almost the same as the proportions of those provisions known to feature in the total population surveyed. Statistical analysis showed no significant difference between returns and the overall distribution of provision for statemented pupils. The questionnaires were completed anonymously and scrutiny showed that the respondents were not necessarily seeking to please us. The parent of a child with specific learning difficulties, for example, said:

> 'I would criticize the time taken in recognizing that a child is in need of special treatment. Once it was agreed that he needed something, things moved quite quickly.'

Another was more scathing:

> 'Our child has not attended school since September 1989. Therefore our opinion of Bedfordshire Education Service speaks for itself!'

Despite the anonymity of the questionnaire, this parent was obviously identifiable. We had a contrasting response from the parent of a child registered at the same special school: 'X School is the best in (town). My daughter has never been happier at school.'

Basic data

The table below shows the type of provision accommodating the respondents' children.

Table 10:1

Type of provision

(a)	Residential special school or college	101
(b)	Special school or college attended daily	330
(c)	Special unit attached to an ordinary (mainstream) school or college	50
(d)	Extra support from a teacher or non-teaching assistant within an ordinary (mainstream) school or college	182
(e)	Home tuition or not known	21
		684

Table 10:2 shows the type of difficulties which parents identified their child experiencing.

Table 10:2

Type of learning or other difficulty

(a)	Severe or profound learning difficulty	99
(b)	Moderate learning difficulty (such as that associated with developmental delay or a general slowness of learning)	376
(c)	Specific learning difficulty (such as that associated with 'dyslexia' or a similar problem with one particular area of learning)	94
(d)	Emotional or behaviour difficulty	148
(e)	'Autistic condition'	16
(f)	Physical difficulty (such as associated with a mobility or manipulation problem)	100
(g)	Health problem (such as associated with a medical condition or frequent illness)	55
(h)	Visual difficulty	47
(i)	Hearing difficulty	49
(j)	Speech or language problem	160

It will be noticed that many parents identified their children as having needs associated with more than one area, since Table 10:2 provides a total considerably larger than the number of respondents.

When we looked at the ages of the children when assessed and the present ages of the children, they appeared to be consistent with the overall distribution in the LEA. This tended to support the reliability of our sample of responses.

What did the parents say?

We asked the views of the parents about the issues in relation to the assessment of their child's needs.

Table 10:3
Parents' views of the standard of assessment

		YES	NO	NEITHER/NOT APPLICABLE/OR UNSURE WHICH
(a)	Reasonable advice from central LEA staff	248	235	201
(b)	Reasonable advice given by teacher(s)	442	135	107
(c)	Reasonable advice given by doctor	207	233	244
(d)	Reasonable advice from EP(s)	451	113	120
(e)	Views taken into account on provision	498	82	104
(f)	Child's needs fully considered in reaching a decision	505	81	98
(g)	Provision offered was what was really wanted	456	118	110
(h)	Assessment completed in reasonable time	427	159	98
(i)	Provision arranged in reasonable time	470	115	99
(j)	Contents of statement and reports were clear and helpful	501	83	100

The Education Department and doctors did not achieve sizeable 'Yes' votes. Elsewhere the clients appeared to be happy. The information on the database was further interrogated and showed that the advice given by doctors was more highly rated by parents with children with physical disabilities (chi-square 30.2, df1, p<.001) or health problems (chi-square 8.4, df1, p<.01) than by parents of other children. Perhaps other special needs are not really the responsibility of doctors, although the large 'No' response may indicate that many parents felt their child had medical requirements which were not attended to. Parents of children at residential school were least happy with the advice given by teachers in connection with the assessment but were significantly happier (chi-square 4.3, df1, p<.05) with the provision offered at the end of the assessment.

There was a sizable number of parents who were concerned about the time taken to complete the assessment. The parent of a mainstream child with moderate learning difficulties remarked that:

> 'The duration of time taken to statement our child caused considerable stress and anxiety to all of the family and I feel this was completely unacceptable.'

On the whole, parents of children in mainstream with additional support were very happy with the advice given by teachers. However, they indicated their concern about the time taken to arrange the provision.

We asked parents for their comments concerning the standard of the provision made for their child.

Table 10:4
Standard of provision

		YES	NO	NEITHER/NOT APPLICABLE/OR UNSURE WHICH
(a)	Teachers skilled at dealing with special needs	535	56	93
(b)	Teachers sympathetic towards child's problem	570	26	86
(c)	Teachers help child to behave well	436	33	215
(d)	Suitable size of group in which child is taught	564	56	64
(e)	Protective or less stressful environment	434	71	179
(f)	Sufficient specialist equipment or			

	other facilities	337	130	217
(g)	Access to enough specialist support from speech therapist	185	143	356
(h)	Access to enough specialist support from physiotherapist	144	85	455
(i)	Access to enough specialist support from an occupational therapist	100	95	489
(j)	Child making reasonable progress with his/her learning in school	536	75	73
(k)	Child progressing in independence	522	60	102
(l)	Child is reasonably happy and relaxed	571	49	64
(m)	Child has reasonable social contact with other children	561	63	74
(n)	Child has a reasonable choice of friends	494	96	94
(o)	Access to a full range of school subjects	515	46	123
(p)	Reasonable access to out-of-school activities	401	131	152
(q)	Reasonable preparation for the next stages of education	376	85	223
(r)	Reasonable preparation for work or life after school	276	92	316
(s)	Transport to and from school satisfactory	497	47	140

It came as no surprise that the Health Authority services were somewhat criticized. Indeed, this criticism is accepted by the managers in our Health Authorities: even where we have designated provision for language impairment there is still a concern expressed about speech therapy support. There are however, some surprises. First of all there was a concern about specialist equipment. This was expressed by parents of children with extra support in mainstream schools. Secondly, parents of children at boarding schools appeared to be better pleased than other groups with access to out-of-school activities and preparation for work or life after school.

Finally, there was something very pleasing about the responses in this section. Questions in relation to teaching and learning brought about a consistently positive response and, after all, that is the central function of the education service.

Table 10:5

Measuring progress

		YES	NO	NEITHER/NOT APPLICABLE/OR UNSURE WHICH
(a)	Child's teachers keep parent reasonably informed about progress	545	79	60
(b)	Child's teachers readily available for discussion	611	18	55
(c)	Annual reviews of child's statements are of satisfactory quality	511	57	116
(d)	Further specialist advice readily available from a school doctor	231	139	314
(e)	Further specialist advice readily available from an EP	277	120	287
(f)	Positive encouragement and advice given to help promote your child's development at home	392	147	145

Again doctors appeared to be lowly regarded. Educational psychologists too did not receive outstanding acclaim. However, as happened previously, when sub-groups were analyzed, the doctors got a clean bill of health with the client groups most relevant to them: parents of children with physical disabilities and health problems. For our psychological service, we really do need to look further at the responses. What does the client want? What does the client get? A more detailed follow-up is now required, perhaps using interviews.

The teachers seemed to highly regarded. However, a large number of respondents appeared to be of the view that they were not getting encouragement and advice to promote the child's development at home. The responsibility for this may lie with a variety of agencies, depending on the child's age, the nature of his or her needs and the provision made. It is something that we have to look at.

Comments from the parents

We allowed space at the end of the questionnaire for parents to write any comments they wished. 349 took us up on this. Common themes arising were that there was a need for more staffing, teachers, psychologists, speech therapists and physiotherapists. This was perhaps unsurprising, as was the call for more material resources. Other requests were for more information and better advice, earlier recognition of special needs and earlier intervention, and a reduction of the time taken to complete assessments and arrange provision. Of those completing this section, 15% said that special education should be focused more definitely on mainstream schools with integration a top priority, 6% stressed a need to continue with special schools, whilst 10% indicated a need for special schools to link with mainstream schools.

We had some specific complaints, reflected in the data in Table 10:3 and the 82 who said that their views were not taken into account in arriving at provision, the 81 who said that their child's needs were not fully considered in reaching a decision and the 75 who said that their child was not making reasonable progress with his or her learning in school. Sadly, we had a group who sustained a negative tone throughout their responses; generally these were parents of children with profound learning difficulties, or specific learning difficulties. Of the last group, one comment serves as an example:

'For our Authority to pretend (presumably for budget reasons) that dyslexia does not exist is part of the reason for my child's problems. As a general statement, help from teaching staff has been practical, thoughtful and caring. The educational psychologist, though readily available, confines herself to long reports concluding that there is a problem. This is useless.'

Who completed the form?

We asked this question. Predominantly it was the mother, either alone or in conjunction with the child's father. The table below shows the full picture:

Table 10:6

Person completing the questionnaire

(a)	Child's mother	367	(c) Child's father	72
(b)	Both parents together	217	(d) Another person	22

Conclusions

Somehow we needed to summarize all of this and establish what lessons had been learned. Some were easy: for example, one question was 'Was reasonable advice given to you by Education Department from County Hall?' We were already aware of our limitations here because of earlier feedback from parents and schools. We had already appointed two statementing officers and they are now having a good effect in giving advice to parents. Also, through them, we are trying to reduce the time taken for assessment, and by and large we are completing assessments within the six month period that the DES suggests is acceptable. Most parents with children at boarding schools, both within the LEA and 'out-county' appear satisfied. Their reasons for being satisfied may need further examination. At the same time, our own LEA boarding schools are under-full and we are currently looking at the implications of this.

A measure of support came through for special schools but there was an even more strong demand for integration. Shall we be able to sustain both in a viable way or will an increase in integration lead to a demise of the special school and a lack of viability? This is a key question for our policy review.

We have plenty of indications as to what the parents want us to do:

(i) ensure early intervention;

(ii) make the assessment as speedy as possible;

(iii) listen carefully to what the customer wants in relation to provision;

(iv) be able to offer a choice of special school (day or boarding) or mainstream school;

(v) ensure that statements in mainstream schools are effective, in particular in relation to security, continuity and the standard of equipment;

(vi) have available a high level of expertise;

(vii) ensure that the health services deliver what they are expected to;

(viii) improve special educational provision in mainstream schools;

(ix) examine the communication between home and school to make it a more viable and responsive partnership.

A lot of this takes money and it is well known that this is no longer abundantly available to LEAs. So can money be found from within the system? Can we take the opportunity to bring about an organized abandonment of the obsolete in order to fund the modern requirements?

One of our most expensive items is the funding of residential school places. We have to ask if it is reasonable to strengthen our day provision by reducing our boarding provision when the parents of children in boarding schools were very positive about this. A further question mark lies over whether we can offer a choice of day special school or mainstream school with additional support and ensure that both alternatives are educationally and financially viable. The parents have answered one set of questions. Most of these are resourced-related; they revolve around the finite amount of money which is available to meet our customers' requirements.

Final notes

This was a first attempt by our County Education Service to obtain the views of one of its client groups about a particular service. There is no doubt that the methodology could have been improved. No special arrangements were made for non-English speaking families. Neither were any other special arrangements made for any families who might have a low level of literacy skills. Another time we will do better in this respect.

We may have underestimated the skills and enthusiasm of our parents and could probably have asked more sophisticated questions. The response rate was nearly 50%; this was higher than expected but it might be that the other 50% would have told us something different. However, what is abundantly clear is that we now have a duty to respond to our 684 sets of parents and use their observations in determining the way forward. We also need to remember that many parents were sufficiently interested to tell us what they wanted. As noted earlier, the 1981 Education Act requires us to take into account the views of the parents. We must not overlook them, individually or collectively, in determining in the ways in which provision is sustained and developed.

Finally, in research like this, parents so often express themselves well and with feeling, conveying to us what the teacher's and the school's job is about. The parent of a child attending a school for children with moderate learning difficulties made a comment which says it all. We quote it as it was written:

> 'Special education has turned my boy into a responsible adult and without it I feel he possibly would have become an irresponsible adult all because he has had the correct tuition needed by caring teachers.'

Chapter 11

A support service's response to the 1988 Act

Ruth MacConville

The 1988 Education Act has been described as the government's attempt to 'modernize' the education system, with its emphasis on economy, efficiency and effectiveness. In this chapter I intend to explore a number of the issues that have arisen for a support service in response to the Act. We are, of course, still in the process of dealing with many of the changes but we do have some clear indicators of where we intend to get to.

For mainstream schools, it looks as if self-management is here to stay. LEAs have already been relieved of much of their previous function as direct providers through the processes of purchasing, organizing and repairing. LEAs will have decreasing choice regarding which services they have left or, perhaps more importantly, whether schools use them. If schools have a choice, then support services have to be marketed. Although the power of 'image' and 'reputation' have never been in question, the difference now is that economic realities make successful marketing a precondition for future survival. The current and crucial question is: 'How will a service be perceived in comparison to the alternatives?'

Sometimes it seems as though we are expected to turn into advertising executives overnight, and as a profession we are suffering from could be termed 'curriculum planning blight'. Whereas we used to have discussions about inspiring pupils we are now using business-speak, talking about 'products', 'mission statements' and 'quality control'. The budget is in danger of replacing the curriculum as the centre of everything we do. It is perhaps significant that Pauline Perry, Director of the South Bank Polytechnic, was recently introduced on Radio 4's discussion programme 'Any Answers' in terms of having made a substantial profit for the institution since her appointment. The new words signal new priorities, indicating a significant shift in the way we think.

The immodest business of advertising.

The requirement to begin to consider their service in marketing terms is distasteful and even abhorrent to many support teachers. Members of a service tend to have high levels of commitment to its cause and its values. The general feeling is that management should be unnecessary, let alone marketing. There is the strong suspicion that professionalism is undermined by being associated with the blatantly immodest business of advertising.

Teachers usually consider themselves to be rational and are generally looking for steady progress in their professional endeavours. The stereotype of advertising people, by contrast, is that they are almost always egotistic and impulsive, looking for large and quick rewards in their quest to make the world a more convenient place to shop. For many, advertising is seen as synonymous with marketing, with all that implies. At a recent in-service training session which I conducted, two main misgivings were identified and explored by members:

(i) the close association of marketing with advertising and the inherent fear that as a profession we are only a step away from the pursuit of visible affluence;

(ii) the high level of concern with what clients want, and the assumption that this means going down on our knees to them.

The feelings of many teachers can be summed up in the comment 'I don't want to be in that sort of business'. In short, although for many the world of marketing may appear glamorous, it is also rather suspect.

Underpromise, overdeliver

The 'product' of a support service is empowerment and thus there is a high level of human and organizational risk inherent in an inability to come up with the goods. The moment a client says 'Can you . . .?' we should be prepared to say 'Yes' provided, of course, that the request is related to what we set out to do. People like doing business with people who keep their word. The hallmarks of a service must be credibility and genuine concern, and these are incongruent with advertising promises that cannot be kept. The car that will give us freedom on an open road, the perfume that will make us instantly desirable, are examples of 'overpromise'. Our working objective is to underpromise, and overdeliver.

Specialist teachers are already an extremely scarce resource. In their view the caseloads are usually quite big enough already. One of the biggest sources of stress for support teachers is taking on too much responsibility and feeling that children's lives would be worse if they did not intervene and support them. I have looked at the issues surrounding the phenomenon of the 'very large caseload' in terms of teacher stress elsewhere (MacConville, 1991). In this context, size of the case load confirms and validates the missionary zeal which can become associated with support service members.

Large caseloads imply large demand. It is important to note, however, that currently most services are 'free' to users. What somebody appreciates at the moment may not be what they will actually pay for; and anyway, those who appreciate or value a service may not be the people that will actually be in a position to decide to use it when budgetary considerations prevail.

Marketing and advertising cannot be synonymous. If we adopt a super-ficial approach to marketing, using widespread advertising literature, this can only lead to an uncomfortable level of consumer disenchantment and ensure that the rhetoric of the service does not match up to the reality of what is on offer to schools. In the present climate this can only be an extremely dangerous state for a service to find itself in. Peters and Waterman (1982), the gurus of successful American companies, remind us that students will never say of a college, 'Its got a great budget'. Similarly, no school or parent will ask, let alone pay, for our service just because of a glossy brochure.

The client is always right.

The view that marketing is concerned with giving clients what they want also fills many support teachers with horror. The frequently encountered and highly stress - inducing expectation of schools is that the visiting teacher is there to take 'the problem' away. In the worst case, we can be presented with a definition of the problem together with a solution for 'human rubber stamping' on the first visit to a school. This usually takes the form of being asked to agree to and then recommend a child's transfer to a special class. We have to modify the general axiom of marketing. The client is always right - but only up to a point. Our job is to work out, with the client, what that point is and to go on from there. The eventual aim is partnership.

From selling to marketing.

As a service we have had to resolve these basic misgivings and work on developing a construct of marketing stripped of the current 'loadsamoney' images. Two main traits of successful organizations identified by Peters and Waterman (1982) were closeness to the customer and a firm belief in teamwork. Putting our clients at the centre of everything we do and recognizing that the team is our most important resource in getting the job done has led to fundamental changes of attitude and ways of working. Paradoxically, marketing has become an ethical issue concerned with standards and with accountability. It is about:

    (i) diagnosing needs;

    (ii) developing appropriate responses;

    (iii) ensuring that the responses are meeting the identified needs.

Diagnosing needs.

The process of diagnosing needs demands simply that, as a service, we talk to schools and find out what it is they want. As Handy (1988) has observed, people don't talk to people. Life is not that simple. People in roles talk to other people in roles. Currently one of the major stumbling blocks in communicating with schools is the confusion caused by the inadequacy of the term 'special educational needs' (SEN) to describe such a complex concept.

Differentiating special educational needs.

If Eskimos have one hundred words for snow and Arabs almost as many for sand, there is a similar requirement to differentiate the term 'special educational needs'. One only has to utter the term to be aware of the hazy notions that it usually conjures up. This is not surprising since the concept is subjective, relative and context-bound. It would appear that nobody really knows what it means. Perhaps more worrying is that it can mean whatever it suits anyone to mean. Definitions in the context of a 'whole school approach' tend to be particularly vague, leading to such trite phrases as 'a special need is an unmet need' or 'every teacher is a teacher of children with special educational needs'.

It is true that the use of a new term or the new definition of a concept is often the necessary challenge to other ways of thinking or an indication of new and alternative ways of conceptualizing issues. The term 'special educational needs' was introduced to work against an unfair system of labelling. It has, however, produced a number of undesirable outcomes, particularly with regard to general attitudes to learning difficulties. The term 'special' tends to have certain connotations relating to difference in a negative sense. If the child is outside the range of acceptability for the teacher, then the child is special. The question becomes: 'whose problem is it: the teacher's or the pupil's?' Also contentious is the term 'need' which implies that the child is needy and consequently powerless. The vagueness of the term itself permits it to be applied with justification to almost any pupil the teacher finds problematic.

Parallel systems.

Galloway (1985) has pointed to the anomalies created by the parallel systems of special and mainstream schools. One problem lies in the divisive salary structure, which discourages special teachers from returning to the mainstream and discourages mainstream teachers from extending their skills to meet the special educational needs encountered in their work. It is perhaps unfortunate that the related concept of the 'whole school approach' has usually been introduced to mainstream schools by special needs advisory staff. The movement to a whole school approach involves the specialist in being more than a good teacher; he or she has to be an advocate, an adviser and a shaper of attitudes (Bowers, 1987). The existence of separate SEN teams, departments, and resource allocations encourages teachers to consider these pupils as someone else's problem. The approach is more likely to be successful if it is underpinned by a whole LEA approach to SEN (Dessent, 1987), but this requires central funding and central steering.

Empowering: the ability to get things done.

The process of empowering schools to get things done requires the consultant to understand what life looks like and feels like for staff. Understanding and assessing organizational culture, combined with effective communication skills, are essential to getting the message across. Like the late Ray Kroc of McDonald's fame, the consultant must help others see 'beauty in a burger'.

Bowers (1989a) distinguishes three fundamental approaches to consultancy: the expert consultant, the doctor consultant and the process consultant. The whole school approach is largely based on the SEN teacher operating as process consultant. Rather than retaining expertise and being seen as indispensable, or just setting out to make things better for the school, the process consultant aims to achieve change by helping the school look at problems in fresh ways and opens up a variety of options for its members to take. The process consultant aims to enlighten and to change. Unfortunately, however, life is not usually that simple. Mainstream teachers often like to think of SEN staff as 'gatekeepers' who control access to information and know things that they do not know. The stark simplicity of a do-it-yourself whole school approach to special needs is frequently unpalatable and disconcerting and all too often the advisory teacher lacks the appropriate power tools of support, information, resources and, especially, time to get the job done.

The dilemma of teamwork.

Even when teamwork seems the most logical approach to take, making the process work effectively is not easy. Two inequalities detract from successful teamwork.

(i) Imposition of hierarchy. The whole school approach is often regarded as a top - down initiative and the advisory teacher comes to be seen as the LEA's agent and gatekeeper of information and resources.

(ii) Knowledge and personal resource gap. The specialized and unfamiliar concepts associated with special needs frequently have the effect of making teachers feel 'overloaded'. Coping strategies include withdrawing, filtering (screening out the complexity) and displacement (unburdening oneself of the complexity). Such mechanisms can work for the individual teacher. Plenty of 'busy work' effectively keeps more complex problems at bay. Issues remain unresolved, however, and there is a growing accumulation of strategic issues that cannot be ignored at school and LEA level.

Alongside the rhetoric of a whole school approach, traditional views of special education continue to exist. Inevitably, this creates confusion which is often reflected in the day-to-day practice of schools.

Developing appropriate responses.

In the process of developing appropriate responses it is a mistake, therefore, to assume or try to guess what it is that schools want. They are usually more than willing to tell you. The real challenge is in making it easy for them to do so. If you can do this, the school will tell you how to provide a good service.

A short questionnaire entitled 'Support Services: their involvement in your school over the last two weeks' was recently distributed to mainstream primary schools within a London borough. It focused on the most important aspects of working with support services from each school's point of view. The findings, followed by extended response interviews, provide insight into the type of support schools currently value and what they would be prepared to purchase in the future.

Special educational needs are no longer current.

General comments from the survey indicated that schools are all working from very different interpretations of what do and do not constitute special educational needs. Despite the very large numbers of children involved, in some cases between a quarter and a third of the school's population, head teachers do not seem to be demanding support for this area as a priority. This appears to conflict with Mittler and Pumfrey's (1989) assertion that the concept of SEN is undoubtedly one of the most powerful value - driven educational developments this decade and has served as a rallying cry uniting pressure groups in their search for resources. There was not one head teacher in our survey who would not be more than happy to trade in a general SEN training day for half a session with an educational psychologist. SEN seems to be no longer a highly charged issue for schools. As one head teacher commented: 'The 1988 Act demands a far more explicit and accountable system'.

The current focus for schools is statementing. Figures in our LEA indicate a sharp increase in the number of children being referred for formal assessment and these reflect the national trend. Schools' populations can be divided into those children with a statement, those without a statement and those firmly in the process of being formally assessed. Members of this last group can be further identified by the Warnock stage at which they are currently being assessed.

From the school's point of view the fact that a statement has been issued, not the extent of the learning difficulty, is the significant feature. A child with a learning difficulty or a behaviour difficulty is less likely to be referred for formal assessment than a child with a moderate sensory impairment. The latter may experience less difficulty in the classroom situation but is more likely to be granted the protection of a statement.

Evidence from the survey suggests that the decision to request formal assessment is frequently contingent on the future of a support service. The tendency is for schools to proceed with caution and take a 'better safe than sorry' approach. Being unsure whether the service will still be there in a few months' time means that a statement is regarded as the way of guaranteeing additional resources for the school.

'The educational psychologist is a must'

The survey indicated that the service most widely in demand is that provided by the educational psychologist, who is described as offering schools three valued items:

(i) Assessment; and they can't get enough of it. Schools want to know 'what is wrong with the child/children', and consider that it is the educational psychologist who will be able to tell them.
(ii) Information and advice on the process of formal assessment.
(iii) Consultation with parents. Head teachers value the support of educational psychologists in their dealings with parents, particularly in explaining to parents the nature of their child's difficulties and the details of the statementing process.

'Experts' and 'specialists'

Head teachers' responses indicate that they place high priority on the support that they currently receive from 'experts' and 'specialists'. Generally these would appear to be services that are identified for work with individual children, particularly those with sensory impairment or specific learning difficulties. Even though these professionals generally offer support within the class situation the schools value the reassurance that they can 'do the specialist bit' if required. However, there appears to be one notable exception to this general trend. This is looked at next.

'Children with behavioural difficulties need classroom assistants'.

The survey indicated that there is currently a potential educational chasm into which children with statements in mainstream schools are likely to fall. Increasingly the LEA is appointing classroom assistants to support children with emotional/behavioural difficulties. There seems to be a 'continuum effect' at work: the more complex the child's needs, the higher the level of non-teaching support the child is likely to be given and, almost as a direct consequence, the less direct support from a qualified teacher, either the class teacher or a visiting specialist, the child is likely to receive.

Any confusion that exists in a mainstream school about addressing special educational needs is necessarily extended to classroom assistants. An increasing number appear to find themselves working under the direction of class teachers who are not familiar with strategies of classroom management or pedagogy to meet special educational needs either in general terms or, more vitally, in relation to the specific needs of individual children with behaviour difficulties.

The new role of the 'support teacher' has been examined by a variety of teachers and researchers (Quicke, 1985; Bowers, 1989a). Many of the classroom situations that are reported as unsatisfactory in the studies by teachers are also reported to be unsatisfactory by classroom assistants. Assistants' responses expressed the feeling of being 'on the fringe' of the classroom, sitting and helping one pupil with no previous knowledge of the lesson, being marginalized from the teaching objectives for the class, and an absence of time for discussion.

Classroom assistants appointed to support individual children frequently seem to find themselves, therefore, in the position of offering 'non-specific support', contributing only in general terms to the well-being of the class by 'providing another pair of hands'. Ouvry (1991), observing the phases in curriculum development, describes the first stage in new initiatives as that of providing 'tender, loving care': getting to know each other but not sure yet quite what to do. Classroom assistants are frequently appointed, it would appear from this study, solely on their ability to 'get on' with children. The LEA's response, although relatively costly and popular with schools, does not in itself appear to address the real issues in terms of providing training, information or specific behavioural management, counselling or instructional skills to meet the child's needs. There is a certain level of tension involved as the schools report that they have a strong vested interest in maintaining this type of support: there is a consciousness that classroom assistants cannot be expected to have higher - order skills, but still a desire for as much help as they can get even though they know it is unlikely to meet pupils' real needs.

'We don't have the expertise'.

Head teachers' responses generally indicate with that they will in future only be prepared to purchase support that cannot be provided by the school's own staff. Head teachers currently value, and in the future will be prepared to purchase, 'niche services', or services that can be described as having a monopoly of expertise. The services of the educational psychologist received the highest rating, followed closely by services for sensory impairment and specific learning difficulties. There are five main items that head teachers want to purchase from 'niche' services:

    (i) information;
    (ii) assessment;
    (iii) treatment (sessions for individual children);
    (iv) joint consultation time with parents;
    (v) training directly related to classroom practice.

He who pays the piper calls the tune.

How would head teachers require support services to operate in the future? There appears to be a demand for:

    (i) prompt action;
    (ii) tighter contracts with negotiated and agreed objectives;
    (iii) speedy return of reports;
    (iv) practical advice relevant to classroom practice.

The views of many head teachers are reflected in the comment: 'If services are purchased, I want value for money and results from every session purchased'. The notion of 'value for money' for many head teachers involves purchasing the direct services of a named person from a support service. If schools are going to be paying the bill they want to be in control of what and who they are getting. Comments had a common thread, of which a typical one was:

'My choice of services also presupposes a choice of actually who will be employed'. This was, without exception, a named teacher who had previously worked within the school and had given good service. 'A proven track record equals value for money' was the remark made by one head teacher.

An agenda of economy.

The findings of this small study suggest that the 1988 Education Act, by providing an extremely strict agenda of economy, is likely to succeed in a number of areas where the 'whole school approach' has failed. The 1988 Act demands that schools differentiate pupils' 'special educational needs'. Global terms and references to individual differences are no longer current, particularly at the chalkface. The process of describing a child's difficulties, then conceptualizing them in terms of the likely effects on classroom management and curricular areas, enables informed decisions to be made regarding the appropriate type and level of resourcing required.

The fact that a number of LEAs are now making levels of funding available for children in mainstream schools according to Warnock's five stages of assessment has put this procedure firmly on the agenda of many schools. This is encouraging because it establishes a continuum of resources available to schools and also cements the process of working together within a school. When members of staff sit down together and say: 'We have a problem, what shall we do about it?' the strategies are more likely to work. The answer itself is not all-important; the process of asking each other the questions is of equal significance. It follows that schools are more likely to get what they want from support services if they know what they want; or at least if they think that they know what they want.

The demand for specialists and experts to provide technical solutions to children's difficulties, indicated by this study, makes successful working relationships between schools and services all the more crucial. The current requirements expressed by most schools is for what amounts to doctor/patient, expert/client relationships (Bowers 1989a) and this must be our initial stance. The challenge for a support service, however, is to survive and progress as consultants. The ethos of entitlement to access to the entire National Curriculum must be maintained and at some point the curriculum challenge has to be tackled by all teachers. It may be that support services will find themselves increasingly concerned with quality control as funds for statemented children become delegated to schools; if so, we have to ask if an inspection function is compatible with the task of the consultant, or whether the two need to be separated in some way.

Ensuring that responses are meeting the identified needs

Our extended dialogue with schools has necessitated a careful examination of current practice and has led to a fundamental change of attitude and ways of working. Needless to say, 'putting our cards on the table' with regard to existing practice has not been easy. The traditions of professionalism remain strong in teaching, particularly in specialist areas. Tenure, the privacy of the classroom and the right to express one's own views in one's own way do not sit easily with being explicit about values, or with a management style that reflects the pursuit of excellence. There are huge issues of accountability within all of this but if a service is to be efficient and effective then the traditions of an individualistic profession have to be largely abandoned.

Procedures but not rules

The challenge of the 1988 Act means that there are now many tasks that are too complex for individual teachers to address alone. Hence staff are now keen to group themselves and to accept a much higher level of organizational discipline.

An essential component of ensuring that our responses are meeting identified needs is being clear about what it is we exist to do. An afternoon is set aside each week to allow the staff to attend team meetings. Meetings are the systems and quality development drivers of a service. A high level of commitment has been achieved through communication and explanation. Our values, aims and objectives have to be understandable and each member of the team must appreciate his or her role in achieving them. If the essence of successful relationships with schools is effective communication then it is necessary to be concerned with the quality of internal communications. The conduct of our own meetings therefore says as much about our values as the contents of the agenda. We have put a great deal of energy into developing systems, problem solving through group consultation, and training and re-training in the processes of consultancy.

The contract underpins the mission statement

For change to occur in organizations, staff require a vision of where they are going: a mission statement. Its purpose is to inspire and underline our cause rather than direct daily activity. Daily activity requires something more tangible: a set of specific tasks to be tackled in support of the cause.

The contract is a way of setting clear, realistic targets for change and working out strategies to reach the targets. Contracts complement the mission statement and our wider aims by providing a small, step at a time, formal structure for organizational change. Involving teachers in a process of prioritizing the workload, agreeing objectives and determining ways of working towards them leads to success. We seek to work from the point of view of the client's needs and do not assume that our product in itself is coherent, understandable and self legitimizing. This, we have discovered, does more for image and reputation than advertising. A small change sustained is more certain to produce a positive outcome than the distribution of a glossy brochure.

The process of teacher, classroom assistant and support teacher forming a contract goes a long way to dispel the commonly held expectation that the visiting teacher is there to take the 'problem' away. The process of forming a contract requires negotiation, and the development of shared understanding about, on the one hand, the needs of the school and an understanding of its culture, and on the other an awareness of the knowledge and skills that the visiting professional can offer.

The contract system mirrors the guidelines for effective team participation set down by Kanter (1983). A task should:

(i) comprise meaningful, manageable tasks with clear boundaries;

(ii) be set within an established time frame and set of reporting relationships;

(iii) provide a mechanism for involving all those with a stake in the issue;

(v) provide a mechanism for providing evaluation and recognition for the team effort.

To return to the findings of our survey, the contract system matches the way that head teachers reported they would require support services to operate in the future. Contracts make it easy for schools to complain constructively. The service may have an excellent system but if how we operate is a mystery to schools they are likely to be confused at best, or angry at worst. It is important to explain to schools how things are done. Contracts are an efficient, shorthand way of explaining to schools how a service operates. They:

(i) encourage careful planning;

(ii) enable both school and service to evaluate their work;

(iii) can empower people and create shared success by setting objectives for change.

The 'contract' approach to support is expensive. It demands time. On the surface this does not appear to be compatible with the prevailing requirement for economy. We have had to reconsider our notions of what is economical. If the workload of the service is only considered in quantitative terms, with large caseloads to get through and more or less the same for every child who is referred to us, then the problems are likely to remain.

In conclusion

The common ground between pupils with learning difficulties and the majority of pupils is far larger than the areas separating them (Galloway, 1985). What we as a service can offer specially to some children is likely to have relevance for all and can highlight general problem areas. A consultancy approach with the contract between two individuals as the basis of the working partnership can improve the quality of teaching and learning for all, and can considerably improve our chances of survival as a service.

Part IV

Developing services
in a climate of delegation

Part IV

Developing services
in a climate of delegation

Chapter 12

Progressing educational psychology practice

Arno Rabinowitz

A potted history: then to now

When, in 1913, Cyril Burt was appointed to be educational psychologist to the LCC, the first such appointment in this country, he had the great good fortune to be allowed to write his own job description. His appointment marked the beginning of what have come to be known as Schools Psychological Services (SPSs). The appointment also had two other long-term consequences: it firmly located the work of EPs within Local Education Authorities (LEAs) and set a standard for the function that is still being haggled over today.

The initial appointment was part-time and the remit Cyril Burt, coming from his academic base in University College, took unto himself was an interesting mixture of work with individual children, research and providing information for his employers. He was commissioned to carry out surveys of children in LCC schools, to examine and report on individual cases of 'educational subnormality', individual gifted children, and on delinquency, and to study and report on the psychological aspects of specific educational problems such as entrance and scholarship qualifications.

By the time the Education Reform Act became law in 1988, every LEA had a service of educational psychologists. Although the extent and range of their services had broadened enormously since Burt's original appointment, what had not changed substantially appeared to be the nature of their occupations. In their report on Educational Psychology Services in England, 1988-9, HMI (1990) described the range of services offered by an educational psychology service as: 'Typically about 60% of time is given to all forms of assessment, advice, treatment, review and writing, 20% to administration and travel and 20% to INSET and other undertakings' (p.7). At first sight it appears that all that had been changed since 1913 was some time for travel, administration and INSET.

The reality is of course different. By the time of the HMI report, psychology services had developed from a service of lone practitioners working independently, often in Child Guidance Clinics, into complex hierarchies situated within education departments and responsible for an ever-increasing range of provision and duties. Every service supported a variety of special and ordinary schools in various ways. Approaches to work had been developed which ranged from the application of psychodynamic approaches in educational settings to the application of methods of behaviour modification. Specialisms had become developed and extended, psychologists had become an integral part of all matters to do with assessment for special education and the evaluation of schools, and their work had been recognized in various Acts as being legally necessary. Many SPSs had established connections and joint appointments with local university-based training courses for educational psychologists and were regular publishers of academic material.

Advantages of SPSs for schools and children

Schools benefited from SPSs by having free and ready access to sources of advice and support for dealing with problems as they encountered them. At its best this support was non-evaluative and supportive of the institution. It provided ways of dealing with problems that schools found painful or intractable. It provided a way of referring children to a wide variety of other services. Many SPSs either controlled or had access to groups of teachers for children with specific learning difficulties or emotional problems. Staff could be supported both in and out of school and INSET tailored to the school's specific needs. The service was free and easily accessible and psychologists could be thought of as colleagues rather than as inspectors or advisers who might be more intimidating.

Children could have the help of someone who was their advocate, whose interest in being in school was the child's interest, where cost was no factor in the amount of time, effort, energy and commitment that could be brought to the aid of an individual child and that child's family. Families could be sure that the psychologist was there to ensure that their child derived the best from the education that was on offer.

Practitioners

Psychologists derived enormous benefit from working within local education authorities. At the most basic level, their pay and conditions of service were good and not linked either to their effectiveness nor to the amount of actual work performed. They could spend as much time as was needed in helping individual children, parents and schools. Resources were not normally a great problem. Supervision, planned professional development and in-service training were regularly available. The profession had reasonably high status and was usually well regarded by schools and political members. The freedom to act on behalf of individual children enabled many to benefit from education who otherwise would not. There was ample opportunity to develop areas of personal interest and to apply these to work.

The profession provided a good career structure with opportunities for moving into academic, inspectorate or administrative work. Added to that, job satisfaction was generally high.

The disadvantages

The reality, of course, is very different. For children, schools and the psychologists themselves, working within local education authority structures brought many unperceived disadvantages. These disadvantages negated in many ways the admirable job concept that lay behind the first appointments: work with individual children, research, reviews and bringing intellectual and research-based influence to bear on policy.

Most services had developed into complicated and considerable hierarchies which attempted to weld together numbers of individual workers. Working within a service and within a joint ethos was not always possible and many services had become simply loose associations of autonomous professionals. This situation required the conception, construction and implementation of management structures designed to enhance and organize the work of disparate individuals into a coherent, consistent framework. In most services this proved to be a difficult process and one which always continued to pose problems for EPs and to absorb energy. Typical structures were those of straight line management, steep in gradient, with administrative ranks characterized by status-laden titles. Straight line management led quickly to a variety of debilitating side effects. One was the primacy of the needs of senior management, both within and without the service, characterized by Ball (1987) as 'top dog' (p.5) theories which reflect the particular interests and needs of administrators and mangers.

In their 1990 report, HMI commented that 'The quality of management of the services varied considerably across LEAs. In a minority of services management was regarded as extremely important and senior members had undertaken personal training and devised management strategies to try and ensure the most efficient and effective use of personnel and resources' (p.p.23-24). Many services remained as basically loose agglomerations of concerned individuals. This, HMI (1990) asserted, was due to the prevalence of a service view that because psychologists were equally qualified all should have a high degree of autonomy. This situation, they suggested, could often be traced back to earlier times when there had been few members of the service.

The professional journals of educational psychologists abound with articles about service delivery, its organization and management. It is clear that there are many questions to be resolved and paths to be cleared. Booker (1991), in one of the most recent of such articles, summarizes his paper as a description of a 'framework for the management of a psychological service that potentially incorporates the complexity of service activity and the necessary professional autonomy of psychology while offering specific principles for management' (p.3). Children and schools are not mentioned at all: organizing a service has become a productive activity of its own. The time, energy and resources that this absorbs are not available to schools.

Similarly, embedding SPSs within LEA structures has other debilitating consequences. One is the challenge of who constitutes the client - for whom does the psychologist work? The other is that of the influences that are brought to bear on the LEA psychologist by the very fact of being an LEA psychologist. Booker (1991) points out that in the current climate the principal client could be considered the holder of the resources: the Education Officer (Schools), and that LEAs, becoming more hard pressed financially, have defined far more explicitly what they are prepared to pay for. The principal client is clearly the provider of fees, the LEA, which has its own order of both financial and policy imperatives. The influence of these factors is most clearly seen when there are clashes between psychologists and their employing LEAs.

Under the 1981 Education Act, parents have a right to receive verbatim copies of professional reports considered by an LEA when their children's special educational needs are being assessed. In one midlands LEA, from 1984 onwards, professionals were instructed to leave certain items of infor- mation out of reports and encouraged instead to write 'covering memos' which would be kept secret from parents. One particular psychologist believed that it was his professional duty to inform parents of the constraints under which he had to write his reports on their children. He was required to resign but was subsequently reinstated in a well-publicised case. What this illustrates is how notionally autonomous professionals are in fact directly controlled by their clients, in this case the LEA.

In many similar ways, the work of EPs is constrained, contained and curtailed by LEA practices and administrative cultures. One independent group of psychologists, of which I am member, was involved in the reviews of children placed in an independent special school in the south of England. These reviews are the responsibility of the LEA in which the child resides but its current rules allow EPs to travel outside county borders only with special permission. Children have to be seen at home during vacations and there is no opportunity for the County EP to see the child functioning in an educational environment or to discuss, at first hand, the child's progress with those who are dealing with him or her directly.

This type of situation arose because, as Booker (1991) and many others have pointed out, management structures for EPs endeavoured to be psychological in perspective and purpose but actually remained embedded in a straight line, business orientated, budget driven managerial style. Needs for support, travel and equipment become measurable only through scales of productivity and cost/value analysis. Unquantifiable energy expenditure is unacceptable. Thus preventative work which, by its very nature, is hard to quantify, becomes difficult to accept as productive work. Work has to be measured by some sort of output and this, to be measurable, has to be observable. Outcomes like the speed or number of statements of special educational needs being processed become more acceptable desiderata than does the subtle, supportive and largely invisible work that constitutes a large part of the work of EPs.

The managerial culture in which an EP works can very quickly act as a lens which distorts an individual's view of the essential nature of the job. Instead of being able to see one's position as child-centred, with research aiding the LEA to make appropriate decisions or find better ways of helping, the EP begins to see work in a way which satisfies the needs of the organization and thus relieves stress on the individual worker. The culture takes over from the professional perspective very quickly and the client in need outside the administrative headquarters is seen as of second order importance. Sometimes the ability to complete a form, fill in a travel claim, know which is the appropriate route for papers, keep one's demands on the organization low and unpressing, and be the cause of no complaints or adverse comments, become more acceptable indicators of personal professional worth to the organization than do work with individual clients and the depth of commitment to the cause of the needs and rights of individual children.

Finally, embedment in an LEA structure can be confusing and worrisome for schools, parents and children. EPs are often seen as agents for or servants of the Authority. This perspective is understandable. EPs almost always work for LEAs. The professional and trade union of educational psychologists, the Association of Educational Psychologists, will only accept as full members those who are in LEA employment. Others have to be mere affiliates. EPs are almost always seen in terms of their LEA status and not in terms of professional ability. This makes it difficult for schools to know if advice is child or LEA-centred, if advice about schools depends more on a knowledge of LEA financing possibilities than on individual need, and if a reluctance to comment on curriculum or materials is due less to a lack of knowledge than to an unwillingness to tread on the toes of colleagues who have these things as much more specific remits in their own job descriptions.

Carolyn O'Grady *(Times Educational Supplement, May 17 1991, p.41)* relates how 'A child in Ealing, for instance, is 30 times more likely to be sent from its home area to an independent special school than a child in Leeds'. Such variations can only be due to differences in LEA policies, not to differences in professional practice or the distribution of disability in the population. In a huge variety of ways EPs in LEAs are constrained and not liberated by the base of their employment.

LMS

The ever-rolling incoming tide of the implementation of LMS has brought with it, for the first time, the possibility that SPSs could become disestablished and required to sell their services to schools and individual clients. DES Circular 7/88 describes LMS as 'One of the key reforms of the Education Reform Act' (p.1). National Curriculum notwithstanding, LMS is the centrepiece of the Act. Nobody should be under any illusions about the transformation that LMS is designed to bring about; its introduction marks a complete break with the past.

The Coopers and Lybrand (1988) report stated unequivocally that LMS requires a new culture and philosophy of education at the school level, and various Secretaries of State have repeated that the Act is about competition, choice and freedom. LMS is designed to shift the school system from a 'community culture' to an 'enterprise culture'. Although the position of EP services is still not finally decided it seems clear now that in many instances EPs will soon become suppliers of services to purchasing clients, no longer assured of a continuous and certain role in relation to schools and having to examine the basis of their work and its content with rigour and candour if they are to survive.

At one stage almost all qualified educational psychologists worked for local education authorities. But over the past three years, and especially since the abolition of the Inner London Education Authority, the number of EPs who have opted for independent educational work has increased greatly. Across the country there are now independent educational psychologists working either singly or in small practices offering a range of services.

In a typically small practice, the range of work incorporates:

(i) working with independent mainstream and special schools (because funds for statemented children are not delegated, LEA schools still cannot use us);

(ii) providing opinions for lawyers and guardians ad litem;

(iii) helping parents in negotiations about special educational provision and accompanying them to appeals;

(iv) helping them appeal to the Secretary of State if local appeals fail;

(v) providing second or expert opinions for Local Education Authorities;

(vi) providing assessments of individual children at parents' request;

(vii) arranging in-service training for schools or groups of teachers;

(viii) helping in 'audits' of independent mainstream and special schools;

(ix) screening the populations in special schools;

(x) providing a service to the new range of grant-maintained schools and City Technology Colleges and to Social Services Departments.

This range of work is much wider than the normally available to LEA-employed psychologists and is achieved without a heavy administrative or managerial setting. Work is organized through a leaderless group which meets every ten days to plan, share experiences, jointly support and supervise, plan allocations, share new knowledge and discuss equipment purchase. Each participant provides her or his own office and material, accepts referrals and processes them. The only obligations are openness, honesty, mutual professional respect and participation in the regular meetings. Common expenditure is limited to letterheads, brochures, legal and accounting costs of the group. Individual members account for their own fees and manage that side of the work entirely by themselves. Exclusion of or admission of new members can only be achieved by 100% consensus. The final obligation is to participate in the group professional idemnity insurance and to maintain a high standard of work.

Independent practice

Apart from the need to provide oneself with a space in which to work and the wide range of technology and assistance that an LEA routinely provides, there appear to be only a few disadvantages to the practitioner in working independently. One is that the work is, essentially, more lonely than it would be if working with a group of colleagues in a daily collegiate atmosphere. Another is the need to learn and to acquire a wide range of commercial skills and to bear these in mind during practice. Time is money and it needs to be conserved and costed. This can, if allowed to do so, sometimes interfere with ideas of the correct amount of time to spend on an individual case. There is a need to understand the professional nature of one's involvement with clients and the fact that follow-up work is a necessary concomitant of all involvement and cannot be curtailed or separately billed.

These disadvantages, once apparent, are easily overcome. Isolation can be avoided by simple use of all the professional opportunities to meet. Commercial skills are straightforward to acquire and there is a great deal of literature available to assist the process. Accountants and lawyers become other co-professionals whose services are there to be used. Professional stagnation is another danger but this, like isolation, is avoidable through a view of professional development as essential for personal nurture as well as protection. Finding opportunities for development is not difficult and caring colleagues ensure that it happens.

For the psychologist, another potential disadvantage is the limited view which schools have of the range of work they really want him or her to do. An emphasis on full assessment for statementing to the exclusion of all else is a typical example. This is avoidable in two ways. First there is the simple right, not available to LEA EPs, to refuse to do such work at all or to limit the amount that one is prepared to do. The other is to demonstrate the worth of one's other professional skills to such an extent that the school demands and appreciates this range of other work of which an EP is capable.

Another similar danger area in independent work is the relationship between the EP and the best users or payers for services. Collusion has always been a hazard for professionals and the temptation to tailors one's work to please those with whom one comes into contact has always been strong. If one's livelihood depends entirely on customer satisfaction then the strength of this temptation increases exponentially. Again, like rocks when at sea, recognizing this hazard takes one halfway to avoiding it. The other major means of avoidance arises from the growth in professional self-esteem that successful independent work brings with it.

Advantages

The advantages of independence thoroughly outweigh any apparent disadvantages. Schools receive truly independent advice focused on the child and the school's need, and separate from any LEA political perspectives or imperatives. The relationship between school and educational psychologist changes quickly: the school becomes used to dealing with an independent professional who is able to exercise freedom and choice in giving advice. This enables the school to be less discreet about the sort of advice and support it requires. The obvious and total separation of the EP from any other LEA function makes the role of the EP clearer to the user and enhances personal and professional relationships.

Not only the school, but also parents and children, can feel that the person with whom they are in contact is working for them and no other employer at that time. There is no suspicion that there is a hidden agenda in operation behind an otherwise bland professional relationship.

All consumers are able to purchase exactly the services they need at the point at which they need them. They do not pay for a vast range of other services maintained in case of need from other sources. This too enhances the school and client's ability to conceptualize and express problems so that the use of valuable and costly services is maximized.

Advantages for EPs

Educational psychologists themselves benefit from this new style of relationships. First there is the luxury of total freedom to work as and when one wishes and with whom one likes. This may seem trivial, but the liberation of spirit that it causes is tremendous. It is comforting to have the knowledge that one need never again work within a school that has a system one throughly dislikes or with a client group with whom one has never enjoyed success. Work immediately becomes more stimulating.

There is the adrenaline-producing situation of knowing that future work depends upon the excellence of one's current work. This, as a motivator, is much more powerful than any organizational or system-generated set of rewards. There is also a wider range of work available and again the stimulation, interest and motivation is enormous. Schools, parents, children and psychologists all benefit from a situation in which referral and conceptual skills are increased, enthusiasm on the part of both buyer and provider of services is enhanced, and the quality of input is improved because it is purely psychological and not concerned or corrupted by political or organizational dynamics.

Response of LEA SPSs

LEA SPSs, not unnaturally, have been spirited in their defence of their establishments and concerned to enure that services remain centrally funded and available 'free' to all schools. Typical defences rely on the tradition of service, the advantages of liaison with other LEA services, and the cost and availability of service to individual schools. The relative quality of psychological advice and support is seldom quoted either by the Association of Educational Psychologists or individuals SPSs as a reason for retention of central services.

Typical of the defences offered is that of Challoner et al (1991). Their case for the central retention SPSs is based on the following:

    (i) SPSs are not expensive;
    (ii) there will be no duplication of services;
    (iii) devolution might lead to a concentration on statutory work;
    (iv) schools might be forced to choose on commercial grounds;
    (v) only the fittest and best organized independent psychologists would survive a devolved system;
    (vi) there could be an emphasis on safe, conventional case work if services were devolved.

If SPSs are retained centrally, they assume that:

    (i) all schools and children will have an equal opportunity of access;
    (ii) the approach of the SPS will be integrated with that of the LEA;
    (iii) quality of personnel will be assured;
    (iv) there will be a wide range of services;
    (v) the use of resources would be efficient;
    (vi) quality, flexibility and preventative work would be encouraged.

In fact all these can be argued as advantages of a devolved system. The assumed disadvantages of devolution, centred within the fear of disestablishment, show the pervasiveness of the managerial and organizational ethic. Coffield (1989), talking about schools in a way which is totally applicable to SPS and LEA management, points out that most management texts used in education tend to be trite condensations of business school manuals which are transferred without adequate reflection. When the empirical grounding is examined closely it can be found to derive from the study of hamburger manufacturers or cartoon film makers. The organizational status quo which is defended is of dubious pedigree. In my view, the systems of control, organization and management within the LEA ultimately diminish and downgrade the quality of the service that can be offered to those in need.

There has been a failure, too, to consider real, different alternative models of organization. The presumption has been that, if disestablished, EPs will dissolve into single or small group practices, all fiercely competing for the same client group and inevitably succumbing to a competitive, 'dog-eat-dog' approach to professional work. Some SPSs have responded by offering menus of services, tailored on a notion similar to dental charges, for which schools would pay on demand. Again, such notions deny the dynamic relationships that must exist between schools, clients and EPs and the way in which the nature of the job demands flexibility. It is not possible to bring to menus the same considerations of portion control, reliability, speed and efficiency of service, courtesy of providers and absolute replicability of performance that characterize such firms as McDonalds. Even if it were, the idea of applying fast-food principles to services provided by caring professionals is a highly questionable one.

EPs take up the profession because of their interest in working with and facilitating the lives of children and others who attend institutions of education. What is required is an organization and system which offers EPs the opportunity to work freely with clients in a way in which their professional skills are appreciated, extended and enhanced outside the debilitating and inefficient management systems of LEAs. Pleas such as that of Booker (1991) for different styles of management should not really be necessary: the mere act of creation of that article is witness to the inefficiency of the system and the amount of energy it consumes.

Models for the future

David Galloway has put forward a model for independent organization that might well prove to be a practicable basis for the future: a type of service akin to a well organized practice of General Practitioners. This would be staffed by Chartered Educational Psychologists and be recognized (and perhaps licensed) by the DES and inspected by HMI. It would be equally available to parents and schools, be able to house a range of associated services and to concentrate above all on delivering an effective service. Galloway (1990) suggests that such a service would be independent of LEA control, would have a sharper and more limited focus on assessment and advice on individual children than many services do at present, and that it would be more open to market forces. Parents as well as schools or LEAs could decide which of the available services to use. In practice the choice would probably be greater in urban than in rural areas, but this would only reflect the provision of services of most kinds.

There are many flaws in this model and many more models are waiting to be described. What is important is that a new perspective be adopted, one which is concerned to find models of organization in which EPs could function independently in the new market rather than trying always to sustain, retain, redescribe and mildly modify existing structures. New models will have to develop which recognize the specific needs of psychologists within organizations. There will need to be increased emphasis on the importance of individual participants. Competitive advantage, for this will be a commercial world, will need to be seen as lying in speed, flexibility and know-how. Quality, not scale, will be recognized as crucial and enabling people to work with maximum efficiency will be taken as the key to the sustainability and ultimate profitability of the service.

Groups which are dependent on their human and intellectual capital will have to recognize that consistency between corporate and individual values encourages maximum commitment and efficiency. Flatter organizational structures will need to replace hierarchical structures. Leadership in the new organizations will be based on shared values and behaviour styles rather than on command. Clearly standards of behaviour, consistent with participants' own beliefs, will encourage corporate decisions and promote speed and initiative and, in the end, provide users with a better service and psychologists with a more satisfying workplace as independent professional workers.

Chapter 13

A possible solution to the management of a Special Educational Needs Support Service under LMS

Gill Carter

In 1989, my LEA, an outer London Borough, was one of only a handful of LEAs that chose to delegate special needs funding (including money for statements) directly to schools, thereby making the maintenance of a large support service, centrally funded, an impossibility. What follows includes a brief historical perspective of the team, an outline of what actually happened in terms of the planning and organization of the team's response to LMS, and more importantly, a discussion of the issues raised by the Agency system finally devised as a way of meeting the new funding constraints.

In 1989, when LMS first became a reality, the Special Educational Needs Support Service (now known as the SENSS Team) numbered some 39 full-time equivalent staff. Like Topsy, the team, founded in 1970 as a remedial reading service had 'just growed' until the early 1980s, when it had been the subject of a review which gave the Special Educational Needs Support Service (SENSS), as it was now to be known, a definite role in helping schools to develop whole-school policies and resources as well as a clearly defined brief in identifying, assessing and supporting individual children experiencing learning difficulties of any kind.

The team was to have a clear career structure, with a head of service, three deputies and six cluster co-ordinators (on 'B' Allowances) all allocated on a regional basis and expected to act in an advisory capacity to a group of between six and ten primary schools. These new posts were to replace the former team leader and one or two arbitrarily determined promoted posts that had characterized the remedial team. Other team members remained on the main professional grade, and had a narrower range of responsibilities than the management team. At this stage it was expected that the team would continue to work only in primary schools.

This new structure was finally put in place in April 1986, with the remedial team leader appointed as head of service. Those who had been on promoted posts over the years had to apply for the new posts in the management team, and with the appointment of further expert staff from outside the Authority to fill the other vacancies, the SENSS team made a confident start in its new role.

The leading of INSET had been a clearly defined requirement for all those in the management team, and SENSS quickly began to make an impact in the development of special needs work throughout the LEA, with courses for school-based special needs co-ordinators, support for the teaching of literacy to children with learning difficulties, the Coventry SNAP programme (Ainscow and Muncey 1984) and courses on maths and behaviour management, to name but a few. INSET for team members continued, too, with two mornings per term being set aside for whole-team meetings. Usually, outside speakers were invited, but there were opportunities, too, for the team to work together and share expertise in such matters as record-keeping, the organization of resources and assessment. All members were invited to a brief induction course on joining the team and were encouraged to take the courses offered by the management group when they could. Gradually, the team was becoming a skilled and highly regarded force in the Authority, looked upon favourably by schools and seen as making a definite contribution to the meeting of special needs.

LMS

The original Head of Service retired in 1988, and the post was admirably filled by one of the deputies in an 'acting' capacity until I took up my appointment in September 1989. At the interview in March, there seemed to be little certainty about what changes LMS would bring, and it was only two months after my starting work in September 1989 that I was sent for by the Chief Education Officer to be told that the Authority's LMS planning would entail the reduction of SENSS from 40 full-time equivalent posts to 4. Rumour had previously been rife and anxiety levels high, and the Director's announcement did little if anything to lower them. The proposal was that all team members, except the head and deputies, would be taken on to the staff of the schools where they were currently working. This hit particularly hard at the 'B' allowance cluster co-ordinators, all of whom were holders of qualifications in SEN, and who worked a maximum of .7 in any one school and at least .3 in an advisory capacity in a cluster of schools and made a valuable contribution to INSET in SEN throughout the LEA.

There seemed little likelihood that schools would want to take them on with their 'B' allowances to do special needs work: schools had anxieties about managing their budgets and were uncertain about the future. The possibility of finding two schools to pay them at 'B' allowance rates, so as to give them a full timetable, gave rise to painful anxieties about split contracts and there was the prospect of a major loss to special needs in the Authority if these six posts disappeared. It seemed highly unlikely that schools would be willing to allow the teachers out to be involved in day-release training if they were being paid for out of delegated budgets and morale dropped to an all-time low as career prospects crumbled and uncertainty became widespread. The agony of the situation was compounded as some schools made it clear that they could not afford to take even a main scale SENSS team member on to their staff, despite direct delegation of money for SEN. Small schools were particularly badly affected and there was a widespread feeling (never substantiated) that schools were beginning to have a vested interest in doing badly in the screening procedure used to allocate funding for non-statemented special needs under the LEA's LMS formula. The Authority was already maintaining a generous percentage of statements, and the high level of demand continued unabated as the Borough's LMS plans became known.

Early 1990 brought a spate of meetings with teacher unions and the Assistant Director of Education, and hours of individual counselling with team members before the notion of setting up a Special Needs Agency was eventually formulated. The idea was that the ten management posts would be retained on a scheme that involved everyone working partly for one or more schools and paid for out of schools' delegated budgets, and partly for the central advisory service, funded directly by the LEA. The amount of time spent on advisory work would vary according to the seniority of the post, with the Head of Service working in a school for only .1 of her time, and the 'B' allowance members being school-based for as much as .7 of their time. The LEA showed its confidence in us by offering an extra full-time post at the centre, bringing the total number up to 5 rather 4 full-time equivalents. It also guaranteed to take full responsibility for the payment of all allowances.

Former SENSS team members who wished to retain their association with the service would, if their schools were happy with the arrangement, become SENSS Agency teachers, appointed by SENSS but paid for and managed by schools out of delegated funding, usually on one-year contracts. SENSS, now operating largely as an employment agency, would, in return, continue its professional support and training of Agency teachers, allow them access to its generous and well organized resources bank and endeavour to respond flexibly to schools' requests for additional SENSS staffing as needs and demands fluctuated during the year.

An audit was made of exactly what team members wished to do. Many preferred to go directly on to the staff of schools where they had been working, several returned to full-time class-teaching positions, but a substantial core chose to remain with SENSS in its new guise, and head teachers were supportive in opting for the Agency, despite its being new and untried.

There were inevitably a few cases that refused to fall in to any category, and required many hours of patient negotiation with officers, unions and individual schools. Particularly difficult to resolve was the case of a teacher who was on a protected allowance because of previous redeployment, but the number of individual difficulties reduced as schools gradually became more confident about their own budgeting and team members were lost by natural wastage or career development, and 1st April 1990, the start of LMS funding, came and went without any major catastrophes.

Early experience

A particular problem for the entire LEA during that first term was the lack of clarity in the computer printouts issued to schools with their budgetary information. Special needs money was initially itemized separately but later included as part of the general delegated budget. Money for statements, still much sought after, did appear as a separate item and was also included in a letter accompanying pupils' statements (appearing as a funding band - an uncanny reminiscence of pre-Warnock categorization), thereby making itself even more attractive. Generally though, the financial information given to schools has taken many months to clarify, and problems continue.

Heads opting to have SENSS Agency teachers in that first term did more than respond positively to our first marketing leaflet. They took a real step in the dark, since we had no real idea of how the financial arrangements were going to work. Our initial advertising drive spoke of payment for Agency teachers being at average Main scale rate, but as yet we had little idea whether that was to mean the average over the whole LEA, payment at the median spinal point or average of all the teachers on the Agency. The LEA's Teachers' Staffing Department, which normally deals with all such difficulties, was inundated with work, so for the first term many schools were simply not charged for their teachers, thereby adding to the administrative complexity of what was already a financial morass.

Despite the problems, interest in the Agency increased, and a survey of schools carried out in the summer term of 1990 highlighted the need for a staffing expansion. From September 1989 it had been intended to extend our area of work to the secondary sector, but it was not until April 1990 that we were able to appoint an experienced head of a secondary special needs department to replace one of our deputies who was leaving us for a job in publishing. Her input and expertise quickly made the secondary schools also look to us to provide staff, and by the end of the summer we were advertising for new staff. We had increased from 23 to 28 full-time equivalent posts. New staff taken on at that time were offered only one year contracts.

Our lack of experience led us to fail to draw up adequate contracts with schools buying in to the Agency. We soon realized the importance of making sure we had more than half a term's notice either of requirement for new staff or cessation of contract. We also found we needed a laid-down procedure for interviewing staff and planning for a shared interview with the school, to be certain that the teacher we were to provide was acceptable to the school as well as to us. Before we had those arrangements properly organized, we had some difficult experiences where schools decided at very short notice that they could no longer afford our services, and we were left with a naturally aggrieved and anxious teacher for whom we could not find work. We were saved from worse problems by the fact that recruitment in the area is currently difficult, and there are usually other jobs to be had either within the Borough or in neighbouring LEAs. We try now to insist that schools commit themselves for a minimum of one year, and are hoping to work towards a three year contracting arrangement.

September 1990 found us with demand for Agency teachers still flourishing and schools continuing to be supportive of our enterprise, though we continued to benefit from the team's good name in the past rather than any strenuous marketing efforts of our own. What was quickly becoming obvious was that our best selling point was the provision of reliable, experienced teachers and we had fortunately inherited a strong team.

The financial arrangements for our service remained to be formalized, though. Again, we had good support from the Resources and Teachers' Staffing departments, but the final task was carried out by one of our deputies who has a particular interest in accountancy procedures. Precise calculations had to be made about Agency teachers' points on the pay spine, number of hours worked per week, changes in employment location over the year, increases and decreases in time allocation and recoupment of money made by the LEA on behalf of out-Borough pupils taught by Agency teachers. Additionally, provision had to be built in for long-term sickness cover and for the eventuality of our finding we had no work to offer a teacher for part of his or her one-year contract. From this complex web of information an average salary was worked out and information about the system was passed to heads at a meeting in February 1991. Charges were finally made to schools in March and despite one or two remaining problems, the system seems set to continue with annual amendments as staff change and school requirements vary.

At the request of the Authority, a business plan has been drawn up for the future, which includes potential costing for the rent of premises, postage, telephones, resources, etc. in case we one day have to leave our comfortable niche in the Teachers' Centre, or at least, have to finance it more directly. It is now planned that the Agency model which we have devised will be extended to the music service, and perhaps eventually to other peripatetic services.

Policy changes within the LEA

As well as the changes being forced upon the service by national legislation and outside factors, there were simultaneous changes within the LEA that also brought pressure to bear. The Special Needs Adviser who had been on the 1985 Working Party and very much involved with the development of the service, left in April 1990 and there was an interregnum when the post was unfilled. The Special Needs Support Service's brief and status in relation to other special needs provision in the Borough had been spelt out clearly in the Working Party's Report of 1985, as had its relationship with the Adviser:

> 'A major resource to help meet the needs of the . . 15% of children with special educational needs in (the LEA's) primary schools, is, of course, SENSS.'
> 'The service falls within the responsibility of Assistant Director of Education (Schools) who will be advised by the Special Educational Needs Adviser.'
> 'Senior members of the service . . . would assist with diagnosis of difficulties and the development of resources and strategies in collaboration with Educational Psychologists and the Adviser for Special Needs.'
> 'The placement of the Service teachers in schools will be made on the recommendations of the Adviser for Special Needs.'

The replacement of the Adviser by a Senior Inspector for SEN brought about a change of relationship to the team, without any such policy change ever having been formally spelt out. The prevailing ethos and policy of the LEA in relation to special educational needs is now, in common with all recent DES guidelines, one which insists on access to a broad and balanced curriculum for all pupils and sees SEN as a mismatch between the child and the curriculum. This philosophy was clearly outlined to head teachers at a series of one-day conferences in the Autumn of 1990, though as yet it remains to be clearly brought home to SENSS Agency teachers via specific documentation and training.

Such a change of outlook must have a bearing on SENSS within the Borough, but so far what seems to have happened is a certain loss of prestige for the team, with it generally not being consulted or involved in policy change. Previously it had been used as the instrument for change within the LEA, especially through the INSET it ran for school special needs co-ordinators and other mainstream teachers. The dynamic role of instituting change has moved to the Inspector, the Principal Educational Psychologist and the Assistant Director of Education, with the occasional involvement of the SENSS management team as supporters of the process.

The LEA is currently working on the advice offered in DES Circular 7/91, but has not yet developed a 'clear and coherent authority-wide policy' for meeting SEN. The HMI Report (1991) produces as its major finding the need for an agreed policy setting out the important aims and objectives for special educational needs provision, emphasizing the importance of co-ordination of the work of advisory teachers for SEN with that done by other services within the LEA.

For us, the 1985 guidelines have yet to be replaced, and we are currently operating in a vacuum. Obviously, LMS has brought administrative change and control of teachers employed on an Agency basis is different from control of teachers employed as a central team. What we now need is clear professional guidance from our LEA about its precise expectation of us. We have been involved in assessment at the Warnock Stage 3 referral procedure. This involvement means that we have direct access to all schools, and we now await the development of other new initiatives. The difficulties and frustration we currently experience are shared by support teams in many other LEAs, and we seem to be further along the path to reorganization than other neighbouring authorities. The speed with which the LMS legislation has had to be introduced has simply not allowed for a systemic, layer by layer approach to installing new management structures.

Issues raised by the Agency system.

(i) Funding

The Agency system of operating under LMS raises various fundamental issues. First and foremost among these is that of funding. It is hard to make predictions and to indulge in forward planning without knowing what school requirements are likely to be for the following year. Similarly, a change in central policy on delegation could mean that schools might have to be charged for the management team's allowances and administrative costs which could price us out of the market. So far, we have received a budget for such training and resources as we have been able to provide: should that source dry up, we would again be vulnerable to having to increase our changes and being over-priced.

(ii) Staff contracts

Although the Authority shows real enthusiasm for the Agency system, and supports us in our desire to make permanent, full-time appointments from now on, the problem of landing ourselves with teachers we cannot 'sell' remains a very real one. We have only limited support for unemployed teachers built into our financial plan, and could not sustain any prolonged period of payment to a teacher not being funded by a school's delegated budget.

We therefore prefer to continue our system of offering short-term contracts, despite the concomitant problems of not being able to attract suitably qualified career teachers or to offer them adequate opportunities for professional development. This remains a major issue to be resolved for the future.

(iii) Marketing

So far, we continue to benefit from SENSS's good reputation, built up over many years, and from the expertise of our advisory team, who are well known and respected in the LEA. The current lack of clear policy for SEN in the Borough, together with a lack of definition of SENSS's role, makes our marketing potential vulnerable. One thing, however, is clear: the best advertisement for our service is the quality of our teachers, and issues about contracts and training must be urgently resolved if we are to ensure the high professional standard of staff essential for our survival.

(iv) Management/control issues

Because SENSS Agency teachers are directly funded by schools for the time they spend actually teaching, they are presumably directly managed by schools also. It is obviously vital for teachers to meet the requirements of the schools in which they operate, but it is frustrating for us not being able to initiate change where teachers are being required to fulfil the old 'remedial reading teacher' role, or where the expertise of our advisory team in bringing about curriculum innovation is not recognized or made use of because the school has its own preconceptions about the role of the special needs teacher. Similarly, it is difficult for SENSS to ask schools to release staff to receive or participate in INSET, and we have lost the flexibility of our former system of operation. Directed time is at the discretion of school heads, and we are at risk of losing our team identity for sheer lack of opportunity to be together.

(v) Training needs

Training is one of the most serious issues of all those raised by the Agency system. If Hounslow SENSS is to move away from the guidelines laid down in our 1985 Working Party Document towards our still undefined role as a curriculum accessing service, there must be an opportunity for retraining.

We are painfully aware, both from what we read and from the talk we hear within the Authority, that we need to spend time as a management group in the first instance, and later with all the Agency staff, in reformulating our aims and objectives to conform with a policy appropriate for the 1990s. Much progress has already been made towards the consultancy model (c.f. Bowers 1989a); now we need to take on the role of effective learning consultants, facilitating access to the National Curriculum for all pupils. We are trying to be proactive in making sure the LEA comes up with a written policy soon and in insisting that time and money be found for us to work together on strategies to implement it. The matter has been raised with the SEN Inspector, who acknowledges the management problem of who 'owns' the SENSS Agency teachers, and hopes to negotiate our status, if not our funding, so that we can develop more autonomy.

At a more basic level, we have done our best to continue our own training programmes for team members through putting on courses based at the Teachers' Centre. We have tentatively restarted a twice-termly meeting for all SENSS Agency teachers (though at least one of these must be after school time) and we ask head teachers' support in allowing SENSS Agency teachers to attend one meeting in school time. So far, the response has been very positive. We offer heads the additional incentive either of attending the meeting themselves, or of sending along their SEN co-ordinator, unit teacher or any other interested teacher who can be spared. However, despite our intimate involvement with LMS, we have not been invited to join LMS training of any kind and are only just beginning to be included in head teachers' meetings.

A final identified training need is that for help with the development of computer skills. A splendid and high-powered machine was delivered to the service in 1990, as part of the computerization of the Authority, but there has never been any software provided and despite constant requests we have never been involved in the training offered to other heads on the use of the SIMS package. Such software as we have, we have provided from our own slender resources, and have taught ourselves to use it. We remain, though, 'incompatible' with schools.

(vi) *Increase in administration time*

The increase in workload has perhaps constituted the major problem of the entire Agency system. SENSS is the only support service in the Authority to be entirely without clerical help, and the enormously increased amount of clerical work brought about by the Agency operates very much to the detriment of the professional services that can be offered to schools. The heaviest burden tends to fall on the Head of Service and the Deputies, who are far too often prevented from sharing their expertise in special needs by the shackles that bind them to the office computer. It seems a peculiar irony that the Head of Service, especially, should be paid such a high rate for addressing envelopes, writing letters and making telephone calls.

Plans for the future

If the Agency is to continue (and so far it shows signs of operating success-fully), future plans must involve dealing with the issues considered in the previous section. The exact amount of central funding available needs to be announced well in advance, so that plans can be made for training, the development of resources and the giving of INSET. Any shortfall will have to be charged to schools, and this will certainly have to be the case for secre-tarial help in the future. We have resisted the urge to charge schools for anything but teaching time, but now that we seem to be successful, we can perhaps risk including at least a nominal amount to cover a few hours' clerical help per week.

Once the Borough's SEN policy is set, and we have a clearer idea of our place within it, we shall be in a better position to draw up contracts for the work our staff do in schools, to set realistic goals, and to operate within a more coherent framework. We hope to move towards longer or permanent contracts for all staff, draw up guidelines for the management of Agency teachers and set up appropriate training programmes, so as to ensure proper professional development for all. Like schools, we want to have our own Institutional Development Plan, with long-term planning a reality in which we are able to share. We are trying to draw up a list of relevant performance indicators and to evaluate our achievements. Until very recently, the way ahead for us seemed so uncertain that forward planning was only a remote possibility; now it is beginning to look as if our unusual *modus operandi* is going to become the norm rather than the exception.

Conclusion

Paragraph 108 of DES Circular 7/91 reads:
'Whilst the Secretary of State believes that there is scope for the delegation of the costs of centrally managed SEN support teams, LEAs will wish to consider carefully the impact of such delegation. Judicious use by schools of specialist teachers employed in central teams, and the expertise available centrally and through outreach from certain special schools, can be an effective way of enabling schools to meet a wide range of SEN, thus obviating a tendency to make excessive use of the formal procedures associated with LEA assessment and determination of provision under the 1981 Act.'

It is encouraging to read that the DES is not recommending wholesale, unconsidered delegation of support services. Our Agency model is a viable one, but we could be far more effective if we were able to operate a two-tier system, with a larger, centrally funded, full-time advisory team with proper clerical support, plus the Agency, funded from schools' delegated budgets. With more central funding we would have more time to deliver INSET, develop policy and give staff and schools the support they need, as well as to manage the Agency more efficiently. At present, we simply have not enough time available to visit and help Agency teachers, or to give them opportunities for professional development.

It is apparently too late to change the Authority's LMS planning. The next two years or so will prove whether the current arrangements can be truly successful. We have plans afoot for starting to re-train staff, and are also interested in trying to introduce the idea of an incentive plan, where the LEA may pay a small percentage of the Agency teacher's salary, so as to encourage take-up of the Agency system. It will be interesting to see if ours becomes the model for other LEAs to follow; perhaps this chapter will allow them to learn from our experience.

Chapter 14

Support service developments: horses for courses

Ann Mattey

Setting the scene

Two years ago the Integrated Support Service was developed in Kent to support schools in identifying, assessing and meeting the individual needs of children. The strategic planning process in Kent has produced a Support Service which is essentially involved in promoting differentiation; during those two years we have attempted to help schools implement the county policy for SEN by supporting a broad, balanced and differentiated curriculum accessible to all children. We have supported schools through a complex time-allocation formula, taking into account the size of the school, the level of need within the school and various other factors, but following an entitlement model to all schools in the area.

We now seem to be approaching a crossroads. We may be forced, through political pressures, along the devolution route, being bought in by schools. Alternatively there may be local forces developing which will steer us in yet another direction. The LEA policy for SEN is presently being reviewed through further strategic planning and this could also have significant implications for the Integrated Support Service.

How can we plan for our development given these uncertain tendencies? As a team, we believe that while responding to an increasingly business-orientated support model we must maintain our professional standards and judgements. We therefore decided that as an interim exercise we should look closely at the needs of the individual schools in our area whilst still maintaining the thread of differentiation. In so doing we would have the necessary strategies and procedures available to implement whatever further changes were facing us, together with clear information on which to base any future developments.

Two features

Two developments in Kent have led to greater awareness and a heightened profile for special educational needs: the SEN Audit and the development of 'cluster meetings'. The SEN Audit was set up to establish a formula for the distribution of resources to support pupils with special educational needs in the mainstream school. It was designed to provide an alternative to the widely adopted practice of linking schools' levels of SEN resourcing, through the non-age weighted element of the formula, to free schools meals. The intention was that it would more directly reflect the actual special educational needs of pupils rather than the level of take-up of an income-related welfare benefit. Its scope therefore includes all children who 'have a learning difficulty which calls for special educational provision to be made for them' in the terms of the 1981 Education Act. Bi-lingual children, gifted and travellers' children are excluded as groups from the audit. Individual children in these groups may of course have special educational needs arising from causes other than belonging to such a group and then will be included.

A copy of the SEN Audit appears on the next two pages. Schools have been asked to identify three things: (i) the general areas of a child's SEN; (ii) the target areas of the child's learning or learning environment to be worked on as priorities in the next year; and (iii) those elements of special educational provision which should give adequate support for the child's SEN. The back of the form offers guidance on the level of resource required to meet the identified need satisfactorily. It defines Level One intervention, where pupils are supported within the school's resources, Level Two where a member of the Integrated Support Service gives additional support within the school, and Level Three where additional support is sought. The same allowance is paid through the LMS formula for each primary school child regardless of their intervention level. In secondary schools, different payments are made for children at different intervention levels. To ensure consistency across all schools in the LEA a three stage moderation process has been developed. These stages involve: a) local moderation, b) area moderation and c) county moderation.

The other significant development has been the multi-agency gathering (we've called ours 'cluster meetings') to enable the education services and other agencies to offer a systematic and co-ordinated approach to identification and assessment, intervention strategies, advice, integration options, support, options for provision, review, and all consequent decision-making which has financial implications. In the event of a child's lack of progress, despite support through the Levels of Intervention, the school can consider referring the case to the cluster meeting. This group, made up from represen-

Figure 14:1 Kent SEN Audit

KENT LEA : SPECIAL EDUCATIONAL NEEDS AUDIT 1991 - 1992

Name of School ....
Name of Pupil .... D.O.B ....
Class Group .... National Curriculum Year Group...........................
Date of Audit ....

N.B.   This form should only be completed for a pupil who "has a learning difficulty which calls for special education provision to be made for him / her." A child has a "learning difficulty" if he / she has a disability which prevents or hinders him / her from making use of education facilities of a kind generally provided in schools within Kent LEA. (1981 Education Act).

AREAS OF NEED

Circle as appropriate each area in which support is required :

LEARNING   **PHYSICAL / SENSORY**   **BEHAVIOURAL / EMOTIONAL**

The following target areas are related to the pupil's learning and / or learning environment. Tick those which you will be working on as priorities in the next year.

TASK / MOTIVATION		SUPPORT FOR PHYSICAL / MEDICAL CONDITIONS	
Attention to task			
Comprehension of task		Adaptation of classrooms	
Completion of task		Adaptation of school	
Confidence in execution of task		Access to medication	
		Access to therapy	
RELATIONSHIP		Access to medical aids	
		Access to adapted aids	
Relationship with other pupils (M/F)		Access to sensory aids	
Relationship with adults (M/F)		Access to information technology	
BEHAVIOUR		**RESPONSE TO TEACHING**	
Outwardness and Sociability		Age appropriate independent learning	
Co-operation		Working well in group	
Stability		Motivation during whole class lessons	
SKILLS AND COMPETENCES		**EXTERNAL INFLUENCES**	
Age appropriate development		Support from home	
Motor control		Regular attendance	
Personal organisation			

NATIONAL CURRICULUM TARGET AREAS

> **Which aspects of provision for the pupil's learning need to be improved / enhanced ?**
> **Box (A) - What the pupil should receive.   Box (B) - What this pupil is receiving.**

LEVEL 1 MINOR CHANGES	A	B	LEVEL 2 SIGNIFICANT CHANGES	A	B	LEVEL 3 MAJOR CHANGES (including formal assessment)	A	B
SUPPORT AGENCIES Occasional ISS support Occasional Sensory Impaired Service support Occasional agency support e.g. EWO Occasional advice from school Special Needs Co-ordinator			Regular ISS support Regular Sensory Impaired Service support Regular consultation with support agencies e.g. EWO, Speech Therapist, EPS Regular consultation with school SEN Co-ordinator			Substantial ISS support Substantial Sensory Impaired Service support Substantial support by specialist service e.g. Speech Therapist, Physiotherapist, Occupational Therapist, EPS		
CURRICULUM DIFFERENTIATION Modification of material / recording Small scale individual programme Materials to facilitate learning in the presence of poor process skills Modification of style / grouping to allow for pupil pace			Structured intervention programmes for two or more curriculum areas			Structured programmes or support for most areas of the curriculum Substantial modifications to the National Curriculum Non-literacy based approaches		
DIRECT PUPIL SUPPORT Occasional individual help Short periods of pastoral contact Occasional counselling			Regular classroom support for short periods for individual group work or direct teaching / monitoring Regular counselling			Needs a scribe In-class individual support in excess of two hours per week		
ADDITIONAL AIDS Aids shared with a larger group e.g. designated school setting (time limited).			Aids shared with a small group of other pupils (1 - 4)			Personal technical aid		
TIME AND LOCATION Greater than normal parent contact Short period of observation Greater than normal monitoring and recording Shadowing of pupil / staff Release time for staff to attend case conferences			Regular use of pastoral / welfare support system Regular use of sanctuary Extended periods of observation			Structured learning context / environment Continuous level of support needed to avoid pupil causing considerable emotional and physical distress in others Continuous level of support needed to avoid pupil causing considerable personal emotional and physical distress Placement in off-site or on-site centre Reintegration programme		

Signature confirms audit consistency within the school.

SEN Co-ordinator and / or Headteacher...

Audit must be completed by 25th October 1991.

tatives of the school, the Integrated Support Service, the Special Needs Management Team, the Educational Psychology Service, the Educational Welfare Service, the Social Services and other relevant professionals, and of course the parents, can consider and prioritize options for meeting needs, realign assistance from support services and consider recommendations to start the formal assessment procedure. The intention of this structure is to channel the various agencies into an effective force to support the school, the child and the parent by delivering an agreed course of action through a 'one stop shop' with a carefully constructed assessment, intervention and review procedure that is dependent upon close working relationships across all the agencies.

Market research

Paragraphs 108 and 109 of DES Circular 7/91 suggests that 'there is scope for delegation of the costs of centrally managed SEN support teams and LEA delegation. Judicious use by schools of specialist teachers employed in central teams, and the expertise available centrally . . . can be an effective way of enabling schools to meet a wide range of SEN'. This very positive statement comes shortly after the HMI (1991) report which acknowledges that 'If pupils with SEN are to be given equitable provision and maximum curricular access, advisory work in classrooms and schools will be necessary for some time to come . . . LEAs must carefully consider how best they can use advisory services for SEN in contributing to the monitoring and imple-mentation of the Education Reform Act' (paragraphs 73 and 75).

Armed with these heartening and encouraging messages we set about our task. First we needed to ask the schools to define their needs in terms of outside advice available to them from specialists. We devised a very straight-forward questionnaire identifying the areas of expertise we could offer to schools which they might be likely to purchase should the SEN budget be fully or partly delegated to schools. We asked the schools to prioritize their needs and to indicate which they would 'buy in' and the frequency of visits they would require.

Having worked with the schools for two years, providing a consistent support model wherever possible, we have gained some credibility with our colleagues in the schools through our collaborative work in curriculum planning and differentiation, as well as the provision of specialist advice and support for SEN. We are now of the opinion that we need to develop further our role as the 'consultant' and offer support to the schools in areas where they may not yet have developed these resources in-house. To do this we are fully aware, as Bowers (1989a) has pointed out, that 'credibility is vital . . .

unless a parent, teacher or a school sees the support teacher as an expert - a person who has skills to deal with the issues that concern them - then they are unlikely ever to approach that person' (p.38). Nevertheless we should not be attempting to carry out the role as a sort of 'Trojan horse' (Dyson, 1990) but facilitating transformations in colleagues' attitudes and thinking about provision for children with special educational needs.

We embarked upon the compilation of a 'skills directory' of all the team members, and having fully analyzed the information, decided there were seven areas where we could offer expertise and be certain that we could do the job properly. To address these areas we have staff qualified through MAs, first degrees, diplomas and advanced diplomas in all aspects of special needs, with some staff qualified in more than one area.

The areas we decided we could offer were:

(i) support for specific learning difficulties;

(ii) support for emotional and behavioural difficulties;

(iii) support for children with exceptional abilities;

(iv) individual support for statemented children (through the LEA);

(v) assessments and assessment-led provision;

(vi) resourcing;

(vii) training.

To provide specialist support in the identified areas effectively and economically we needed to look carefully at the ways in which we organized and allocated our support staff to the schools. Having a clear picture of the skills and experiences within the teams we decided to move towards stratified support which we designated 'Consultant Specialists' and 'Support Staff'. The highly skilled staff within the team would negotiate contracts or agreements with the schools to provide advice, specific INSET, individual programmes etc., and the Support Staff would carry out the teaching or other programmes devised and designed by the Consultant Staff. Whether or not future SEN budgets are delegated or partially delegated, schools will be able to choose the level of support they need and require of us and be assured they will be receiving a value-added service to meet the identified needs.

In preparation for the future we are now piloting different models of support, having created new teams which still adhere to the geographical areas served in West Kent but are defined by the type of support which they provide. These consist of four Primary Teams, whose new ways of working are outlined below, and a cross-regional Secondary Team, which will continue to work to the old model of support through assessment, devising individual programmes, advising colleagues and providing INSET.

The Consultancy Model: Team A

(Team Leader and 4 team members)

Three Consultant Specialists have been allocated a case-load of schools. Other team members' and classroom assistants' time will be allocated to schools to carry out the individual and support programmes identified and negotiated with a consultant to meet the needs of children at any intervention level. This will be established through the annual Special Needs Audit.

The whole team will construct a skills list of all personnel resources available to each school: integrated support service (ISS) teachers, classroom assistants, parents, volunteers etc. Wherever possible and appropriate these resources will be built into the support programme for each school, thereby maximizing the capability of each school to meet the individual needs of its children. The training of all non-professional colleagues will be undertaken as part of the consultant's role.

The consultant will visit each school on his or her caseload and will discuss with the school's head teacher and SENCO the particular needs to be addressed across the following term, The school and the consultant will decide which items on the support 'menu' they will require for which classes and individual children. The support 'menu' could include:

advice through collaborative work in the classroom;
developmental influences on classroom management and organization;
observation, assessment, evaluation, monitoring and reviewing procedures;
INSET provision;
developing differentiation strategies;
resourcing for differentiation;
individual programmes for specific needs;
developing partnership with parents.

Having decided upon the targets for the term, a clear contract/agreement will be drawn up to identify the role of the ISS, the role of the parents and the role of the classroom assistant in meeting the agreed objectives. A review meeting will be built in as part of this.

The School-controlled Model: Team B

(Team Leader and 3 team members)

One of the means by which support services may be managed in the future is by being controlled by the schools themselves. A devolved budget may be made available to schools to organize support on a local level. In order to provide us with some experience of working in this manner, Team B will allocate each member of the team to 4 schools for one term.

The team leader will take part in a meeting with four head teachers to negotiate the time allocation for each school. These will be aware of the level of need within their own schools and their group of schools through the SEN Audit already described. It is anticipated that head teachers will enjoy the benefits of working together in a small consortium to meet the needs of their own children. Further developments may involve community action in supporting children with emotional and behavioural difficulties and their families, incorporating support from, perhaps, the Social Services Department. The team member will play a substantial role in resourcing this small cluster of schools and should be an effective agent for co-ordinating the maximum use of available resources as well as providing useful and practical ways of extending differentiated materials to access the curriculum for those children having difficulties.

Having negotiated the team member's time in each school, the head teachers will then decide how the team member will be directed. Into this timetable will be built monitoring time by the team leader, a review meeting with the head teachers and resourcing time for the team member.

The 'School-needs-led' model: Team C

(Team Leader and 3 team members)

In order to be a vehicle for change the Integrated Support Service has, to date, enthusiastically promoted and implemented the philosophy and policy for special educational needs outlined in the LEA documentation. To do this we have been engaged in an intensive programme of INSET to help schools establish and implement whole school policies for SEN and have actively supported schools in cross-curricular planning and resourcing for differentiation in addition to supporting individual needs.

The emergence of LMS and all the other possibilities confronting us have encouraged us to look closely at schools' needs as they identify them. This has involved an area-wide questionnaire and a cluster-based individual school approach by the team leader of Team C. An interesting outcome of the research is that the schools have asked for the style of support that was previously on offer, i.e. curriculum planning, assessments followed by specific short-term programmes, resourcing and regular consultation.

Having carefully identified the particular needs of all the schools, the team will endeavour to plan individual school programmes to be delivered by the team members and our classroom assistants, bearing in mind the numbers and spread of children identified on Level Two intervention, the geographical spread of this rural area and allowing some flexibility within the timetables to respond quickly to any crisis or special requests.

Time-allocation model: Team D

(Team Leader and 4 team members)

The allocation of support time to schools, given the ratio of support staff to the number of schools within the clusters, has always been a contentious management issue. The information provided through the Audit has been very helpful but we have also tried to incorporate other school situations and influences into the formulation of our caseloads, such as the number of children on roll, class size, crisis circumstances or short-term response to specific needs. This method of support allocation has not always been successful and the schools and the team have been aware of some anomalies, despite various attempts to put the resources where needed.

Schools have been asked to identify from the 'menu' those areas of need where support is required. Team D has attempted to develop a formula for apportioning the maximum time available to schools through a percentage of a combination of these factors:

a) The number of children identified by the school in agreement with the ISS - firstly children who need individual programmes involving target-setting and direct support broadly relating to Intervention Level Three, and secondly, statemented children requiring target-setting, individual programmes devised by ISS and liaison between ISS and an appointed supporter. These criteria do not exclude children at Intervention Level Two, but focus time allocation on more specialized areas of the continuum and create an initial list of priorities for action.

b) The relationship of the above identifications to the Audit, minus leavers at Year 6 (Junior schools), Year 4 (First schools) and Year 2 (Infant schools).

c) The size of the school expressed in the number of classes. There is a greater time implication in supporting six children in 4 classes than in supporting six children in 1 class.

d) Distribution of identifications in numbers of classes. Where this is less than 3 there is a need to correct the balance using appropriate weightings.

e) Class size. The average numbers in classes range from 8 to 30. SEN children who are one of eight clearly receive more teacher time than those who are one of thirty.

f) Adjustment at the team leader's discretion. The reasons for this adjustment could be that the Audit figure is considered too high, the use of support in the school is poor, there is an exceptionally high level of need not reflected in the Audit figures, or that there are too many identifications in comparison with other schools of a similar size/needs.

By making appropriate allocations for each of these factors, a formula can be employed to determine time allocations to schools. Thus if:

Identifications = X

Relationship of Identification/Audit = R

Size of school = S

Distribution of Identifications = D

Class sizes = C

Adjustment = A

Time allocation proportion = X x (R x S x D x C x A)

Each school's figure is converted to a percentage of the whole, and this percentage is allocated from the total support available. The percentage is then expressed as hours of support across the term. Each school is then approached and asked for their preference for patterns of support - weekly, fortnightly, in intensive blocks - to be tailored to the school's requirements. Finally, the team leader attempts to combine all the stated preferences into the timetable, matching the team members' skills to the needs of the schools.

The prospect

By developing these various styles of support we hope to be fully prepared for whatever developments we consider most appropriate, or to equip ourselves to be able to respond to whatever the national and local market forces impose upon us. We intend to evaluate very carefully the full implications of our projects so as to be able to present calculated data and evidence of success or setback, whilst conserving and implementing our philosophy of supporting schools in their duty to provide for the individual needs of all children.

Chapter 15

Change and opportunity: setting up an independent consultancy

Andrea Clifford

Setting the scene

After 24 years in state education, sixteen of them in special education, I left my post with the ILEA to become an independent educational consultant and counsellor. This chapter seeks to share my experiences of such a venture and to offer some advice and cautions to others who may be thinking of taking the same course of action.

One of the certainties of life is change. The bulk of my teaching career was spent in special education as the Teacher in Charge at the Child Development Centre, Charing Cross Hospital. When I was appointed in 1974 it was still the trend for children with special needs to be withdrawn from the mainstream classroom for appropriate help and indeed for children in special schools who needed additional help to be withdrawn from the special classroom. At that time there were also few support services for teachers. Most schools shared the time of an educational psychologist with several others and visits by the few advisory teachers and inspectors available were never frequent enough in the view of many class teachers. A constant stream of children came to the Child Development Centre with all kinds of special educational needs. Children were assessed by an inter-disciplinary team and intervention was offered usually by the teachers, but sometimes by the occupational therapist or the psychologists, such inter-vention involving the child coming to the Centre often on a weekly basis during school time. There was close liaison on the Centre's part with the child's school, the Centre at that time often acting as a resource and support to the child's teacher. Change first began to come with the Warnock Report (DES, 1978) and later with the 1981 Education Act, both of which focused attention on meeting children's special educational needs within ordinary schools. A change in ways of working became apparent. Instead of special classes or pupil withdrawal, the concept of 'support' within the classroom became widely accepted. The Warnock Committee argued that children with and without learning difficulties should be educated in a common setting as far as possible. In the chapter on special education in mainstream schools they concentrated on different forms of integration and outlined the necessary conditions for their success. This included specialist training for teachers responsible for children with special needs and advocated integration as an alternative to provision in special schools.

During the mid 1980s there was a rapid establishment of support from advisory teachers and a focus of attention on assessing children's educational needs within school. Clearly this brought dramatic change to the work of the teachers in the Child Development Centre. Although there continued to be a steady flow of children referred for initial assessments, ongoing teaching and support could now be offered within the child's school. I had developed a particular interest and expertise in emotional factors associated with learning difficulties and continued to work at the Centre individually and in groups with children who could not be maintained fully in mainstream classrooms and who needed the kind of therapeutic intervention that could only take place in a one-to-one situation.

Another change, reflected in the work of people such as Williams and Muncey (1982) and Ainscow and Tweddle (1979), was the increasing use of structured objectives, not only in work with people with severe learning difficulties, but also with people with minor learning problems who attended mainstream schools. This approach became much more fashionable than the psychodynamic approach which underpinned the philosophy of the Child Development Centre. This philosophy argues that we learn about the world and ourselves from the moment we are born and continue to do so throughout our lives. Learning in infancy and for a considerable period thereafter takes place within a dependent relationship with another human being. It is the quality of this relationship which will deeply influence both the hopefulness required to remain curious and open to new experiences, and the capacity to perceive connections and discover their meanings. Affective and cognitive aspects of learning are therefore closely linked and interdependent, with an exploration of the child's personal relationships being seen as essential to understanding any learning difficulty.

Because there was a tendency for work in the Child Development Centre to become increasingly specialized, its orientation clashed with the more simplistic notions which underpinned the vogue of objectives (subsequently eschewed by Ainscow and Tweddle, 1988), and was met with frequent demands for justification. However, the psychodynamic work done both with children and teachers continued to prove fruitful and the teachers who came to the Centre felt that they received a kind of support that they had not received elsewhere (Clifford, 1980).

Further change came with the demise of the ILEA. By this time the number of referrals to the Centre had become considerably reduced. It was increasingly difficult to find an accepted role for my skills, which were predominantly psychoanalytic, within the educational system. However, change invariably brings opportunity; although the Borough of Hammersmith offered to continue the work at the Centre after the ending of ILEA, I decided to take the alternative of redundancy. This was done with some trepidation, but experience led me to believe that there was still an important role for teachers trained and experienced in psychodynamic approaches and consultancy skills and that such teachers could fill a much needed gap in statutory provision. I was encouraged by the enthusiastic response my work, including lectures, received from teachers and I therefore decided to work freelance as an educational consultant and counsellor. A year later, with further cuts in education spending, it seems that many other specialist teachers are finding themselves in the same position and are thinking of launching an independent career. The purpose of this chapter is to help such a teacher to focus his or her thinking.

So you want to be an independent consultant

The term consultant can mean almost anything anyone decides to make it into. It is essential to have a clear definition of what kind of consultant you feel you are going to be. Bowers (1989a) outlines clearly the different natures of consultancy. In general terms he describes consultancy as: 'a helping relationship which is provided by individuals or groups who have a particular range of skills. These skills will assist those with whom they work to understand more clearly what they are trying to do and how they can become more effective' (p.35).

Whilst I realize that many readers may not choose to take the path to becoming an independent special needs consultant, I will address those who do. In order to help you to define what kind of consultant you feel you can be, you need to make assessments, both of yourself and of the educational market.

Assessing yourself

It may seem simplistic to suggest that you look carefully at what you've done to date, examining your experience. However, it is essential to have an immediate grasp of how rich and varied and how specialized your background is in the general field of education. Your experience both opens up and limits your marketability. Credibility is all. You cannot expect people to purchase your expertise simply because you are selling it and feel it is worth marketing. It is therefore important to prepare a detailed curriculum vitae and look carefully at how it reads. For example, it may well be, in spite of considerable experience, that some formal qualification in an area is still needed before you are likely to be consulted as an expert. It may be that you have both considerable experience and qualifications but have to date not published on any aspect of your work which may give you formal credibility. The writing of an article, chapter or even book may be an early priority.

Next, think about what you're good at and what you enjoy doing. One of the initial fantasies of going freelance is that it will only involve doing work you enjoy. What you're good at and what you enjoy are likely to be the same thing, and identifying such areas will help you to focus your consultancy. It is also important to think about what you want from your consultancy. What is your level of ambition? Are you seeking world fame as a renowned expert in a particular area of education or would you be content to be earning a living equivalent to that if you had stayed in more secure employment? Level of ambition has to be fuelled and matched by level of energy. Take into account your age and family responsibilities and try to reconcile available energy with ambition. Ask yourself how much effort you want to put into your consultancy. Are you prepared to work whatever hours, social and antisocial, that appear to be requested or do you consider that a regular working schedule is what you are looking for? Such questions will help you to define which areas of your expertise you can most exploit. It is perhaps important to say here that there is a place for people at almost every level. There is a lot more demand for individual tuition after school than there is for world-wide lecture tours.

Assess the market

Firstly, look at the way that education is going. Is it in sympathy with or against the tide of your thinking? Either way there could be a role for you, but it is important, in knowing where your work is going to come from, to have a clear idea of current trends. For example, if you are hoping to be mainly consulted by state schools, perhaps buying in your services through their delegated budgets under LMS, then it may be important to have a way of working which is in harmony with the National Curriculum. However, if you are hoping to offer some specialist service that parents and a small proportion of teachers want but which is now out of fashion in educational thinking, you may attract most work from independent special needs centres. You should try to think of three alternative plans of action before selecting the prime aim. This is a good self-discipline, encouraging objective thought about the potential of the plan chosen. A first idea is not necessarily the best.

Test assumptions about the market. Having established that there is a market for your skill and expertise, the next step is to try and evaluate your worth in that market. Are others following the same path? Is there an already well established independent service in the area, and if so is it likely to view you as a competitor or to embrace you as a colleague? How much scope is there in the future for the kind of consultancy that you are offering? If you are hoping for a lengthy career it may not be wise to aim your consultancy at an area of education that is likely to become of decreasing importance, or for which it is known there is going to be more than ample funding available to LEAs and therefore little scope for private work within the foreseeable future. It is important to test out assumptions by talking to head teachers, advisers, education officers and class teachers. Assess their responses to the service you are thinking of offering. Try to get the views of parents. Do they feel that the service you are proposing would fill a much needed gap in their child's education? Is it one on which they would be prepared to spend money?

Assess each sector of the market against your own position. It may be that testing your assumptions about the market uncovers gaps in the education service which need to be filled but which did not come into your original thinking. It is important to assess not only the areas in which you have knowledge and expertise but those in which you could rapidly gain them. If you are going to be successful, one thing is sure: you will have to be flexible and adaptable, and prepared to develop skills in areas of education which are topical but not necessarily at the moment within your range of experience. Assess how rapidly you could gain expertise in other areas before deciding where to focus your consultancy.

Having surveyed the whole field of education, and having matched your skills, or ability to gain skills, with each sector of the market, you must now reflect upon whether or not your would enjoy working in particular spheres. Assess whether there are areas in which you quite definitely do not want to work. There may be areas of special education in which you do not wish to develop skills. Some consultants have expertise in, and are comfortable working with, any kind of learning problem, be it severe learning difficulties or emotional and behavioural disturbances. They are also prepared to work in any kind of setting. I prefer to specialize in one particular area; in my case this is the area of emotional difficulties. This preference may involve turning down work and even going without work for a period. Would you be prepared to do that? Alternatively, it may be that in order to get contacts for work that you would enjoy you initially have to work in some area that you do not enjoy. In the final analysis it may come down to a choice between job satisfaction and financial survival, a tough decision which you may not have to make if you do not work freelance.

So you've decided to be an independent consultant.
Develop a plan for getting work.

Perhaps the most anxiety-provoking thought in instituting a freelance consultancy is 'Where will the work come from?' Anxiety can decrease with structure and it is therefore important to develop a plan for attracting work. Existing contacts are invaluable. Talk to people at all levels in your existing educational structure. Tell them what you are going to do and try to identify a clear role for yourself in their field when you begin the conversation. Be prepared to spend time following up contacts they may give you - even if they not fruitful.

A well-produced, competently printed leaflet or brochure is essential. It looks professional and gives the impression of a well-established consultancy. Although the response can be slow, it is essential to identify your target market, which may be schools, education authorities, clinics, doctors, etc., before beginning to circulate your leaflet/brochure. In Chapter 9 of this book, Tony Bowers expands on this notion of effective market segmentation. Schools may well file and store your brochure for several months but then suddenly remember it when an appropriate occasion arises. My experience is that my brochure can also lead to a 'Could you also . . ?' phone call, perhaps asking me to work in or develop an area that I had not originally considered. For example, as a result of sending my brochure to a local G.P., I was asked to supervise psychiatric social workers working with children in a child guidance clinic.

It could well be worthwhile contacting your local paper and requesting an interview. A general article, which you have seen prior to publication, highlighting and outlining the nature of your work, can bring much positive publicity. It may also bring crank replies, but these are a necessary price to pay. I have already referred to professional credibility and this can only be enhanced by the publication of articles and papers in educational journals. These can lead to requests for lectures which in turn can lead to requests for individual consultancies. Writing may seem time-consuming and sometimes bothersome to the action-orientated consultant, but it is a necessary and productive way of reaching the wide number of potential clients.

Although time consuming, face-to-face interviews can in the long run be more fruitful than the written word. If you feel that there is a definite market for your skills in a particular region, such as a particular school or authority, it is always worth writing and enclosing your curriculum vitae, following up such a letter with a phone call requesting an interview.

While important, it is not enough simply to have strong existing contacts. You are going to have to be prepared to *sell* your services. The key to this is to believe that you can provide them in a way that is better than other people in your field can do.

So you've worked out what you are going to do

Having established that there is a market for your skills and that you now know how to approach it, the time has come to assess the risks and the financial implications involved in setting up a freelance consultancy. The first thing to think about is expense. How much is it going to cost to run your consultancy? Remember to include not only incidental expenses such as your car and any typing you don't do yourself, but also professional insurances and personal pension plans. Whilst your initial expenses may be higher in the first year than in the later running of your consultancy, it is also worth bearing in mind that expenses during the first year may be higher than you estimate. It is almost impossible to think of everything before beginning, and during the first year you will meet unbudgeted for expenses. Assessing the expenses helps to gauge an appropriate fee for services. If you are offering one skill, for example lecturing, this is a relatively simple task, although there again bear in mind that you will always need to charge more than you initially thought and that you may not want to put up your prices to existing clients at the end of your first year. However, if you are offering more than one service, (e.g. teaching, lecturing, counselling), it is more difficult to arrive at the most expedient way of deciding your fee. It is possible to charge a set fee per hour for services, regardless of the skill involved; for example, individual special needs teaching would cost the same per hour as running a workshop. This establishes clearly what your time is worth. It may, however, restrict the number and variety of clients taken on, since individual parents are unlikely to be able to afford the same fee as a large institution. Alternatively, a sliding scale of fees which depends upon the skill involved as well as a time and distance factor could be introduced. For example, you may charge more per hour for a consultancy that takes place away from your base.

Earlier in the chapter I referred to levels of ambition and energy, and these two points are important in deciding on fees. Think not only about how much you need to live on, but how quickly you need to reach that amount. Particularly within education, and perhaps even more particularly within special needs education, it is important to remember vacations. You may feel prepared to work during the school holiday, but the reality may be that if your clients are children, schools or other educational institutions, work may not be forthcoming during much of that time.

The final factor to consider is how far you can start your consultancy before giving up your existing employment. It is possible that as a result of your present job you have already been asked to do some consultancy work, and it may be feasible to develop this work and the contacts it brings further before you give up your existing job. It is also worth looking at government schemes, such as the Enterprise Allowance, which give financial help to encourage small businesses to develop. It is important to explore such schemes before you give up your existing employment, as the way in which you leave your current post may effect for eligibility for such a scheme.

What happens next?

The excitement and stimulation of setting up your own consultancy cannot be over-emphasized, but neither can the anxiety. After 24 years of a regular income I found it very difficult to live on a day-to-day basis, swinging from the euphoria of chunks of work coming in to the agony of the 'phone not ringing for days on end. Whilst I have emphasized the necessity of marketing your skills, following up contacts and making new contacts, you also have to be prepared for a large number of what in the business world are called 'false leads'. Time and time again, hopes of work or opportunity can be raised by someone agreeing to or offering an interview, only to find that on meeting them there is no basis for collaborative work or that their motives for contacting you seem unclear. I was rung up and asked to visit a school to be told on arrival that, while they never had children with emotional problems, they were interested to meet me because I was within an hour's travelling distance.

This chapter has so far concentrated on the external skills and strategies required for setting up your own consultancy. What are also essential are good internal resources. Freelance work can be accompanied by an intense sense of loneliness. Bowers (1987) has looked at this in relation to the external consultant, pointing to the need for SEN support staff to be able to cope with isolating conditions. There may be no established group of colleagues to bring with them both stimulation and frustration. This can engender a powerful sense of 'the buck stops here'; confidence in your own judgement is essential. It may be necessary, particularly during the first year, to include in your consultancy expenses an element which allows you to consult a consultant in a similar field for whom you have respect. Along with a strong degree of self-reliance and confidence in your own professional judgement comes the demand for flexibility and adaptability. The workload can be relentless: letters and telephone calls have to be dealt with immediately, bills sent out promptly, reports written, contacts made, and so on. Time off becomes a precious commodity. It is likely that most the time you will be preparing for work, thinking about work or doing one of the thousand mundane, routine administrative jobs that accompany running a consultancy.

It almost goes without saying that a strong sense of self-discipline is essential. It is vital to be able to motivate yourself and to be able to generate your own creativity. It is important to think in terms of 'having a job' and avoid accepting invitations to meet friends or family socially during what you define as work time. Whilst this may not be understood by people seeing you as 'free' it is very important to sustain a disciplined sense of working. There will always be things to do.

You may have a tremendous sense of urgency for work, in which case the slowness of response to projects necessitated by sending out brochures and requesting interviews can be frustrating. Even more harrowing are bad debts. There is nothing more frustrating than doing the work and then not getting paid. I am fortunate in that it has not yet happened to me, but I am advised by almost everyone known to me who runs a personal consultancy that one day it is bound to happen. It is worth looking at the reasons for the bill not being paid. It may be that the agreement was somehow inappropriate. Whilst contracts do not have to be in writing, or even formal, it can help to send a letter after an initial meeting setting out your understanding of the nature of the contract from both sides. Obviously such a letter should allow the client to be able to disagree with or modify the contract.

Selling

The importance of being able to sell yourself has already been discussed. Everyone has their own style of selling and for a lot of people it will be a difficult component of any project. It is often hard to strike a balance between being over-confident and not confident enough. This is a problem which everyone has to resolve for themselves. My recommendation, provided the work is compatible with the consultancy you have set up, is that you take on any project you are offered and worry about it later! There is invariably someone who has the skills which you may need to acquire whom you can approach for help, advice and, if necessary, assistance. This may involve having to do work which you might not particularly want to do and which may seem menial. If you are aiming to run workshops at the local university, then teaching special needs one afternoon in a local school may seem a long way from the target.

Try to assess how much it is necessary to do such work in order to stay afloat financially and how much such work detracts from the main aim of the consultancy. The gamble taken in the above example is that by committing oneself to teach special needs, time may be taken up that could later be used to run workshops at the university. On the other hand, the university may well turn out to be looking for a person with recent 'hands-on' experience. Through such processes there is also the problem of perhaps getting a name as a specialist for an area of special needs that you don't particularly want to specialize in. For example: a teacher may get many requests for private educational assessments. If these are well done, word will spread among parents, bringing a flurry of referrals which may detract from a main aim of, say, running courses for teachers. This may at times seem frustrating, but all change brings opportunity and there may be the opportunity to introduce the area of skill and expertise you want to develop into the work offered; for example, a particular style of special needs teaching may lead to a consultancy with the staff of that particular school. It really comes down to how much you believe in what you're doing and how well you are prepared to sell your expertise.

Finance

It is highly likely that in initially setting up a consultancy you will be working from your own home. It goes without saying that the professional advice of your bank manger, accountant and solicitor are essential. Another essential is a reliable telephone answering machine; my own experience leads to the suggestion that a separate telephone line is useful, though probably not essential. Using home as a business base can be both an advantage and stressful. One source of stress is never being sure whether a 'phone call is business or social, whatever time of day or night it arrives. In working in the area of special needs it has to be accepted that parents, teachers, etc., may be highly emotionally charged by the problems they are asking for advice on and may therefore not be sensitive to the times or lengths of their telephone calls.

Word processing and keyboard skills are invaluable. The ability to produce your own letter and reports immediately is a great asset. However, if it is necessary to rely on the skills of outside workers such as typists, it is of course vital to ensure that the providers of such services have the same high professional standards as you do. Much time can be wasted checking and re-checking badly typed or spelled copy and it is essential that telephone messages are accurately reported if you are to appear efficient to clients.

A month before I was due to leave my permanent teaching post I visited my bank manager to discuss the financial aspects of setting up my consultancy. I went prepared with facts and figures, ready to be questioned about my financial viability during the coming year. It therefore came as a tremendous surprise to me when his first question was 'How does your partner feel about you going freelance?' He stressed to me an important factor to consider: the effect on family and social life. It is essential to have emotional and social support, particularly when working without colleagues, and to have those supports readily accessible. It may have to be accepted that social life may be virtually non-existent during the first year. The support of the people you live with, and the sacrifices they may have to make, cannot be stressed enough.

Some final points

Setting up your own consultancy can be the most exciting phase of your professional career. You need drive, initiative, flexibility and adaptability, together with an abundant sense of humour. It is essential to have a clear idea of your own skills and expertise, and to have confidence in them. You should enjoy the excitement of sharing those qualities with other people who may not always be co-operative. Resistance on the part of clients, explored by Bowers (1989a), is at times inevitable; the effective consultant will recognize this and know how to cope with it. You have to be able to cope with unfairness. A particular consultancy may not go well through no mis-management of yours and yet that client may discourage other clients from using you. The reverse, of course, is always true; I have found word of mouth to be the best publicity. Above all it is vital to keep a clear definition of where your consultancy is going. Keep reviewing where you hope to be in six months' time, what kind of work you hope to be doing and assessing whether your current work is leading you in the direction that you want to go. If it is not, then look at the work carefully and see how you can develop the skills you want to promote within the work that is available. The alter-native is to reappraise the venture entirely; keep your options as open as possible, and don't forget that if one thing isn't working you may have to get out and try again with something else.

References

Adams-Chapman, M.E. (1986) Marketing the college: Some benefits and barriers. *Educational Management and Administration* 14, 107-111.

Adey, S. (1991) 1981 and all that. *Head Teachers Review,* Spring, 3-4.

Ainscow, M. and Muncey, J. (1984) *Special Needs Action Programme: Workshop Leader's Guide.* Cardiff: Drake Educational.

Ainscow, M. and Tweddle, D.A. (1979) *Preventing Classroom Failure: An Objectives Approach.* Chichester: Wiley.

Ainscow, M. and Tweddle, D.A. (1988) *Encouraging Classroom Success.* London: Fulton.

Allen, N. (1990) *Making Sense of the Children Act.* Harlow: Longman.

Audit Commission (1989) *Losing an Empire, Finding a Role: The LEA of the Future.* Audit Commission Occasional Paper No.10.

Baker, M.J. (1987) *The Marketing Book.* London: Heinemann.

Ball, S.J. (1987) *The Micro-Politics of the School: Towards a Theory of School Management.* London: Methuen.

Bird, P. (1991) Micros: Hit or M.I.S? *School Governor,* February/March, 29-31.

Blissett, M. (1972) *Politics in Science.* Boston: Little, Brown.

Booker, R. (1991) Responding to the needs of the context: Some principles for the management of psychological services. *Educational Psychology in Practice,* 7, 3-10.

Bowles, G. (1989) Marketing and promotion. In B. Fidler and G. Bowles (Eds.), *Effective Local Management of Schools.* Harlow: Longman.

Bowers, T. (1984) Power and conflict: facts of life. In T. Bowers (Ed.), *Management and the Special School.* London: Croom Helm.

Bowers, T. (1987) Internal and external support: roles and definitions. In T. Bowers (Ed.), *Special Educational Needs and Human Resource Management.* London: Croom Helm.

Bowers, T. (1989a) From support to consultancy. In T. Bowers (Ed.), *Managing Special Needs*. Milton Keynes: Open University Press.

Bowers, T. (1989b) Marketing services. In T. Bowers (Ed.), *Managing Special Needs*. Milton Keynes: Open University Press.

Bowers, T. (1991a) Four 'c's in consultancy: Clients, contracts, collaboration and change. *Year Book of the Scottish Learning Difficulties Association,* 1990-91, 10-15.

Bowers, T. (1991b) *LMS in Special Schools* (materials pack). Cambridge: Perspective.

Bowers, T. (1991c) *LMS and SEN Support Services* (materials pack). Cambridge: Perspective.

Bowman, P. and Ellis, N. (1977) *Manual of Public Relations*. London: Heinemann.

Buckton, C. (1989) Teamwork in the primary school. In T. Bowers (Ed.), *Managing Special Needs*. Milton Keynes: Open University Press.

Casteel, V. (1984) Special needs and school-focused in-service education. In T. Bowers (Ed.), *Management and the Special School*. London: Croom Helm.

Challoner, M., McCaffrey, T. and Stokes, E. (1991) Educational entitlement for all. *DECP Newsletter*, No.43. Leicester: British Psychological Society.

Chisnall, P.M. (1985) *Marketing: A Behavioural Analysis*. Maidenhead: McGraw-Hill.

Clayton, T. (1989) The role and management of welfare assistants. In T. Bowers (Ed.), *Managing Special Needs*. Milton Keynes: Open University Press.

Clifford, A. (1980) A support group for teachers. *Therapeutic Education*, 8, 31-35.

Coffield, F. (1989) Caught in the Act: ERA, 1988-? In F. Coffield and T. Edwards (Eds.), *Working Within the Act: Education Reform Act 1988-?* Durham: Educational Publishing Services.

Coopers and Lybrand (1988) *Local Management of Schools: A Report to the DES*. London: DES.

Coulson-Thomas, C. (1979) *Public Relations: A Practical Guide*. Plymouth: McDonald Evans.

DES (1967) *Children and Their Primary Schools* (The Plowden Report). London: HMSO.

DES (1978) *Special Educational Needs: Report of the Committee of Enquiry into the Education of Handicapped Children and Young People* (The Warnock Report). London: HMSO.

DHSS (1983) *Report of the NHS Management Inquiry* (The Griffiths Report). London: HMSO.

DoH (1989) *Working for Patients: A Summary*. London: HMSO.

Davies, B. and West-Burnham, J. (1990) Marketing Schools. In B. Davies, L.

Ellison, A. Osborne and J. West-Bunham, (Eds.), *Education Management for the 1990s*. Harlow: Longman.

Dessent, T. (1984) Special schools and the mainstream: the resource stretch. In T. Bowers (Ed.), *Management and the Special School*. London: Croom Helm.

Dessent, T. (1987) *Making the Ordinary School Special*. London: Falmer.

Drucker, P.F. (1973) *Management: Tasks, Responsibilities and Practice*. London: Heinemann.

Dry, A. (1991) The truant's charter. *Education*, 2nd August, 88.

Dyson, A. (1990) Effective learning consultancy: A future role for special needs co-ordinators. *Support for Learning*, 5,116-127.

Evans, J. and Lunt, I. (1990) *Local Management of Schools and Special Educational Needs*. London: Institute of Education.

Farrar, M.R. (1987) Visitors are welcome . . . but. *British Journal of Special Education*, 14, 2, 71-72.

Fielding, M. (1991) Desperately seeking a just solution. *Times Educational Supplement*, 7th June, 26.

Frain, J. (1986) *Principles and Practice of Marketing*. London: Pitman.

Galloway, D. (1985) *Schools, Pupils and Special Educational Needs*. London: Croom Helm.

Galloway, D. (1990) The Education Reform Act and educational psychologists: the beginning of the end or the end of the beginning? In M. Gledhill and R. Reason (Eds.), *Effective Applications of Psychology in Education*. Leicester: British Psychological Society.

Glatter, R. (1984) Managing for change. *Management in Post-compulsory Education* (Block 6). Milton Keynes: Open University.

Gold, K. (1991) Silver service. *Times Educational Supplement*, 7th June, 16-27.

Gray, H. and Freeman, A. (1989) *Organizing Special Educational Needs: A Critical Approach*. London: Paul Chapman.

HMI (1990) *Educational Psychology Services in England, 1988-1989*. London: DES.

HMI (1991) *The Work and Professional Development of Advisory Teachers for Special Educational Needs*. London: DES.

Handy, C. (1989) *The Age of Unreason*. London: Hutchinson.

Henry, T. (1991) Quality counts. *Perspective*, 16, 13-15.

Hill, D., Oakley-Smith, B. and Spinks, J. (1990) *Local Management of Schools*. London: Paul Chapman.

Kanter, R.M. (1983) *The Change Masters*. New York: Simon and Schuster.

Krachenberg, A.R. (1972) Bringing the concept of marketing to higher education. *Journal of Higher Education*, 43, 369-380.

Longhorn, F. (1988) *A Sensory Curriculum for Very Special People*. London: Souvenir Press.

Lunt, I. (1991) Local management of schools and education services. In H.

Daniels and J. Ware (Eds.), *Special Educational Needs and the National Curriculum*. London: Institute of Education.

Luthans, F. (1989) *Organizational Behaviour.* New York: McGraw-Hill.

MacConville, R.M. (1991) A service's response to the 1988 Education Act. *Year Book of the Scottish Learning Difficulties Association*, 1990-91, 16-22.

Masidlover, M. (1979) The Derbyshire language scheme: Remedial teaching for language delayed children. *Child*, 5, 9-16.

Matthews, A. (1991) Services for sale. *Perspective*, 16, 7.

Mittler, P. (1991) Prospects and pitfalls for pupils with special educational needs. *Head Teachers Review*, Spring, 1-2.

Mittler, P. and Pumfrey, P. (1989) Peeling off the label. *Times Educational Supplement*, 13th October, 29-30.

Morris, G. (1991) Heads' pay deal does not fit in with LMS. *Times Educational Supplement*, 22nd March, 20.

NCC (1990) *A Curriculum for All*. York: National Curriculum Council.

National Children's Bureau (1990) *Working with the Children Act, 1989*. London: National Children's Bureau.

Nicholson, S. (1991) What about special schools? *Head Teachers Review*, Spring, 12-15.

Ouvry, C. (1991) *The Curriculum Challenge*. London: British Institute of Mental Handicap.

Peters, T.J. and Waterman, R.H. (1982) *In Search of Excellence: Lessons from America's Best-Run Companies*. New York: Harper and Row.

Prus, C. (1989) *Making Sales*. Newbury Park, California: Sage.

Quicke, J. (1985) Initial teacher training and the role of the support agencies. In J. Sayer and N. Jones (Eds.), *Teacher Training and Special Educational Needs*. London: Croom Helm.

Rab, F. (1989) Teacher-parent communication in the special school: The head as manager and researcher. In T. Bowers (Ed.), *Managing Special Needs*. Milton Keynes: Open University Press.

Sharron, H. (1991) Goodbye to all that (the Fallon interview). *Managing Schools Today*, 1, 16-18.

Touche Ross (1990) *Extending Local Management to Special Schools. A Feasibility Study for the Department of Education and Science*. London: DES/HMSO.

Vuori, H. (1989) Research needs quality assurance. *Quality Assurance in Health Care*, 1, 147-159.

Watts, P. (1990) Changing times: Changing services? *Support for Learning*, 5, 6-12.

Williams, H. and Muncey, J. (1982) Precision teaching before behavioural objectives? *AEP Journal*, 18, 116-124.

Wolfendale, S. (1987) *Primary Schools and Special Educational Needs*. London: Cassell.

Glossary of initials

The abbreviations listed below have been used in this book. Expansions are provided here and, where it is thought necessary, a brief definition is given.

AMG   Annual Maintenance Grant. The amount of money paid each year to a grant-maintained school.

ASB   Aggregated Schools Budget. The amount remaining from the GSB, after deduction of excepted items, to be shared among schools on the basis of each LEA's formula.

AWPU   Age-Weighted Pupil Unit. The finance-carrying element attached to each pupil within the LMS formula; resources are allocated according to a school's pupil population, with the actual entitlement varying in relation to particular age groups.

CEA   Cambridge Educational Associates. An educational consultancy offering services to LEAs and schools.

CMO   Community Medical Officer.

DES   Department of Education and Science.

EBD   Emotional and Behavioural Difficulties.

EP   Educational Psychologist.

ESW   Education Social Worker.

EWO   Education Welfare Officer.

FE   Further Education.

GEST   Grants for Education Support and Training. Central government-funded initiatives, in which LEAs may bid for a share of earmarked money. LEAs themselves have to make a contribution to the allocated sum.

GMS   Grant-Maintained School. A school 'opted out' from LEA control.

GP   General Practitioner or family doctor.

GSB   General Schools Budget. The element of an LEA's overall budget available in a financial year for all schools covered by a scheme of delegation.

HMI   Her Majesty's Inspectors of Schools.

HV   Health Visitor.

IT   Information Technology.

LEA   Local Education Authority.

LFM   Local Financial Management.

LMS   Local Management of Schools. A system in which resources are allocated to schools in accordance with a formula established by the LEA.

LMSS   Local Management of Special Schools.

MLD   Moderate Learning Difficulties.

PR   Public Relations.

PSB   Potential Schools Budget. That proportion of the GSB which has been identified in Circular 7/91 as generally amenable to delegation to schools.

SAT   Standard Assessment Task. A nationally-determined form of assessment of children's performance in elements of the National Curriculum.

SEN   Special Educational Need(s).

SENCO   Special Educational Needs Coordinator. Teacher with overall responsibility for SEN in a school.

SIMS   Schools Information Management System. A set of computer programs designed to facilitate a variety of areas of information management.

SLD   Severe Learning Difficulties.

SPS   Schools Psychological Service.

SSA   Special Support Assistant. An ancillary worker in a special school, or one assisting children with SEN within a mainstream school.

SWOT   Strengths, Weaknesses, Opportunities and Threats. A marketing acronym.

Index